Success with C++

Kris Jamsa, Ph.D.

a division of Kris Jamsa Software, Inc.

Published by
Jamsa Press
2821 High Sail Ct.
Las Vegas, NV 89117
U.S.A.

For information about the translation or distribution of any Jamsa Press book, please write to Jamsa Press at the address listed above.

Success with C++

Printed in the United States of America.
98765432

ISBN 0-9635851-7-7

Publisher
Debbie Jamsa

Copy Editor
Paul Medoff

Composition
Kevin Hutchinson

Cover Design
Jeff Wolfley & Associates

Layout Design
Phil Schmauder

Technical Editor
Ken Cope

Illustrator
Phil Schmauder

Indexer
Ken Cope

Cover Photograph
O'Gara/Bissell

Dedication

To Triggerhill's I'm So Happy,
My best friend...

Acknowledgments

When futurists ponder the information superhighway and how information at one's fingertips will change our work habits, they should have the opportunity to witness the editorial process at Jamsa Press. I am very fortunate to have the opportunity to hand-pick the industry's best technical editors, copy editors, illustrators, and designers to work on Jamsa Press books. My selections focus on quality of work and are not constrained by geographic bounds. As we enter the electronic era, the brainstorming sessions that once took place at the coffee bar now take place using electronic mail and a barrage of faxes.

When I finish a chapter, I immediately forward the text using electronic mail to the book's technical editor. Depending on the project, the editor might be across town, across the state, or even across the country. After the technical queries are resolved, the technical editor forwards the manuscript electronically to the copy editor, without the delay of U.S. Mail or even the fastest on-time delivery service. This manuscript's electronic excursion continues as it moves to the illustrators, the proofers, and finally into page layout. With the computers in my office serving as the hub for the book's travel, you can hear the chatter of modems and faxes at all hours of the day and night.

Without the delays one would normally experience when shipping hardcopy manuscript from one editor to another, the Jamsa Press production team receives a constant flow of chapters. I am very fortunate to have team members who are not merely talented and dedicated, but also unselfish, with their expertise and time. Everyone on the Jamsa Press production team unselfishly gives their expertise to improve the quality of the book. And they do so all day and (often) all night long throughout the duration of a project. Please take time to note the team members who worked on this project. It is their efforts that ensure this book's quality and that makes Jamsa Press truly a computer user's best friend. I cannot thank them enough for their effort.

Technical Editor	Copy Editor	Illustrator	Page Layout	Indexer
Ken Cope	Paul Medoff	Phil Schmauder	Kevin Hutchinson	Ken Cope

Table of Contents

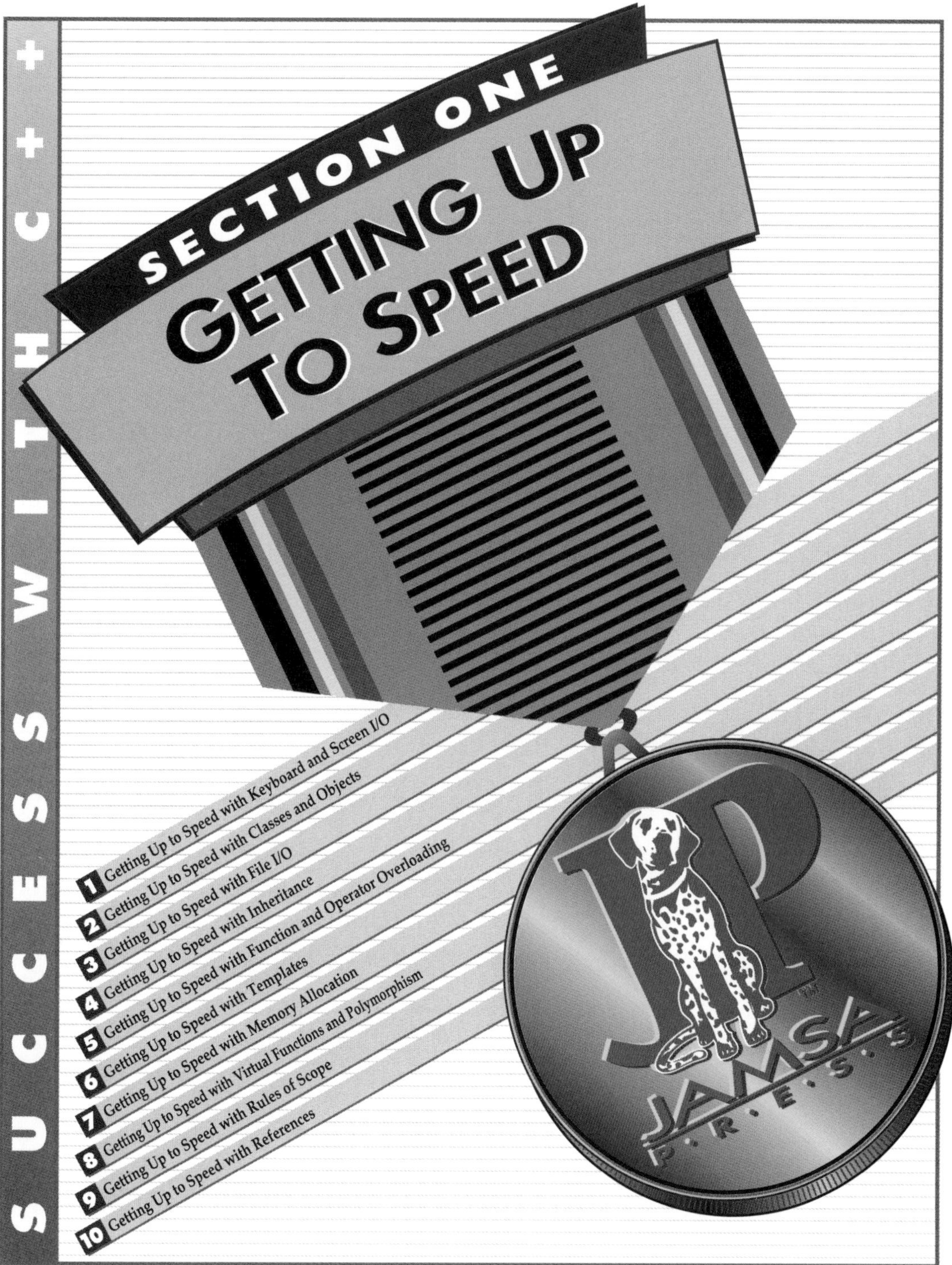
SUCCESS WITH C++
SECTION ONE
GETTING UP TO SPEED
1 Getting Up to Speed with Keyboard and Screen I/O
2 Getting Up to Speed with Classes and Objects
3 Getting Up to Speed with File I/O
4 Getting Up to Speed with Inheritance
5 Getting Up to Speed with Function and Operator Overloading
6 Getting Up to Speed with Templates
7 Getting Up to Speed with Memory Allocation
8 Getting Up to Speed with Virtual Functions and Polymorphism
9 Getting Up to Speed with Rules of Scope
10 Getting Up to Speed with References
JAMSA PRESS

Chapter 1
Getting Up to Speed with Keyboard and Screen I/O

Every program you create, regardless of the its purpose, will perform some type of input and output operations. Thus, this chapter reviews C++ keyboard input and screen output in detail. By the time you finish this chapter, you will have learned

- What an I/O stream is
- How your compiler uses a header file
- Why *cin* and *cout* are so important
- How you can format input and output
- What a manipulator is
- Some uses of input and output stream member functions
- How to perform buffered output

If you are familiar with C++ I/O operations, you might want to review quickly the manipulators presented in this chapter. Chapter 11 examines the I/O classes in detail. At that time you will examine the I/O classes and methods. If you are just learning C++, take time to experiment with each program presented in this chapter—change each program and note your results.

Understanding I/O Streams

In the simplest sense, an *I/O stream* is a sequence of flowing characters written to the screen display or read from the keyboard. When you perform standard input and output operations in C++, you normally use the I/O streams *cin* for input and *cout* for output. As it turns out, C++ defines I/O streams as classes. You should find the definitions within the header file IOSTREAM.H or within ISTREAM.H and OSTREAM.H, depending on which compiler you are using. If you examine the file's contents, you will find declarations for various class methods and the input and output operators. You might want to print a copy of the file now so you have it for use a reference. Don't worry if you don't understand all the declarations and definitions that occur in within the file; we will examine the file's contents closely in Chapter 11.

Note: As an example of the compiler differences that you may encounter, Borland C++ uses IOSTREAM.H for most stream-related definitions. In addition to IOSTREAM.H, Microsoft Visual C++ splits these definitions among IOS.H, ISTREAM.H, OSTREAM.H, and STREAMB.H.

Your C++ programs will normally include the IOSTREAM.H file as one of the first statements. The following program, SUCCESS.CPP, for example, uses *cout* to display a message on your screen display:

```
#include <iostream.h>

void main(void)
 {
   cout << "Getting up to speed with C++ I/O";
 }
```

As you can see, the program uses the output or *insertion operator* (the double less-than signs <<) to display the message on the screen. In Chapter 11 you will learn how C++ defines the insertion operator for I/O stream classes. Likewise, in Chapter 11, you will learn where C++ actually defines *cout* as an object.

In a similar way, the following program, GET_NAME.CPP, asks the user to type in his or her first name. The program uses the input or *extraction operator* (the double greater-than signs >>) to assign the letters typed to the variable *first_name*:

```
#include <iostream.h>

void main(void)
 {
   char first_name[64];

   cout << "Type in your first name: ";

   cin >> first_name;

   cout << "Hello, " << first_name;
 }
```

The program uses the output operator to display the prompt for the user's name. The program then uses the input operator to assign the letters typed to the variable *first_name*. As you can see, the program then uses the output operator twice within the same statement to display the message **Hello**, followed by user's name:

```
cout << "Hello, " << first_name;
```

When you output information using multiple extraction operators in this way, C++ displays the information as it appears in the statement from left to right. Experiment with the previous program and type in your first and last name at the program's prompt for your name. As you will find, the program only displays your first name—regardless of the amount of information you type. When you use *cin* to read character strings, such as a name, from the keyboard, *cin* uses whitespace characters to separate one string from another. Should you need to read a line of text from the keyboard, you can use *cin*'s *getline* member function discussed later in this chapter. The following program, FULLNAME.CPP, places two variables in the input statement to read the user's first and last names:

```
#include <iostream.h>

void main(void)
 {
   char first_name[64];
   char last_name[64];

   cout << "Type your first and last names: ";
   cin >> first_name >> last_name;

   cout << "Hello, " << first_name << " " << last_name;
 }
```

The program uses the following statement to read values for two variables at one time:

```
cin >> first_name >> last_name;
```

When you use two or more extraction operators within the same statement, C++ assigns the values typed to the variables from left to right. Also, note the use of the double quotes within the output message to separate the first and last names. If you remove the quotes, the characters of the last name would continue immediately to the left of the first name characters:

```
cout << "Hello, " << first_name << " " << last_name;
```

UNDERSTANDING CIN AND COUT

An I/O stream is a sequence of bytes, either for input or output. When your programs need to display output to the screen display (or standard output device), your programs can insert characters into the *cout* output stream using the insertion operator like this:

```
cout << "Success with C++" << endl;
```

When your programs need to perform keyboard input (or input from the standard input device), your programs can extract characters from the *cin* input stream using the extraction operator like this:

```
cin >> some_variable;
```

REDIRECTING I/O STREAMS

C++ associates the *cout* and *cin* I/O streams with the operating system's standard input and standard output file handles. Thus, you can use these two I/O streams to write programs that support I/O redirection. For example, the following command line directs DOS (or UNIX) to send the output of the SUCCESS program to a file named OUTPUT.DAT, as opposed to the screen display:

```
C:\> SUCCESS > OUTPUT.DAT   <ENTER>
```

The following program, LINE_NBR.CPP, displays a line number in front of each line of redirected input:

```
#include <iostream.h>

void main(void)
 {
   char line[256];
   long line_number = 0;

   while (! cin.eof())                    // Loop until no characters
                                          // are available
     {
       cout << ++line_number << '\t';     // Display a line number
                                          // and a tab
       cin.getline(line, sizeof(line));   // Read a line of text
       cout << line << endl;              // Display the line of text
     }
 }
```

The program uses the *cin* and *cout* I/O streams. However, as you can see, the program takes advantage of two member functions *cin.eof* and *cin.getline.* Remember, *cin* and *cout* are objects and as such, have defined member functions. If you have never used these two functions, don't worry. We will examine them later in this lesson. In addition to using these member functions, the program uses the *endl* manipulator to write each newline (a carriage-return and linefeed).

To display line numbers in front of the program statements in the file SUCCESS.CPP, for example, you would invoke LINE_NBR as follows:

```
C:\> LINE_NBR  <  SUCCESS.CPP  <ENTER>
1 #include <iostream.h>
2
3 void main(void)
4   {
5     cout << "Getting up to speed with C++ I/O";
6   }
```

If you want to save the line numbered output to a file (such as a file named OUTPUT.DAT), you could redirect LINE_NBR's output as shown here:

```
C:\> LINE_NBR  <  SUCCESS.CPP  >  OUTPUT.DAT  <ENTER>
```

Using Other I/O Streams

Most of the C++ programs you will encounter will use the *cin* and *cout* I/O streams. As it turns out, the file IOSTREAM.H also defines the I/O streams *cerr* and *clog*. Table 1.1 briefly describes the different I/O streams:

Stream	Purpose	Example
cin	Keyboard input (stdin)	cin >> name;
cout	Screen output (stdout)	cout << "Hello, world!";
cerr	Standard error device output (stderr)	cerr << "Critical error";
clog	Buffered output to standard error (stderr)	clog << "Error message";

Table 1.1 *Summary of C++ I/O streams.*

Redirecting Your Program Output

When you run a program, C++ associates the *cin* and *cout* I/O streams with the standard input and output devices. By default, the operating system associates the standard input device with the keyboard and standard output with the screen display. If you invoke a C++ program using I/O redirection operators in your command line, you can redirect the program's input or output. In other words, you can redirect *cout* output stream from the screen display to a file or even another program. Likewise, you can redirect the *cin* input stream from the keyboard to a file.

When your program tests for and processes critical errors, you will not the program's error messages redirected from the screen display. In such cases, you should use the *cerr* stream to display the message. For example, the following program, USE_CERR.CPP, displays a message using *cerr*:

```
#include <iostream.h>

void main(void)
 {
   cerr << "You cannot redirect this message";
 }
```

Compile and execute this program using the operating system's redirection operators. As you will find, you cannot redirect messages written to *cerr*. Later in this chapter, you will examine buffered output which is used by *cout* and *clog*.

Understanding I/O Streams

In the simplest sense, an I/O stream is a succession of characters, such as those written to the screen display or those read from the keyboard. The header file IOSTREAM.H defines four I/O streams: *cout*, *cin*, *cerr*, and *clog*. The *cout* I/O stream lets you display output to the screen or standard output device. Likewise, *cin* lets your programs read characters from the keyboard or standard input device. Finally, *cerr* and *clog* let your programs write output to the standard error device. To send output to an I/O stream, you use the output (extraction) operator (<<), as shown here:

```
cout << "Hello, successful world!";
cerr << "Some error message";
```

To obtain input from *cin*, you use the input (insertion) operator (>>), as shown here:

```
cin >> name;
```

C++ lets you place multiple data values and operators in an output stream or multiple variables within an input stream:

```
cout << "Type in your first and last names" << endl;
cin >> first >> last;
```

Understanding Input and Output Streams

Many of the manipulators and functions discussed in this chapter correspond to input and output streams. When you examine the header file IOSTREAM.H, you will find definitions that use *ios* and others that use *istream* and *ostream*. Definitions that use *ios* correspond to input and output streams (hence io). In a similar way, definitions based on *istream* correspond to input streams and those based on *ostream* to output streams. By examining the stream definitions you can better understand each manipulator or member function. In Chapter 11 you will take a close look at the relationships between these classes.

Reviewing the Special Characters

One of the previous programs used the *endl* output manipulator to generate a carriage-return/linefeed sequence. In a similar way, the following program, THREELIN.CPP, uses the *endl* manipulator to display the program's output on three lines:

```
#include <iostream.h>

void main(void)
 {
   cout << "Success" << endl;
   cout << "with" << endl;
   cout << "C++!" << endl;
 }
```

Using the *endl* manipulator several times in the same statement, the following program, THREETOO.CPP, is identical in function, displaying its output on three lines:

```
#include <iostream.h>

void main(void)
 {
   cout << "Success" << endl << "with" << endl << "C++!" << endl;
 }
```

In a similar way, another program presented earlier in this chapter used the **\t** characters to generate a tab. When you perform output to *cout*, *cerr*, or *clog*, you can use the special characters listed in Table 1.2 within your output stream.

Character	Purpose
\a	Alert or bell character
\b	Backspace character
\f	Formfeed character
\n	Newline character (equivalent to *endl*)

Table 1.2 *Special characters available for use with* ***cout, cerr,*** *and* ***clog****.* *(continued on next page)*

Character	Purpose
\r	Carriage return with no linefeed
\t	Horizontal tab character
\v	Vertical tab character
\\	Backslash character
\?	Question-mark character
\'	Single-quote character
\"	Double-quote character
\0	Null character
\ooo	Octal value, such as \033
\xhhh	Hexadecimal value, such as \x1B

Table 1.2 Special characters available for use with ***cout****,* ***cerr****, and* ***clog****. (continued from previous page)*

The following program, SPECCHAR.CPP, uses these special symbols to clear the screen display and then to beep the computer's built-in speaker. In order for the program to clear the screen display, you must have the ANSI device driver loaded. The program uses the special ANSI escape sequence **Esc[2J** to clear the screen:

```
#include <iostream.h>

void main(void)
 {
   // Clear the screen display
   cout << "\033[2J";

   // Sound the computer's speaker
   cout << "Beep\a\tBeep\a\t\Beep\a";
 }
```

The program uses the \a character to sound the speaker and the \t character to advance the cursor to the next tab stop. Many of the programs presented in this book will use different special characters.

You can use the special characters with each of the output streams, as well as the file streams you will use in Chapter 3. For example, the following program, BEEPCERR.CPP, uses the BEEPCERR.CPP, uses the \a character to sound the computer's built-in speaker before displaying a message to *cerr*:

```
#include <iostream.h>

void main(void)
 {
   cerr << "\aSome error message\t\tXXX-11-XXXX";
 }
```

As you can see, the program uses the \a character to sound the computer's built-in speaker and the \t character to generate a tab. In Chapter 11 you will learn how to create your own manipulators that correspond to these special characters.

Working with Manipulators

An I/O stream *manipulator* is an item through which you filter I/O stream output. For example, three common manipulators are *hex*, *oct*, and *dec*, which let you display a value in hexadecimal, octal, or decimal. For example, the following program, MANIPULA.CPP, illustrates how your programs can use these manipulators:

```
#include <iostream.h>

void main(void)
 {
   int number = 1001;

   cout << "Decimal: " << number << "\tHexadecimal: " <<  hex <<
           number << endl;
   cout << "Decimal: " << dec << number << "\tOctal: " << oct <<
           number << endl;
 }
```

If you examine the program's third statement, you will find the use of the *dec* manipulator. You may be wondering why it is necessary to use the manipulator with the decimal value 1001. As it turns out, the *cout* output stream, by default, displays values in decimal. If your program uses the *oct* or *hex* manipulators, however, *cout* will display values in either octal or hexadecimal, based on the last manipulator used. Thus, for the program to display the value 1001 in decimal, the program must use the *dec* manipulator. Take time to experiment with this program, perhaps adding the following statement to end of the program:

```
cout << "Displaying the value 1001: " << 1001;
```

Because the *oct* manipulator was last used by the program, *cout* will display the value in octal, not decimal as you might expect.

Setting the Conversion Base

The *dec*, *hex*, and *oct* manipulators let your programs specify the conversion base an output stream will use to output numbers. For example, the following statement directs *cout* to display the value 255 in hexadecimal:

```
cout << hex << 255;
```

After the statement executes, however, *cout* will use the hexadecimal base for all numerical output until you select a different base. It is not necessary that you output a value to change a base. The following statement, for example, directs *cout* to display values you later output in decimal:

```
cout << dec;
```

Finally, when you specify a base using the *dec*, *hex*, or *oct* manipulators, you only specify a base for a specific I/O stream. The base values for other streams are not affected.

In addition to using the *dec*, *hex*, and *oct* manipulators to set the conversion base, your programs can use the *setbase* manipulator that is defined the header file IOMANIP.H. The following program, SETBASE.CPP, uses the *setbase* manipulator to achieve the same result as the previous program:

```
#include <iostream.h>
#include <iomanip.h>

void main(void)
 {
   int number = 1001;

   cout << "Decimal: " << number << "\tHexadecimal: " <<
           setbase(16) << number << endl;
   cout << "Decimal: " << setbase(10) << number << "\tOctal: " <<
           setbase(8) << number << endl;
 }
```

*Note: If your compiler doesn't include the **setbase** manipulator, you can use the **setiosflags** manipulator. For example, to select hexadecimal, use **setiosflags(ios::hex)**.*

Controlling a Value's Output Width

Several of the previous programs have used spaces within quotes to help format their output. In addition to "brute-forcing" your program's spacing in this way, your programs can use the *setw*

ı number character positions an output field will con-
han you have specified using *setw*, the value will use as
uires fewer characters, however, the additional blanks
s specified in *setw* manipulator is displayed. Unlike *dec*,
nanipulator only effects the next value output. In other
loes not remain in affect. The following program,
manipulator:

```
etw(i) << 12 << setw(i) << 123 << endl;
```

nly remains in affect for the next value output, the pro-
within the same statement. When you compile and ex-
ay the following output:

```
setw(1)
setw(2)
setw(3)
setw(4)
```

As you can see, if a value requires more digits than *setw* has currently selected, the value uses as many digits as it requires. In the case of the first line of output, all three values required at least one digit. Likewise, the second line of output provides a minimum of two digits, the third three digits, and the fourth four. As you can see, the fourth line of output precedes the value 1 with three spaces, 12 with two spaces, and 123 with one space.

Setting the Fill Character

As you just learned, the *setw* manipulator lets you specify the minimum width used to display a field's value. By default, the I/O streams use blank spaces to obtain the proper spacing between characters. Using the *setfill* manipulator, you can specify a different character. For example, the following statement directs *cout* to use a period as the fill character:

```
cout << setfill('.');
```

When you specify a character using *setfill*, the character remains in effect for all subsequent output until you select a different character. The following program, SETFILL.CPP, changes the previous SETW.CPP program to use a period as the fill character:

```
#include <iostream.h>
#include <iomanip.h>

void main(void)
 {
   int i;

   cout << setfill('.');

   for (i = 1; i < 5; i++)
    cout << setw(i) << 1 << setw(i) << 12 << setw(i) << 123 << endl;
 }
```

The prototype for the *setfill* manipulator resides in the header file IOMANIP.H. When you compile and execute this program, your screen will display the following output:

```
C:\> SETFILL  <ENTER>
112123
.112123
..1.12123
...1..12.123
```

A convenient use of the *setfill* manipulator is to create a menu or even a table of contents for a report such as the following:

Table of Contents
Chapter 1 Getting Up to Speed with Keyboard I/O 1
Chapter 2 Getting Up to Speed with Classes 22
Chapter 3 Getting Up to Speed with Files 45
Chapter 4 Getting Up to Speed with Templates 67
Chapter 5 Getting Up to Speed with Inheritance 99

The following program, TABLE.CPP, illustrates how you might use the *setfill* manipulator to create the previous table:

```
#include <iostream.h>
#include <iomanip.h>

void main(void)
 {
```

```
    cout << setfill('.');
    cout << "Table of Contents" << endl;
    cout << "Chapter 1 Getting Up to Speed with Keyboard I/O" <<
            setw(18) << 1 << endl;
    cout << "Chapter 2 Getting Up to Speed with Classes" <<
            setw(34) << 22 << endl;
    cout << "Chapter 3 Getting Up to Speed with Files" <<
            setw(36) << 45 << endl;
    cout << "Chapter 4 Getting Up to Speed with Templates" <<
            setw(32) << 67 << endl;
    cout << "Chapter 5 Getting Up to Speed with Inheritance" <<
            setw(30) << 99 << endl;
  }
```

Controlling Floating-Point Digit Display

When you work with floating-point values, such as 3.14159, you can control the number of digits an output stream displays using the *setprecision* manipulator. For example, assume that your program needs to output the result of the expression 22.0 / 7.0. To control the number of digits displayed to the right of the decimal point, you can use the *setprecision* manipulator, as shown in the following program, SETPREC.CPP:

```
#include <iostream.h>
#include <iomanip.h>

void main(void)
  {
    int i;

    for (i = 0; i < 10; i++)
      cout << setprecision(i) << 22.0 / 7.0 << endl;
  }
```

As you can see, the program loops from 0 to 10, using *setprecision* to control the number of digits displayed. The *setprecision* manipulator prototype is defined in the header file IOMANIP.H. When you compile and execute this program, your screen will display the following output:

```
C:\> SETPREC  <ENTER>
3.142857
3.1
3.14
3.143
3.1429
3.14286
```

```
3.142857
3.1428571
3.14285714
```

*Note: Later in this chapter you will learn how to select fixed floating-point display format using the **ios::fixed** flag. When you use fixed format, the **setprecision** manipulator controls the number of digits displayed to the right of the decimal point, not the total number of digits.*

Flushing Buffered Output

As you have learned, the *cout* and *clog* output streams use *buffered output*, a certain amount of data is stored up in a memory location and is all transferred at once, for more efficiency. Later in this chapter you will examine buffered and unbuffered output in detail. As you will learn, when you perform buffered output, there may be times when you want your programs to *flush* the data (move it from the buffer location) to the screen immediately. To flush output in this way, you can use the *flush* manipulator. The programs presented in that section will explain the *flush* manipulator in detail.

Ignoring Leading White Space on Input

As you have learned, the *cin* input stream uses white space to separate one input field from another. When you perform I/O operations, there may be times when you want *cin* to ignore leading white space that precedes your first field. To ignore leading white space, your programs can use the *ws* manipulator, as shown here:

```
cin >> ws >> field;
```

For example, the following program, SKIP_WS.CPP, uses the *ws* manipulator to ignore leading white space that appears before the text you type:

```
#include <iostream.h>
#include <iomanip.h>

void main(void)
 {
   char text[128];

   cout << "Type in a word preceded by one or more blanks" << endl;
   cin >> ws >> text;
   cout << "You typed >" << text << "<" << endl;
 }
```

Controlling I/O Stream Flags

As you have learned, several of the I/O stream manipulators remain in effect after an I/O operation completes. For example, the *dec*, *hex*, and *oct* manipulators select the base used to display numeric values. To implement these manipulators, I/O streams have a flag field that specifies the current settings. A header file defines different flag settings as an enumerated type, as shown here:

```
enum {
  skipws =  0x0001,       // Skip white space during input
  left =  0x0002,         // Left justify output
  right = 0x0004,         // Right justify output
  internal = 0x0008,      // Pad after sign or base indicator
  dec =   0x0010,         // Decimal base
  oct =   0x0020,         // Octal base
  hex = 0x0040,           // Hexadecimal base
  showbase = 0x0080,      // Use base indicator on output
  showpoint = 0x0100,     // Force decimal point for floating point
  uppercase = 0x0200,     // Uppercase hex output
  showpos = 0x0400,       // Add '+' to positive integers
  scientific =  0x0800,   // Use 3.1415E2 floating notation
  fixed = 0x1000,         // Use 314.45 floating notation
  unitbuf = 0x2000,       // Flush all streams after insertion
  stdio = 0x4000          // Flush stdout, stderr after insertion
 }
```

Using the *setiosflags* manipulator, your programs can control many of these flags. For example, the following program, IOSFLAGS.CPP, uses the *dec*, *oct*, *hex*, and *showbase* flags to display a number in decimal, octal, and hexadecimal:

```
#include <iostream.h>
#include <iomanip.h>

void main(void)
 {
   cout << setiosflags(ios::showbase);

   cout << setiosflags(ios::dec);
   cout << "10 in decimal is " << 10 << endl;

   cout << setiosflags(ios::oct);
   cout << "10 in octal is " << 10 << endl;

   cout << setiosflags(ios::hex);
   cout << "10 in hex is " << 10 << endl;
 }
```

When you compile and execute this program, your screen will display the following:

```
C:\> IOSFLAGS  <ENTER>
10 in decimal is 10
10 in octal is 012
10 in hex is 0xa
```

In this case, the *ios::showbase* flag directs *cout* to display precede octal values with 0 and hexadecimal values with 0x. In some cases, you might want to set more than one flag in one step. To do so, you OR the desired flags, as shown here:

```
cout << setiosflags(ios::showbase | ios::oct);
```

DISPLAYING HEXADECIMAL OUTPUT IN UPPERCASE LETTERS

As you have learned, the *hex* manipulator lets your programs display an value in hexadecimal. By default, I/O streams display hexadecimal values in lowercase letters. If you want your programs to display uppercase hexadecimal values, you can use the *ios::uppercase* flag. The following program, UPPERHEX.CPP, illustrates the use of the *ios::uppercase* flag:

```
#include <iostream.h>
#include <iomanip.h>

void main(void)
 {
   cout << "Lowercase: " << hex << 255 << "   " << 10 << endl;
   cout << setiosflags(ios::uppercase);
   cout << "Uppercase: " << 255 << "   " << 10 << endl;
 }
```

When you compile and execute this program, your screen will display the following output:

```
C:\> UPPERHEX  <ENTER>
Lowercase: ff  a
Uppercase: FF  A
```

LEFT- AND RIGHT-JUSTIFYING OUTPUT

By default, I/O streams display their output justified to the left. Using the *ios::left* and *ios::right* flags, your programs can control output justification. For example, the following program, LEFTRITE.CPP, uses the flags to display output aligned at both left and right:

```
#include <iostream.h>
#include <iomanip.h>

void main(void)
 {
   cout << setiosflags(ios::right);
   cout << setw(5) << 1 << setw(5) << 2 << setw(5) << 3 << endl;
   cout << setiosflags(ios::left);
   cout << setw(5) << 1 << setw(5) << 2 << setw(5) << 3 << endl;
 }
```

When you compile and execute this program, your screen will display the following output:

```
C:\> LEFTRITE  <ENTER>
    1    2    3
1    2    3
```

As you have learned, the previous program could have combined statements, as shown here:

```
#include <iostream.h>
#include <iomanip.h>

void main(void)
 {
   cout << setiosflags(ios::right) << setw(5) << 1 << setw(5) <<
           2 << setw(5) << 3 << endl;
   cout << setiosflags(ios::left) << setw(5) << 1 << setw(5) <<
           2 << setw(5) << 3 << endl;
 }
```

Controlling Scientific and Exponential Output

When you display floating-point values, there may be times when you want to display the values using a fixed decimal format, such as 123.456, while other times you will want to display the values in a scientific (exponential) format, such as 1.23456e2. The *ios::fixed* and *ios::scientific* flags let you control your program's floating-point output. For example, the following program, FIXFLOAT.CPP, illustrates the use of these two formatting flags:

```
#include <iostream.h>
#include <iomanip.h>

void main(void)
 {
   cout << setiosflags(ios::fixed) << 123.45 << endl;
```

```
    cout << 12345.6789 << endl;
    cout << resetiosflags(ios::fixed);
    cout << setiosflags(ios::scientific) << 123.45 << endl;
    cout << 12345.6789 << endl;
 }
```

Note: The program uses the ***resetiosflags(ios::fixed)*** *statement to overcome errors in several of the compilers used to test the programs presented in this book. Experiment with this program using your compiler and determine if you can remove the line.*

When you compile and execute this program, your screen will display the following output:

```
C:\> FIXFLOAT  <ENTER>
123.450000
12345.678900
1.234500e+02
1.234568e+04
```

As you can see, the *ios::fixed* format directs the I/O stream to display the decimal point in its actual location, whereas the *ios::scientific* flag directs the I/O stream to use the exponential format.

Forcing Decimal Point Output

When your programs display the result of an different floating-point operations, there may be times when a stream does not display the decimal point in an exact result. For example, consider the following statement:

```
cout << 10.0 / 5 << endl;
```

Because the result of the division is exact, the I/O stream might display the result as simply 2, as opposed to 2.0. When you need your programs to display the decimal point, you can use the *ios::showpoint* flag. The following program, SHOWPOIN.CPP, illustrates the uses the flag to force the decimal point display:

```
#include <iostream.h>
#include <iomanip.h>

void main(void)
 {
   cout << 10.0 / 5 << endl;
   cout << setiosflags(ios::showpoint) << 10.0  / 5 << endl;
 }
```

When you compile and execute this program, your screen will display the following output:

```
C:\> SHOWPOIN  <ENTER>
2
2.00000
```

Forcing a Value's Sign Display

By default, I/O streams only display a value's sign before negative numbers. Depending on your program's purpose, there may be times when you need the program to precede positive values with a plus sign. In such cases, your programs can use the *ios::showpos* flag. For example, the following program, SHOWPOS.CPP, illustrates the flag's use:

```
#include <iostream.h>
#include <iomanip.h>

void main(void)
 {
   cout << -10 << " " << -5 << " " << 0 << " " << 5 << " " <<
           10 << endl;
   cout << setiosflags(ios::showpos);
   cout << -10 << " " << -5 << " " << 0 << " " << 5 << " " <<
           10 << endl;
 }
```

When you compile and execute this program, your screen will display the following output:

```
C:\> SHOWPOS  <ENTER>
-10 -5 0 5 10
-10 -5 0 +5 +10
```

Restoring I/O Stream Flags

Throughout this section you have learned how to set specific flags using the *setiosflag* manipulator. If your programs perform a large amount of stream I/O, there will be times when you will want to turn different settings on and off. To restore a specific flag to its default setting, your programs can use the *resetioflags* manipulator. For example, the following program, RESETIO.CPP, displays several values in hexadecimal, preceding the values with the 0x hexadecimal base specifier. The program then uses the *resetiosflags* manipulator to turn off the base specifier display:

```
#include <iostream.h>
#include <iomanip.h>

void main(void)
 {
```

```
    cout << setiosflags(ios::showbase);
    cout << hex << 255 << " " << 10 << endl;
    cout << resetiosflags(ios::showbase);
    cout << 255 << " " << 10 << endl;
}
```

When you compile and execute this program, your screen will display the following output:

```
C:\> RESETIO  <ENTER>
0xff  0xa
ff  a
```

Using I/O Flags

The stream manipulators let your programs control different I/O settings. To track these settings, I/O streams maintain a collection of flag bits. Using the *setiosflags* and *resetiosflags* manipulators, your programs can directly control the flag settings. For example, the following statement directs *cout* to display its output right-justified:

```
cout << setiosflags(ios::right);
```

To understand better the I/O stream flag settings, examine the header file that your compiler uses for stream related definitions (such as IOSTREAM.H, ISTREAM.H, or OSTREAM.H). In Chapter 12 you will learn how to create your own output manipulators to simplify the use of these flags within your programs.

Putting Input Member Functions to Work

Most simple C++ programs use the *cin* and the insertion operator to perform input operation. As your programs become more complex, however, there will be times when you need finer control over input operations than the insertion operator can provide. In such cases, your programs can use the I/O stream input member functions discussed here.

Determining the Number of Characters Extracted

When your programs extract characters from an input stream using an extraction operator, there may be times when your programs need to know the number of characters extracted. To do so, your programs can the *gcount* member function. For example, the following program, GCOUNT.CPP, prompts you to type in a line of text. The program then reads the text using *cin.getline*, using the *gcount* member function to determine the number of characters read:

```
#include <iostream.h>
#include <iomanip.h>

void main(void)
 {
   char text[64];

   cout << "Type in a line of text and press Enter" << endl;

   cin.getline(text, sizeof(text));

   cout << "You typed: " << text << " " << cin.gcount() <<
           " characters" << endl;
 }
```

Note: When it is counting a string, ***gcount*** *will include the carriage return—that is, if you type* ***123****, the* ***gcount*** *will be 4.*

Compile and execute this program. Experiment with the *gcount* function by typing in strings with a different number of characters. Keep in mind that the value *gcount* returns will include the carriage return.

Reading a Line of Input from the Keyboard or STDIN

When your programs perform input using the *cin* input stream, *cin* separates values using white-space and end-of-line characters. Depending on the values your programs need to input, you might want to read an entire line of text and let your programs parse out the different fields. To read a line of text, your programs can use the *getline* member function. The following program, GETLINE.CPP, uses the *getline* member function to read a line of text from the keyboard:

```
#include <iostream.h>

void main(void)
 {
   char line[128];

   cout << "Type in a line of text and press Enter" << endl;
   cin.getline(line, sizeof(line));
   cout << "You typed: " << line << endl;
 }
```

By default, the *getline* member function reads characters up to a carriage return or to the number of characters specified. Depending on your program's input requirements, there may be times when you want *getline* to end the input operation when a specific character is encountered. To end an input operation when *getline* encounters the letter X, invoke the member function like this:

```
cin.getline(line, sizeof(line), 'X');
```

When you terminate I/O operations on a specific character, it is important that you understand that the next input operation continues at the first character that immediately follows the terminating character. For example, the following program, STOPON_X.CPP, ends the first input operation on an X character. The program then performs a second input operation:

```
#include <iostream.h>

void main(void)
 {
   char line[128];

   cout << "Type in a line of text and press Enter" << endl;
   cin.getline(line, sizeof(line), 'X');
   cout << "First line: " << line << endl;
   cin.getline(line, sizeof(line));
   cout << "Second line: " << line;
 }
```

Compile and execute this program. At the prompt to enter text, type in a series of words separated by an X. When the program displays its output, the program will display the text that precedes the X on one line and the text that follows the X on another.

Note: The X in this program is case sensitive. A lowercase X will not terminate input for the first ***cin.getline****. Also, until you type X, you may press the* ENTER *key one or more times without terminating input for the first* ***cin.getline****. The input operation for the first* ***cin.getline*** *will be terminated with the first* ENTER *after you have typed X.*

USING CIN MEMBER FUNCTIONS

As you have read, *cin* as a class object of type *istream*. As such, *cin* supports several member functions. The following statement, for example, uses the *getline* member function to read a line of text from the keyboard:

```
cin.getline(line, sizeof(line));
```

By examining *cin*'s class definition within IOSTREAM.H, you can quickly determine the available member functions by reading the function prototypes.

Performing Input Operations One Character at a Time

Depending on your program's input requirements, there may be times when you need to perform input operations a character at a time. In such cases, your programs can use the I/O stream *get* member function. For example, the following program, YES_NO.CPP, prompts the user to type a Y or N response. The program uses the *get* member function until a Y or N character is encountered:

```
#include <iostream.h>
#include <ctype.h>

void main(void)
 {
   char letter;

   cout << "Type a Y or N: ";

   do {
     letter = cin.get();               // Read a character
     letter = toupper(letter);         // Convert to uppercase
   } while ((letter != 'Y') && (letter != 'N'));

   cout << endl << "You typed: " << letter << endl;
 }
```

As you can see, the program simply loops until a Y or N character is encountered. To simplify the test, the program converts each character typed into the upper case.

Keep in mind that your input operations that use the *cin* I/O stream are not restricted to keyboard input. The following program, TO_UPPER.CPP, uses the *get* member function to read redirected input a character at a time, converting the input to uppercase letters until the end of file is encountered:

```
#include <iostream.h>
#include <ctype.h>

void main(void)
 {
   char letter;

   while (! cin.eof())
     {
       letter = cin.get();
       letter = toupper(letter);
       cout << letter;
     }
 }
```

As you can see, the program uses the *eof* member function to detect the end of file (or end of redirected input). Later in this chapter, you will examine the *eof* function in detail.

The following command uses the TO_UPPER command to display the contents of the file TO_UPPER.CPP in uppercase:

```
C:\> TO_UPPER < TO_UPPER.CPP <ENTER>
```

Peeking at the Next Character Input

Depending on your program's input, there may be times when you need to read characters up to, but not including, a specific character. For example, assume that your program is reading a file that contains names followed by phone numbers, as shown here:

Joe Smith 555-1212

John Davis 222-2323

Betty Lou Johnson 333-3343

In this case, your program might read assign the characters that precede a number to a string variable. To read characters up to a specific character, your programs can use the *cin.peek* member function. The function reads a character from the input buffer without removing the character. The following program, TO_DIGIT.CPP, prompts you to type in words followed by a number. The program uses the *peek* member function to locate the digit, assigning the characters that precede the digit to the character string named *line*:

```
#include <iostream.h>
#include <ctype.h>

void main(void)
 {
   char letter, string[128];

   int i = 0, done = 0;

   cout << "Type in a string terminated by a number" << endl;

   do {
     letter = cin.peek();

     if (! isdigit(letter))
       string[i++] = cin.get();
     else
       done = 1;
   } while ((! done) && (i < sizeof(string)));
```

```
    string[i] = NULL;

    cout << "String input: " << string << endl;
  }
```

Note: Most programs that use the ***peek*** *member function can be rewritten to eliminate the program's need to use the function and in turn improve the program's readability. If your program uses the* ***peek*** *member function, you should consider possible ways to rewrite the program code.*

Putting a Character Back into the Input Buffer

The previous program used the input stream *peek* member function to determine the next character in the input buffer. Depending on the processing your program performs, there may be times when the program needs to place a character back into the input buffer or place a character other than the character read into the buffer. In such cases, your programs can use the *putback* member function. The following program, PUTBACK.CPP, reads characters from the input buffer, displaying a count of the number each character read. The program only counts uppercase characters. If a lowercase character is encountered, the program places an uppercase equivalent of the character back into the buffer:

```
#include <iostream.h>
#include <ctype.h>

void main(void)
 {
   int count[26];
   char i;

   char letter;

   for (i = 0; i < 26; i++)
     count[i] = 0;

   cout << "Type in a string and press Enter" << endl;

   do {
     letter = cin.get();

     if ((letter >= 'a') && (letter <= 'z'))
       cin.putback(toupper(letter));
     else if ((letter >= 'A') && (letter <= 'Z'))
       count[letter - 'A']++;
   } while (letter != '\n');

   for (i = 0; i < 26; i++)
    {
```

```
      cout.put((char)('A' + i));
      cout << " " << count[i] << endl;
    }
 }
```

As you can see, if the program encounters a lowercase letter, the program uses the *putback* member function to place the character's uppercase equivalent back into the input buffer. In this way, the program only needs to count uppercase characters.

Note: Most programs that use the ***putback*** *member function can be rewritten to eliminate the program's need to use the function and in turn improve the program's readability. If your program uses the* ***putback*** *member function, you should consider possible ways to rewrite the program code*

Testing For the End of a File

Chapter 3 examines C++ file operations in detail. At that time, you will find that many programs read files from start to end using the *eof* member function to test for the end of a file. When you write programs that support I/O redirection, you can use the *eof* function to determine the end of the redirected input. For example, the following program, LINECNT.CPP, reads redirected input and then displays a count of the number of lines read:

```
#include <iostream.h>

void main(void)
 {
   char line[256];
   long count = 0;

   while (! cin.eof())
    {
      cin.getline(line, sizeof(line));
      count++;
    }

   cout << "Lines read: " << count << endl;
 }
```

After you compile this program, you can redirect input to the program, as shown here:

```
C:\> LINECNT  <  LINECNT.CPP  <ENTER>
Lines read: 15
```

As you can see, the program, like several others presented in this chapter, simply loop until the end of file is encountered.

Ignoring Characters in the Input Stream

When your programs perform I/O operations, there may be times when you want to ignore characters in the input stream. For example, assume that your program needs to read the following file and that your program is only concerned with the social security numbers:

Smith, John 111-22-3333

Lewis, Bill 222-33-4444

Jones, Mary 333-44-5555

Using the *ignore* member function, you can direct an input stream to ignore characters in the input stream. The following statement, for example, directs *cin* to ignore the next ten characters in the input stream:

```
cin.ignore(10);
```

Your programs can also direct an I/O stream to end character discarding if a specific character is encountered. For example, the following statement directs *cin* to ignore the first ten characters or the characters up to an including character letter A:

```
cin.ignore(10, 'A');
```

In this case, the most characters *cin* will ignore is ten. In other words, if the letter A appears in the first ten characters, *cin* will stop discarding characters.

Reading and Saving Different I/O Settings

As you have learned, I/O streams provide several different manipulators and functions that let you control specific settings. For example, the *setw* manipulator lets your program define a field's output width. When your program uses these manipulators to control settings, there may be times when you want to determine the current flag settings so the program can later restore them. In such cases, your programs can use the functions listed in Table 1.3 to read the current settings.

Member Function	Returns
flags	Current flag settings
width	Current field output width
fill	Current fill character
precision	Current precision setting

Table 1.3 *I/O stream member functions that return state settings.*

The following program, SHOWINFO.CPP, uses these functions to display a stream's default settings:

```
#include <iostream.h>

void main(void)
 {
   long flags;

   flags = cout.flags();
   cout << "Default flags: " << hex << flags << endl;
   cout << "Default width: " << dec << cout.width() << endl;
   cout << "Default fill: >" << cout.fill() << "<" << endl;
   cout << "Default precision: " << cout.precision() << endl;
 }
```

When you compile and execute this program, your screen will display output similar to the following:

```
C:\> SHOWINFO  <ENTER>
Default flags: 2001
Default width: 0
Default fill: > <
Default precision: 6
```

Understanding Output Stream Settings

C++ provides several member functions that let you control the stream's spacing and formatting. When you use these functions to change a setting, the change remains in effect until the program ends or you make a second change to the setting. If you examine the header file that your compiler uses for stream-related definitions, you will find that these functions correspond to member variables within the I/O stream class. When you invoke the function, the value of the corresponding member variable is changed. When you later perform an I/O operation to the stream, the I/O operation uses the member variable setting to control the operation.

Putting Output Member Functions to Work

As you have just learned, input streams provide several member functions your programs can use to perform specific I/O operations. In a similar way, this section examines output stream member functions. The following program, PUTALPHA.CPP, for example, uses the *put* member function to display the letters of the alphabet on your screen one letter at a time:

```
#include <iostream.h>

void main(void)
 {
   char letter;

   for (letter = 'A'; letter <= 'Z'; letter++)
     cout.put(letter);
 }
```

When you compile and execute this program, your screen will display the following output:

```
C:\> PUTALPHA  <ENTER>
ABCDEFGHIJKLMNOPQRSTUVWXYZ
```

You may be wondering why the previous program used the *put* member function, as opposed to simply displaying the using *cout*, as shown here:

```
for (letter = 'A'; letter <= 'Z'; letter++)
  cout << letter;
```

If your program declares the variable *letter* as type *char*, you can use either technique to display the letters. However, if your program declares the variable *letter* as type *int*, the second technique will display the numbers 65 through 90 on your screen, instead of the letters A through Z.

Using cout Member Functions

As discussed, *cout* as a class object of type *ostream*. As such, *cout* supports several member functions. The following statement, for example, uses the *put* member function to write a character to the standard output device:

```
cout.put(7); // Sound the computer's built-in speaker
```

By examining *cout's* class definition within IOSTREAM.H, you can quickly determine the available member functions by reading the function prototypes.

Testing the Success of Your I/O Operations

Each of the previous programs have performed their I/O operations assuming the operations were successful. When your programs write simple messages to the screen or read one or two lines from the keyboard, you can normally "get away" with assuming that the operation was successful.

However, as your programs become more complex, you should test the success of your I/O operations using the member functions *good*, *bad*, *fail*, and *rdstate*. Each of these member functions examine status bits within the stream's I/O state flag to determine if an error occurred. Depending on your compiler, the value and meaning of the status bits may differ slightly. However, if you examine the header file that your compiler uses for stream-related definitions, you should find an enumerated type definition that defines the bits, similar to the following:

```
enum io_state {
  goodbit = 0x00     // Set if I/O operations have been successful
  eofbit = 0x01,     // Set if currently at the end of the file
  failbit = 0x02,    // Set if last I/O operation failed
  badbit = 0x04,     // Set if an invalid operation was attempted
  hardfail = 0x80    // Set if an unrecoverable error occurred
 };
```

To determine if an I/O error has occurred, your programs can test the different status bits. The following program, TEST_IO.CPP, for example, uses the *fail* member function to determine whether the program's input and output operations were successful:

```
#include <iostream.h>
#include <stdlib.h>
#include <ctype.h>

void main(void)
 {
   char letter;

   while (! cin.eof())
     {
       letter = cin.get();
       if (cin.fail())
        {
          cerr << "Error reading input" << endl;
          exit(1);
        }

       cout.put((char)toupper(letter));
       if (cout.fail())
        {
          cerr << "Error writing output" << endl;
          exit(1);
        }
     }
 }
```

Assume, for example, that you invoke TEST_IO, as shown here:

```
C:\> TEST_IO < FILENAME.CPP > A:UPPER.CPP   <ENTER>
```

In this case, TEST_IO will read the contents of the file FILENAME.CPP, writing the uppercase equivalent of each character to the file UPPER.CPP, which resides on drive A. If an error occurs when TEST_IO reads the input file or writes to the output file (such as insufficient disk space), the program will display an error message to the standard error file stream and will end. Because your programs may test for a failed I/O operation on a regular basis, the I/O streams define the exclamation mark as an operator that tests for a failed I/O. In this way, the following *if* statements are identical in function:

```
if  (cin.fail())
```

```
if  (! cin)
```

Once an I/O stream encounters an error, the stream's error bit remains set until you clear the flag using the *clear* member function, as shown here:

```
if (cout.fail())
 {
   cerr << "Display some error message" << endl;
   cout.clear();
 }
```

Depending on how your program handles I/O errors, you might want the program to examine the stream's error status flag to determine which error has occurred. To do so, your programs can use the *rdstate* member function, as shown here:

```
io_state = cin.rdstate();
```

To understand better the definitions of these member functions, examine the header file that your compiler uses for stream-related definitions.

Understanding the State of an I/O Stream

When you perform stream I/O operations, your programs can test the operation's success using member functions of the I/O class. If you examine the header file that your compiler uses for stream-related definitions, you will find that the I/O classes contain a state member variable whose bits correspond to the stream's current state. By examining the bits within this variable, your programs can determine the success of a previous I/O operation. Most programs, however, will use the built-in member functions to perform these tests.

Unbuffered versus Buffered I/O

The *cout* and *clog* I/O streams use buffered output. When a stream buffers output, the output is not actually written until the buffer fills, the program ends, and the program flushes the stream, or in the case of *cout*, the program reads input from *cin*. The following program, BUFFERED.CPP, for example, writes output to *cout* and then waits three seconds before ending. When the program ends, the buffered output is displayed, as in this example:

```
#include <iostream.h>
#include <time.h>

void main(void)
 {
   time_t start_time, current_time;

   cout << "Hello C++ world!" << endl;
   time(&start_time);

   do {
     time(&current_time);
   } while ((current_time - start_time) < 3);
 }
```

The program uses the *time* to determine the current time. The program then delays until three seconds have passed.

Flushing a Stream's Output

Depending on your program's processing, there may be times when you want to flush a stream's output before the buffer fills, the program ends, or an input operation is performed. In such cases, your programs can use the *flush* member function. For example, the following program, FLUSH.CPP, writes a message to *cout*, pauses two seconds, flushes the streams output and then delays three more seconds before ending:

```
#include <iostream.h>
#include <time.h>

void main(void)
 {
   time_t start_time, current_time;

   cout << "Hello C++ world!" << endl;
   time(&start_time);
```

```
    do {
      time(&current_time);
    } while ((current_time - start_time) < 2);

    cout.flush();

    time(&start_time);

    do {
      time(&current_time);
    } while ((current_time - start_time) < 3);

    cout << "Done!" << endl;
  }
```

In Chapter 11 you will dig deeper into buffered I/O streams when you examine the *streambuf* and *filebuf* classes.

Using Member Functions to Control I/O Stream Flags

Earlier in this chapter you learned how to control I/O stream output using the *setiosflags* and *resetiosflags* manipulators. In addition to using these manipulators, your programs can gain finer control over these flag settings using several I/O stream member functions discussed here. For example, the following program, IOFLAGS.CPP, uses the *flags* member function to display a stream's flag settings:

```
#include <iostream.h>
#include <iomanip.h>

void main(void)
 {
   cout << "cout starting flag settings: " <<
           hex << cout.flags() << endl;
   cout << setiosflags(ios::showbase);
   cout << "cout ending flag settings: " << cout.flags() << endl;
 }
```

When you compile and execute this program, your screen will display output similar to the following, depending on your compiler:

```
C:\> IOFLAGS  <ENTER>
cout starting flag settings: 1
cout ending flag settings: 0xc1
```

Using the *flags* member function, your programs may want to save a stream's flag settings at different times throughout your program's processing so you can restore the flags to a known setting. For example, the following program, SAVEFLAG.CPP, uses the *flags* member function to first read a stream's flag settings and later to restore the settings to their previous settings:

```
#include <iostream.h>
#include <iomanip.h>

void main(void)
 {
   long flag_settings;

   flag_settings = cout.flags();  // Read the flags

   cout << "Hexadecimal values: " << hex << 255 << " " <<
           10 << endl;

   cout.flags(flag_settings);     // Restore the flags

   cout << "Decimal values: " << 255 << " " << 10 << endl;
 }
```

When you compile and execute this program, your screen will display the following output:

```
C:\> SAVEFLAG   <ENTER>
Hexadecimal values: ff a
Decimal values: 255 10
```

In addition to using the *flags* member function to set I/O stream flags, your programs can use the *setf* and *unsetf* member functions. To set and clear flag settings using these two member functions, you must know the bit settings that correspond to each flag. Using the enumerated flag type previously shown in this chapter, you can determine the proper bit settings. For example, the following program SETCLEAR.CPP, uses the *setf* and *unsetf* member functions to set and clear I/O stream flags:

```
#include <iostream.h>
#include <iomanip.h>

void main(void)
 {
   cout.setf(0x80);       // Show base
   cout << hex << 255 << " " << 10 << endl;

   cout.unsetf(0x80);     // Clear the base display
   cout << hex << 255 << " " << 10 << endl;
 }
```

The program uses the *setf* member function to enable the hexadecimal base display. After the program displays two values, the program uses the *unsetf* member function to turn off the base display. When you compile and execute this program, your screen will display the following output:

```
C:\> SETCLEAR  <ENTER>
0xff 0xa
ff a
```

Putting It All Together

Every program you create, regardless its purpose, will perform some type of input and output operations. Thus, a key to your C++ programming success is understanding the I/O streams and their capabilities. Before you continue with Chapter 2, make sure you have learned the following:

- ✓ An I/O stream is best viewed as a series of bytes.
- ✓ Your compiler uses a header file to define the ios, istream, and ostream I/O streams—the stream's member functions and variables. Take time to print a copy of this file and examine the file's contents.
- ✓ The insertion (<<) and extraction (>>) operators let your programs output and input characters to or from an I/O stream.
- ✓ Manipulators are elements you can place in an input or output stream to control your I/O formatting. The header file IOMANIP.H defines the available manipulators.
- ✓ When your program uses a manipulator to set a stream's formatting, C++ sets bits within the stream's flag field that controls the setting. To better understand the available bits, see the header file that your compiler uses for stream definitions.
- ✓ Input and output streams support different methods that let you control your output format or to perform specific I/O operation. Your compiler defines the prototypes for the available stream member functions in a header file.
- ✓ The *cout* and *clog* output streams perform buffered output, which means their output is not actually written until the buffer fills, the program ends, the program flushes, or in the case of *cout*, the programs performs an input operation.

Chapter 2
Getting Up to Speed with Classes and Objects

It is possible to write a lot of C++ programs and never really fully understand or even use objects, and yet objects and classes are cornerstones to the full power of C++. For those of you who are still not fully comfortable with objects, relax. This chapter starts at step 1 and introduces the key fundamentals you must know. The chapters that follow each build upon the information presented here. In this way, you can learn about the key parts of the object puzzle one part (one chapter) at a time. As before, you should take time to experiment with the programs presented here. By making even simple changes, you can learn a great deal. By the time you finish this chapter you will understand the following:

- What an object is
- How an object-oriented point of view makes a large, complicated program easier to envision and write than a conventional, function-oriented point of view
- How an object can save you lots of time and effort
- What inheritance is
- The advantages of using objects
- How to create an object
- The advantages and disadvantages of inline functions
- How to use two different variables with the same name in the same program
- What class constructor and destructor functions are
- How to assign the value of one object to another

Getting a Feel for Object-Oriented Programming

In the simplest sense, an object is a thing. A dog, a book, and even a computer are all objects. In the past, programmers viewed programs as long lists of instructions that perform a specific task. When you create object-oriented programs, you look instead at the objects that make your program. For example, assume that you are writing a program that implements a simple word processor. If you think of all the functions a word processor performs, you can quickly become overwhelmed. However, if you view the word processor as a collection of distinct objects, the program becomes less intimidating. For example, Figure 2.1 illustrates the major objects in the word processing system.

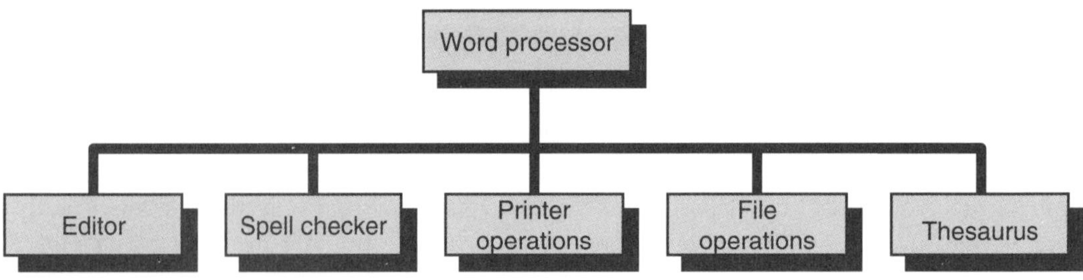

Figure 2.1 Viewing a word processor as a collection of objects.

As you examine each new object, you may find that it too, is also composed of objects, as shown in Figure 2.2.

As you begin to identify the objects used in your system, you will find that many different parts of your program use the same type of objects. As a result, by writing your programs in terms of objects, you can easily (and quickly) *reuse* the code you write for one part in a different part of your program or maybe even in a different program! Here lies some of the power of C++.

The first step in creating object-oriented programs is to identify the objects that make up your system. To better understand how to identify a system's objects, you can turn to the following books on object-oriented analysis and object-oriented design:

- *Object-Oriented Design with Applications*, Booch, Benjamin/Cummings, 1991
- *Object-Oriented Analysis*, Coad & Yourdon, Yourdon Press, 1990
- *Object Data Management*, Cattel, Addison-Wesley, 1991
- *Object-Oriented Reuse, Concurrency, and Distribution*, Atkinson, Addison-Wesley, 1991
- *Object-Oriented Methods*, Graham, Addison-Wesley, 1991
- *An Introduction to Object-Oriented Programming*, Budd, Addison-Wesley, 1991

- *Object-Oriented Software Construction*, Meyer, Prentice-Hall, 1988
- *Object-Oriented Systems Analysis: A Model-Driven Approach, Embley*, Kurtz and Woodfield, Yourdon Press, 1992

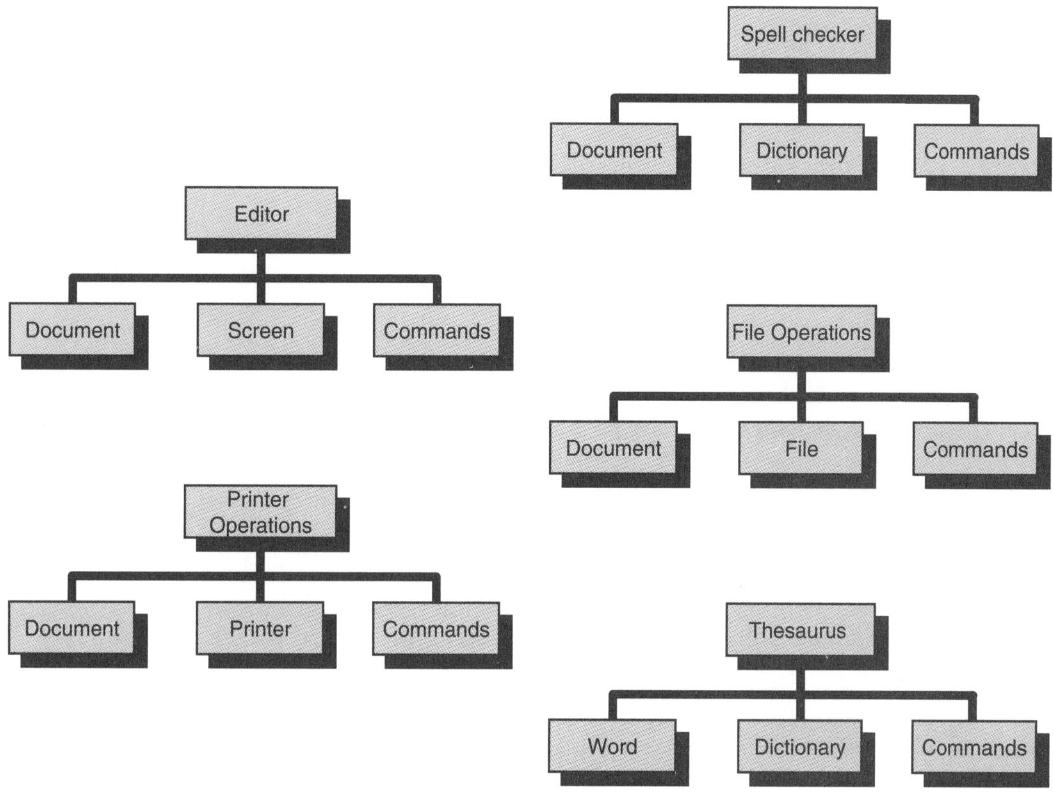

Figure 2.2 *Identifying additional objects within your word processor.*

After you identify the objects, you must determine each object's purpose. To do so, think of the operations an object performs or the operations that are performed on the object. For example, given a *file* object, a program can copy, delete, or rename the file. It is important to note that, in general, these operations apply to each file on your disk, regardless of the file's contents. These operations will become the object's *member functions*, for which you will later write C++ functions within your program. Next, identify the information you must know about the object. In the case of the file object, you must know the filename, size, protection attribute, and possibly the date and time the file was created or last changed. These data items will become the file object's *member variables*. Conceptually, you can now view your file object, as shown in Figure 2.3.

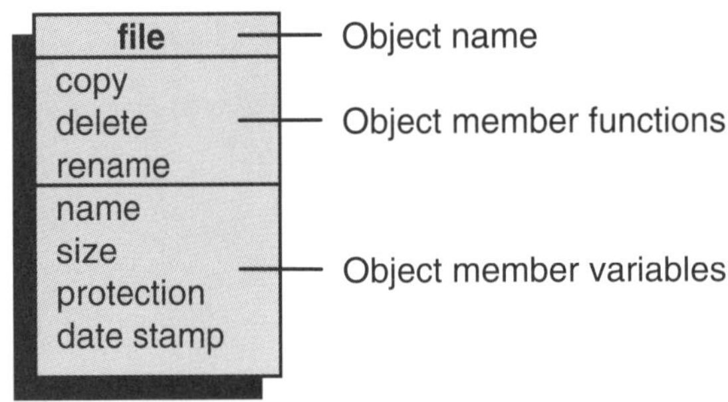

Figure 2.3 A file obect's member functions and variables.

UNDERSTANDING OBJECT ORIENTED PROGRAMMING

Object-oriented programming is based on writing programs in terms of the objects (things) that make up a system. Within a system, objects store specific types of information and have specific operations performed on the information. The first step in creating an object-oriented program is to identify the system's objects, the key object information, and the operations performed on the objects. As you create your first C++ programs, your design will probably stop there. As you become more experienced, you will look for relationships between objects that let you build objects from one another. For now, however, should someone ask you to define a C++ object, simply tell them that an object represents a real-world entity (thing), may hold data (member variables) and has a specific set of operations (member functions) that are performed upon it.

You may be thinking that your program needs to print and display files and that sometimes files contain executable programs that you need to run. As such, you may want to add similar methods to the object definition. Adding these additional methods is not exactly wrong. However, there is a better way to handle special cases.

If your file contains a document, for example, you might want to print and display the file's contents. However, if the file contains an executable program, printing or displaying the file's contents would be meaningless. Likewise, if the file contains an executable program, running the file's contents makes perfect sense. However, if you tried to run a document file, an error would occur. Thus, a better solution is to identify two new object classes, which in this case, could be called *document* and *program.* One way to create these two new classes is simply to add the required fields to each class, as shown in Figure 2.4.

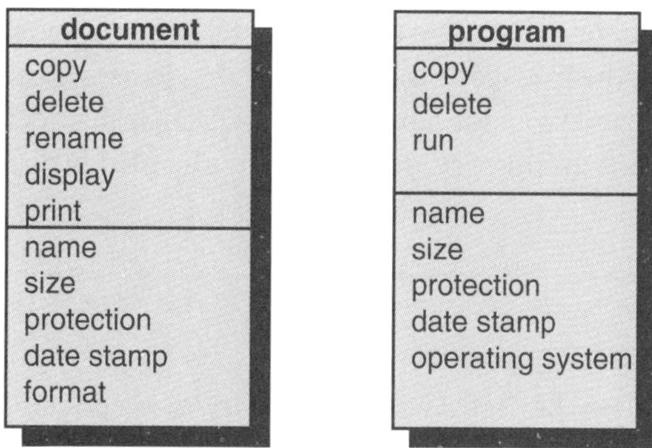

Figure 2.4 Creating stand-alone document and program classes.

As you can see, the *document* object adds the member functions *display* and *print* and the member variable *format*, which specifies the document's internal format, such as Word or WordPerfect. Likewise, the *program* object adds *run* member function and the *operating system* field, which specifies whether the program is DOS, Windows, or UNIX-based.

For the most part, the these two new object classes simply duplicate the *file* class you previously defined. Thus, a better design solution is to build the two new object classes based on the *file* class, as shown in Figure 2.5.

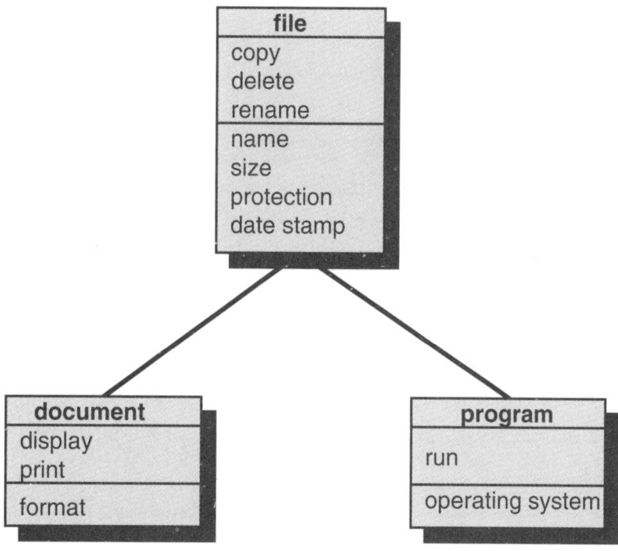

Figure 2.5 Basing the new classes on the existing file class.

When your programs build one class from another in this way, the new class *inherits* the member functions and variables of the base class. In the case of the *document* and *program* classes, the objects you create of these class types not only can use their own member functions and variables, but also those of the *file* class. In this way, your program can quickly display, print, copy, rename, or delete a document file.

Keep Class Definitions Simple

As you begin to define classes, try to keep your definitions general. In other words, the member functions and variables that appear in your first-level (base) class should apply to each and every related class you derive (build) from the class in the future. If you find yourself adding several different member functions or variables to a class definition, you should consider defining a second, more specialized class that is based on the general class.

Building one class from another in this way is the essence of *class inheritance*, which is covered in detail in Chapter 4. You may be wondering why you need to go to so much trouble to design classes in this way. The primary reason for using inheritance is *reuse*, the ability of one program to use code written and tested for another. Assume, for example, that you created the *file* class to support a budget program. Because the class now exists, you can quickly use the class within new programs. Not only does using an existing class save programming, it also reduces the amount of testing you must perform, because the *file* class member functions were previously tested and verified for the budget program.

Understanding Inheritance

Inheritance is the ability of a *derived* class to *inherit* the member functions and variables of an existing *base* class. As you identify and examine the objects that make up a system, you will often find relationships and similarities between objects. In many cases, these relationships let you build one object from another, complete with all of the original's methods. When you design object classes, try to keep your classes as general as possible. As the number of member functions and variables within a class definition increases, your ability to reuse the class or to derive other classes from the class can decrease.

Software Engineering Goals That Drive Object Use

Why should you base you programming around objects? There are several software-engineering terms that are often used to describe this. Although software-engineering community is far from agreeing upon the best use of objects, most software engineers will agree that the use of objects offers the following advantages:

Ease of design and code reuse Once the code works properly, the use of objects increases your ability to reuse a design or code you created for one application within a second application.

Increased reliability Once proper testing has been previously performed on object libraries, the use of existing (working) code will improve your program's reliability.

Ease of understanding By allowing designers and programmers to focus on smaller pieces of a system and providing a framework within which designers can identify objects, the operations performed on the objects, and the information objects must store, object use helps programmers focus on and understand key system components.

Increased abstraction Abstraction lets designers and programmers "look at the big picture"—temporarily ignore underlying details so they can work with system elements that are more easily understood. For example, by focusing only on the word processor objects earlier in this chapter, the implementation of a word processor became much less intimidating.

Increased encapsulation *Encapsulation* groups all of the pieces of an object into one neat package. For example, the *file* class previously defined in this chapter combines the functions and data fields a program needs to work with a file. The programmer who is working with the *file* class does not need to know each piece of the class, only that they need to use the class within their program. The class, in turn, will bring with it all the necessary pieces.

Increased information hiding *Information hiding* is the ability for your program to treat a function, procedure, or even an object, as a "black box," using the item to perform a specific operation without having to know how what goes on inside. In Chapter 1, for example, your programs used I/O stream objects for input and output without having to understand how the streams work.

As we examine different C++ programming concepts throughout this book, you will learn how the concepts relate to these definitions.

Understanding Objects and Classes

Throughout the preceding discussion, the terms *objects* and *classes* have been used very loosely. In general, a *class* provides a template with which your program can later create objects. For example, the *file* class previously discussed describes the member functions and variables that will be used for the *file* objects your program creates in the future. An *object*, therefore, is an *instance* of a class template. In other words, an object is the entity, specific example, or thing with which your programs work.

A class definition is very similar to a C structure definition. For example, the following statements define the *file* class:

```
class file {
public:
  char filename[64];
  long size;
  unsigned protection;
  long datetime;
  int copy(char *target_name);
  int rename(char *target_name);
  int delete_file(void);
};
```

As you can see, the class definition defines the member variables and functions. Note the *public* label that appears at the start of the class. The only way your programs can directly access a class member, be the member of a function or a variable, is if the member follows the *public* label. Later in this chapter you will learn how to use *public* and *private* labels to control how your programs can access the class members. In Chapter 4, you will learn how related classes use *protected* member functions to provide a "middle ground" for member access. For now, however, place the *public* label at the start of each class, making all the class members available throughout the program.

A class defines a template for future object creation. The class itself does not create an object. To create an object, you declare variables of the object type, as shown here:

```
void main(void)
 {
    file source, target;    // Declare two file objects

    // Other statements here
 }
```

Classes versus Objects

As you read articles and books about C++ and object-oriented programming, you will encounter the terms *class* and *object*. A *class* provides a template, which defines the member functions and variables that are required for objects of the class type. An *object*, on the other hand, is an *instance*, or specific example of an object—essentially an object variable. You must define the class prior to the object declaration.

To declare an object variable, you simply specify the class type, followed by the object's variable name, as shown here:

```
class_name   object_name;
```

The process of creating an object is often referred to as *instantiating an object* or *creating an object instance.*

Looking at a Complete Example

The best way to understand C++ classes and objects is to create a simple program. The following program, MOVIES.CPP, creates a class named *movie* and then creates two objects of type movie, named *fugitive* and *sleepless*. The program defines the *movie* class as follows:

```
class movie {
public:
  char name[64];
  char first_star[64];
  char second_star[64];
  void show_movie(void);
  void initialize(char *name, char *first, char *second);
};
```


As you can see, the *movie* class uses three variable members and two member functions. Following the class definition, the program must define the *show_movie* and *initialize* member functions, as shown here:

```
void movie::show_movie(void)
 {
   cout << "Movie name: " << name << endl;
   cout << "Starring: " << first_star << " and " << second_star <<
          endl << endl;
 }
```

```
void movie::initialize(char *movie_name, char *first, char *second)
 {
   strcpy(name, movie_name);
   strcpy(first_star, first);
   strcpy(second_star, second);
 }
```

The class function definitions are very similar to the standard function definitions, however, there are two primary differences. First, the function names are preceded by the class name and two colons:

```
                                   Class name
                                   Function name
void movie::initialize(char *movie_name, char *first, char *second)
```

Second, within the class function, statements can refer directly to class member variables:

```
void movie::initialize(char *movie_name, char *first, char *second)
 {
   strcpy(name, movie_name);
   strcpy(first_star, first);
   strcpy(second_star, second);
 }                                 Function local variable names
                                   Class member names
```

The following statements implement the MOVIES.CPP program:

```
#include <iostream.h>
#include <string.h>

class movie {
public:
  char name[64];
  char first_star[64];
  char second_star[64];
  void show_movie(void);
  void initialize(char *name, char *first, char *second);
};

void movie::show_movie(void)
 {
   cout << "Movie name: " << name << endl;
   cout << "Starring: " << first_star << " and " << second_star <<
           endl << endl;
 }

void movie::initialize(char *movie_name, char *first, char *second)
 {
   strcpy(name, movie_name);
```

```
    strcpy(first_star, first);
    strcpy(second_star, second);
  }

void main(void)
  {
    movie fugitive, sleepless;

    fugitive.initialize("The Fugitive", "Harrison Ford",
      "Tommy Lee Jones");
    sleepless.initialize("Sleepless in Seattle", "Tom Hanks",
      "Meg Ryan");

    fugitive.show_movie();
    sleepless.show_movie();
  }
```

As you can see, the program creates two objects of type *movie*:

```
movie fugitive, sleepless;
```

Class name

Object names

Accessing class members is very similar to accessing structure members in C: You specify the object name followed by the dot operator and the desired member name. For example, to call the *initialize* function, the *fugitive* object uses the dot operator and member function name, as shown here:

```
fugitive.initialize("The Fugitive", "Harrison Ford", "Tommy Lee Jones");
```

Object name

Function name

Function parameters

In this case, the program used the *initialize* member function to initialize the class member variables. Later in this chapter, you will learn how to use *constructor* functions to initialize member variables in a more natural way.

When to use Classes, As Opposed to Structures

If you have programmed in C, you should recognize the fact that the syntax for working with classes is very similar to that of C structures. You may be wondering when you should use classes, as opposed to structures, or even unions. As you know, classes, structures, and unions each let your programs store related data. Your programs should uses classes whenever specific operations are performed on the data. For example, if you simply need to store a date, you can use a value. But if you want the program to format and display the date, file the date, or compare two dates, you should use a class. Likewise, if the choice is between using a structure or a union, the decision should come down to the number of values the data structure must store at any given time. Finally, keep in mind that by default, class members are private, and structure and union members are public.

If you experiment with C++ structures, you will find that they support many of the same features as C++ classes, such as public and private data, member functions, and so on. As a rule, if you are creating objects, use a class.

Accessing Class Members

In the previous program, you used the dot operator to invoke the *initialize* and *show_movie* member functions. When your programs place object members after a *public* label, your programs can access the members using the dot operators. For example, the following program, PUBLIC.CPP, uses the initialize function to assign values to the members of the *fugitive* and *sleepless* objects. The program then displays the different member values by referencing the member using the dot operator:

```
#include <iostream.h>
#include <string.h>

class movie {
public:
  char name[64];
  char first_star[64];
  char second_star[64];
  void show_movie(void);
  void initialize(char *name, char *first, char *second);
};

void movie::show_movie(void)
 {
   cout << "Movie name: " << name << endl;
   cout << "Starring: " << first_star << " and " << second_star <<
endl << endl;
 }

void movie::initialize(char *movie_name, char *first, char *second)
 {
   strcpy(name, movie_name);
   strcpy(first_star, first);
   strcpy(second_star, second);
 }
```

```
void main(void)
 {
   movie fugitive, sleepless;

   fugitive.initialize("The Fugitive", "Harrison Ford",
     "Tommy Lee Jones");
   sleepless.initialize("Sleepless in Seattle", "Tom Hanks",
     "Meg Ryan");

   cout << "The last two movies I've watched are: " <<
           fugitive.name << " and " << sleepless.name << endl;

   cout << "I thought " << fugitive.first_star << " was great!" <<
           endl;
 }
```

Because the class members are *public*, programs can access the members directly. When you compile and execute this program, your screen will display the following:

```
C:\> PUBLIC  <ENTER>
The last two movies I've watched are: The Fugitive and
Sleepless in Seattle
I thought Harrison Ford was great!
```

When a class defines member variables as public, your programs can access the member variables using the dot operators. However, as you will learn later in this chapter, such direct variable member access is not always desirable.

Using Inline Functions

As you have learned, a class contains member variables and member functions. When you define class functions, you have two choices. First, you can define the functions outside of the class definition, as shown here:

```
class movie {
public:
  char name[64];
  char first_star[64];
  char second_star[64];
  void show_movie(void);
  void initialize(char *name, char *first, char *second);
};

void movie::show_movie(void)
 {
```

```
   cout << "Movie name: " << name << endl;
   cout << "Starring: " << first_star << " and " << second_star <<
           endl << endl;
 }

void movie::initialize(char *movie_name, char *first, char *second)
 {
   strcpy(name, movie_name);
   strcpy(first_star, first);
   strcpy(second_star, second);
 }
```

In this case, the class definition must contain prototypes that describe each class member function:

```
class movie {
public:
  char name[64];
  char first_star[64];
  char second_star[64];
  void show_movie(void);
  void initialize(char *name, char *first, char *second);
};
```


Likewise, the function definitions must specify the class name prior to the function name:


```
void movie::show_movie(void)
 {
   cout << "Movie name: " << name << endl;
   cout << "Starring: " << first_star << " and " << second_star <<
           endl << endl;
 }
```

Second, you can define your class member functions within the class, actually placing the function statements within the class declaration. For example, the following program, INLINE.CPP, defines the class member functions inline, within the class declaration:

```
#include <iostream.h>
#include <string.h>

class movie {
public:
  char name[64];
  char first_star[64];
  char second_star[64];
```

```
  void show_movie(void)
    {
      cout << "Movie name: " << name << endl;
      cout << "Starring: " << first_star << " and " <<
              second_star << endl << endl;
    }

  void initialize(char *movie_name, char *first, char *second)
    {
      strcpy(name, movie_name);
      strcpy(first_star, first);
      strcpy(second_star, second);
    }
};

void main(void)
 {
   movie fugitive, sleepless;

   fugitive.initialize("The Fugitive", "Harrison Ford",
     "Tommy Lee Jones");
   sleepless.initialize("Sleepless in Seattle", "Tom Hanks",
     "Meg Ryan");

   cout << "The last two movies I've watched are: " <<
           fugitive.name << " and " << sleepless.name << endl;

   cout << "I thought " << fugitive.first_star << " was great!" <<
           endl;
 }
```

As you can see, when you declare a member function inline, the function statements reside within the class itself:

```
#include <iostream.h>
#include <string.h>

class movie {
public:
  char name[64];
  char first_star[64];
  char second_star[64];
  void show_movie(void)
    {
      cout << "Movie name: " << name << endl;
      cout << "Starring: " << first_star << " and " <<
              second_star << endl << endl;
    }
```

Inline member function statements

```
void initialize(char *movie_name, char *first, char *second)
   {
     strcpy(name, movie_name);
     strcpy(first_star, first);
     strcpy(second_star, second);
   }
};
```

Inline member function statements

An advantage of declaring member functions inline is that the entire class is consolidated at one location within your program code. Unfortunately, using inline functions in this way also increases the size and complexity of your class definitions. Simply put, the larger your class definitions become, the more difficult your definitions are to understand. In addition, the code for inline functions is not shared among similar object types as discussed next.

When you define member functions outside of a class, the C++ compiler creates one copy of each function's instructions, which is later used by every object you create for that class. In other words, if you create 1,000 objects, each object shares the single copy of the function code. Such function sharing is desirable because it significantly reduces your program's memory overhead.

USE OUT-OF-LINE MEMBER FUNCTION DEFINITIONS

When you define your member functions, you have two choices. First, you can define the functions inline within the class so that the function statements actually appear within the class declaration. Second, you can define the functions *out of line*, outside of the class declaration. In most cases, you will want to define member functions outside of your class declaration to reduce your class size and complexity and to ensure that the function code is shared among objects.

If you generate assembly language listings of the programs PUBLIC.CPP and INLINE.CPP, you will find that the compiler does not share the function code for functions that are declared inline.

RESOLVING MEMBER NAME AND PARAMETER NAME CONFLICTS

When you pass parameters to a class member functions, the formal parameter names you use within the function create local variables:

```
void movie::initialize(char *movie_name, char *first, char *second)
 {
   strcpy(name, movie_name);
   strcpy(first_star, first);
   strcpy(second_star, second);
 }
```

Formal parameter names

As you can see, this function uses different names for the parameters and class member variables. When a parameter name conflicts with a class member name, the parameter name is used and the class member name is *hidden*. Assume, for example, that the *initialize* function used the following parameter names:

```
void movie::initialize(char *name, char *first_star,
  char *second_star)
 {
   strcpy(name, name);
   strcpy(first_star, first_star);
   strcpy(second_star, second_star);
 }
```

As you can see, it would be impossible for the C++ compiler to determine which name reference corresponds to a parameter and which corresponds to the class member. As a result, the compiler simply assumes each reference corresponds the parameter.

Because it can be sometimes challenging enough just to come with either good class member names or good parameter names, your programs can take advantage of the global resolution operator (::) to eliminate the need for unique names. When your programs want to refer to a class member, your programs simply precede the name with the class name and two colons, as shown here:

```
void movie::initialize(char *name, char *first_star,
  char *second_star)
 {
   strcpy(movie::name, name);
   strcpy(movie::first_star, first_star);
   strcpy(movie::second_star, second_star);
 }
```

Member name reference

Parameter name reference

By preceding the class member names with the class name and double colons, not only does the compiler know when you are referencing a class member, so too do other programmers who are reading your code.

Resolving Name Conflicts

Within your member functions, there may be times when a class member name conflicts with the name of a parameter passed to the function. By default, the C++ resolves such name conflicts by using the parameter (the local variable) and hiding the existence of the class member. To prevent such name conflicts, precede the class member references with the class name and double colons, as shown here:

```
void dogs::assign_dogs(char *breed, int height, int weight)
 {
   strcpy(dogs::breed, breed);
   dogs::height = height;
   dogs::weight = weight;
 }
```

In this case, the names preceded by **dogs::** correspond to class member names. The other names correspond to the local variables.

Understanding Private Class Members

Each of the classes you have examined so far have declared each of the class member variables and functions as *public*. In this way, your programs can access the class members at any location within your program (where the class is in scope) using the dot operator. Unfortunately, allowing a program to access all class members directly in this way can lead to errors and other problems. Here's why.

As previously discussed, one of the advantages of using objects is that programmers don't have to fully understand the object in order to use it. In other words, programmers can treat the objects as a "black box." To use an object, a programmer should only need to know the object's purpose and a few member functions. As you will learn, many objects have member variables that store important information.

For example, assume you are writing a program for the Pentagon that controls all the nuclear missiles that are housed in silos across the United States. In this case, your program makes use of *silo* objects similar to that shown here:

```
class silo {
   public:
      initialize(int missile_type, char *location);
```

```
        bombs_away(char *password);
        int missile_type;
        char location[64];
        int fire_missiles;    // If 0 don't fire, if 1 fire
        char password[64] = "Hillary";
};
```

As you can see, (for obvious security measures) to fire a missile, the program must specify a password. If the password is correct, the *fire_missiles* flag variable is set to 1, and the missiles are launched. If the password is not correct, the variable remains 0, and we have world peace. Unfortunately, because you have declared all of the class members as public, your program has free access to the members. As such, your program could use the following statement to launch the missiles, bypassing the your secure password-driven *fire_missiles* function:

```
wyoming_silo.fire_missiles = 1;
```

When you use objects, you should restrict access to most object member variables to member functions. In this way, the only way your program can access the *fire_missiles* member variable is by using a member function—you force the program to play by your rules.

To restrict access to class members, you can use *private* members, by placing the *private* label within your class declaration. The following class, for example, restricts access to several of the *silo* class members by making the members *private*:

```
class silo {
   public:
      initialize(int missile_type, char *location);
      bombs_away(char *password);
   private:
      int missile_type;
      char location[64];
      int fire_missiles; // 0-don't fire, 1-fire
      char password[64] = "Hillary";
};
```


In this case, your programs can still access the *initialize* and *bombs_away* members using the dot operator. However, your programs can now only access the member variables using functions such as *initialize* and *bombs_away*. If your program tries to access these variables directly, the C++ compiler will generate syntax errors.

The following program, PRIVATE.CPP, changes the *movie* class previously discussed to use private members:

```
#include <iostream.h>
#include <string.h>

class movie {
 public:
  void show_movie(void);
  void initialize(char *name, char *first, char *second);
 private:
  char name[64];
  char first_star[64];
  char second_star[64];
};

void movie::show_movie(void)
 {
   cout << "Movie name: " << name << endl;
   cout << "Starring: " << first_star << " and " << second_star <<
          endl << endl;
 }

void movie::initialize(char *movie_name, char *first, char *second)
 {
   strcpy(name, movie_name);
   strcpy(first_star, first);
   strcpy(second_star, second);
 }

void main(void)
 {
   movie fugitive, sleepless;

   fugitive.initialize("The Fugitive", "Harrison Ford",
     "Tommy Lee Jones");
   sleepless.initialize("Sleepless in Seattle", "Tom Hanks",
     "Meg Ryan");

   fugitive.show_movie();
   sleepless.show_movie();
 }
```

As you can see, the program has made all three member variables private. When you compile and execute this program, your screen will display the following output:

```
C:\> PRIVATE  <ENTER>
Movie name: The Fugitive
Starring: Harrison Ford and Tommy Lee Jones
```

```
Movie name: Sleepless in Seattle
Starring: Tom Hanks and Meg Ryan
```

Note that this program has removed the messages displayed from within *main* in the program PUBLIC.CPP:

```
void main(void)
 {
   movie fugitive, sleepless;

   fugitive.initialize("The Fugitive", "Harrison Ford",
     "Tommy Lee Jones");
   sleepless.initialize("Sleepless in Seattle", "Tom Hanks",
     "Meg Ryan");

   cout << "The last two movies I've watched are: " <<
           fugitive.name << " and " << sleepless.name << endl;

   cout << "I thought " << fugitive.first_star << " was great!" <<
           endl;
 }
```

Because the member variables are now private, the program cannot access the variables directly using the dot operator. Instead, if your program wants to display such messages, you must create member functions to do so. If you think that creating such member functions is too much work, and that direct member access is preferred, beware—you are opening up the door to difficulties and errors in the future—dooming your programs (and possibly world peace) to the type of errors presented in the previous silo example.

Understanding Private Class Members

When you declare a class, you can define members as public or private (or protected, as you will learn in Chapter 4). Public class members are available throughout your program using the object name and the dot (*class.member*) or indirection (*class_ptr->member*) operators. Private class members, on the other hand, can only be accessed using class member functions. Using private class members, your programs can better control the values assigned to class members and how those values are used. By default, all class members are private. Once you include a *public* label within your program, however, you can specify public members. If you later want to declare private members, you must use the *private* label, as shown here:

```
class some_class {
   public:
      void some_function(char *parameter);              Public class
      void some_other_function(int a, int b, int c);    members
   private:
      int key_value;                                    Private class
     char password[64];                                 members
};
```

In this case, the class member functions are public, while the class member variables are private. Depending on your class, however, you can have private member functions, as well as public member variables. Your job in designing classes is to determine which members need to public and which should remain private.

Understanding Information Hiding

Information hiding is the process of designing functions or classes as "black boxes." In other words, to use a function or class, a programmer does not need to know the box's inner workings, since it brings with it all of its methods, but rather, simply the operation the box performs and how to interface with the box. Within your C++ programs, private class members support information hiding.

Understanding Class Constructors and Destructors

When you create an object, there may be times when you need to allocate memory for buffers used by the object. For example, assume you are working with a *file* object that stores the filename as a character string. When you first create the object, you want the object to allocate memory dynamically (see Chapter 7) to store the string. Before you later discard the object when it is no longer needed, you will want to release the memory. To help your programs perform operations each time an object is created (sometimes called constructed) and destroyed, C++ supports *constructor* and *destructor* functions. Once you get past the terms, you will find that a constructor is nothing more than a function that automatically executes each time you create an object and a destructor is a function that automatically executes when an object is destroyed.

Earlier in this chapter you used the *initialize* member function to initialize the member variables of *movie* class objects. Using a constructor function, you can eliminate the need for your programs to invoke a function such as *initialize*. Instead, your programs simply specify parameter values when you create the object, as shown here:

```
movie fugitive("The Fugitive", "Harrison Ford",
  "Tommy Lee Jones");
movie.sleepless("Sleepless in Seattle", "Tom Hanks", "Meg Ryan");
```

C++, in turn, will automatically invoke the constructor function. Within the constructor, you can assign the parameters to the member fields, just as you did using *initialize*.

A constructor function is unique in that it does not return a value and it is not type *void*. Second, the constructor function uses the same name as the class. In the case of the *movie* class, the constructor function is be called *movie*:

```
class movie {
 public:
  void show_movie(void);
  movie(char *name, char *first, char *second);
 private:
  char name[64];
  char first_star[64];
  char second_star[64];
};
```

Constructor function

As you can see, the function does not specify a return type. Like all class member functions, you can define your constructor function inline or out of line. The following program, CONSTRUC.CPP, uses the *movie* constructor function to initialize objects:

```
#include <iostream.h>
#include <string.h>

class movie {
 public:
  void show_movie(void);
  movie(char *name, char *first, char *second);
 private:
  char name[64];
  char first_star[64];
  char second_star[64];
};

void movie::show_movie(void)
 {
   cout << "Movie name: " << name << endl;
```

```
   cout << "Starring: " << first_star << " and " << second_star <<
           endl << endl;
 }
                                    Constructor function declaration

movie::movie(char *name, char *first_star, char *second_star)
 {
   strcpy(movie::name, name);
   strcpy(movie::first_star, first_star);
   strcpy(movie::second_star, second_star);
 }

void main(void)
 {
   movie fugitive("The Fugitive", "Harrison Ford",
     "Tommy Lee Jones");
   movie sleepless("Sleepless in Seattle", "Tom Hanks", "Meg Ryan");

   fugitive.show_movie();
   sleepless.show_movie();
 }
```

Using constructor functions, your programs can initialize objects when the objects are created, eliminating the need for separate initialization functions.

Understanding Constructor Functions

A *constructor function* is a class member function that C++ automatically executes each time you create an object of a specific class. The constructor function is unique in that the function uses the same name as that of the class. As such, for a class named *dogs*, the constructor function would be named *dogs*. In addition, the function does not return a value and is not *void:*

```
class dogs {
   public:
      dogs(char *breed, int height, int weight);   Constructor function
      void show_dogs(void);
   private:
      char breed[64];
      int height;
      int weight;
};
```

Understanding Destructor Functions

A destructor is a function that automatically runs when an object is destroyed. Like a constructor function, the destructor function has the same name as the class. Also, the destructor function does not return a value and is not the type *void.* Your programs cannot pass parameters to a destructor function. You distinguish the destructor function from a constructor due to the fact that destructor is preceded by a tilde (~) character:

```
class dogs {
   public:
      dogs(char *breed, int height, int weight);
      ~dogs(void);
      void show_dogs(void);
   private:
      char breed[64];
      int height;
      int weight;
};
```

Destructor function

The following program, DESTRUCT.CPP, adds a destructor function to the *movie* class. When the object is destroyed (in this case when the program ends), the destructor function is invoked:

```
#include <iostream.h>
#include <string.h>

class movie {
 public:
  void show_movie(void);
  movie(char *name, char *first, char *second);
  ~movie(void);
 private:
  char name[64];
  char first_star[64];
  char second_star[64];
};

void movie::show_movie(void)
 {
   cout << "Movie name: " << name << endl;
   cout << "Starring: " << first_star << " and " << second_star <<
           endl << endl;
 }

movie::movie(char *name, char *first_star, char *second_star)
 {
```

```
    strcpy(movie::name, name);
    strcpy(movie::first_star, first_star);
    strcpy(movie::second_star, second_star);
  }

movie::~movie(void)
  {
    cout << "In the movie destructor for " << name << endl;
  }

void main(void)
  {
    movie fugitive("The Fugitive", "Harrison Ford",
      "Tommy Lee Jones");
    movie sleepless("Sleepless in Seattle", "Tom Hanks", "Meg Ryan");

    fugitive.show_movie();
    sleepless.show_movie();
  }
```

At first glance, the following function definition can be intimidating:

```
movie::~movie(void)
  {
    cout << "In the movie destructor for " << name << endl;
  }
```

To understand the function header, examine it one piece at a time. To begin, moving from left to right, the first *movie* and double colons specify that this function corresponds to the movie class. Next, the tilde (~) character lets you know that this definition is for a destructor function. Knowing that, you should be able to guess that the name *movie* will follow a second time—because the destructor always uses the class name. Finally, your program can't pass parameters to a destructor so the parameter list is *void.*

As you can see, the program does not actually call or invoke the destructor. Instead, once you define a destructor function, its execution is automatic when the object is destroyed. Normally, the destructor function would release memory or save information to a file on disk. In this case, however, the destructor simply displays a message on your screen. When you compile and execute this program, your screen will display the following output:

```
C:\> DESTRUCT  <ENTER>
Movie name: The Fugitive
Starring: Harrison Ford and Tommy Lee Jones
```

```
Movie name: Sleepless in Seattle
Starring: Tom Hanks and Meg Ryan

In the movie destructor for Sleepless in Seattle
In the movie destructor for The Fugitive
```

As you can see, the program's last two lines of output are written by the destructor functions.

Understanding Destructor Functions

A destructor is a function that automatically executes when objects of a specific class type are destroyed. Destructor functions have the same name as the class, however, their name is preceded by the tilde (~) character. A destructor does not return a value and is not *void*. Your program cannot pass parameters to a destructor. The following *employee* class uses a destructor function:

```
class employee {
  public:
    employee(char *name, int age);
    ~employee(void);
    void show_employee(void);
  private:
    char name[64];
    int age;
};
```

Destructor functions, like constructors, must be public class members.

Using Multiple Constructor Functions

In Chapter 5 you will examine function overloading, in which your program uses multiple functions with the same name. During compilation, the C++ compiler determines which function to invoke, based on the number or type of parameters or the function's return type. When you define constructor functions within your programs, you can specify multiple functions, from which the compiler will select the correct function to invoke based upon your program's use. For example, the following program, MULTICON.CPP, uses two constructor functions for the *message* class. The first constructor assigns the message specified by the parameter message, while the second constructor uses the default "Hello, world" message:

```
#include <iostream.h>
#include <string.h>

class message {
  public:
    message(char *user_message);
    message(void);
    void show_message(void);
  private:
    char secret_message[64];
};

message::message(char *user_message)
 {
   strcpy(secret_message, user_message);
 }

message::message(void)
 {
   strcpy(secret_message, "Hello, world");
 }

void message::show_message(void)
 {
   cout << "The message is " << secret_message << endl;
 }

void main(void)
 {
   message greeting;
   message book("Success with C++");

   greeting.show_message();
   book.show_message();
 }
```

As you can see, the first object creation that creates the *greeting* object does not specify parameters. Thus, the program invokes the *message* constructor that works with *void* or no parameters. When the program creates the *book* object, however, it passes a character string to constructor. Therefore, the program invokes the constructor that supports a string parameter. When you compile and execute this program, your screen will display the following output:

```
C:\> MULTICON  <ENTER>
The message is Hello, world
The message is Success with C++
```

Using Default Arguments with Constructor Functions

In Chapter 5 you will learn how to specify default parameter values for functions. As you will learn, if you invoke a function without specifying values for each parameter, you can specify default values. The following program, DEFPARAM.CPP, for example, uses a default parameter value for the *message* class constructor function:

```
#include <iostream.h>
#include <string.h>

class message {
  public:
    message(char *user_message = "Hello, world");
    void show_message(void);
  private:
    char secret_message[64];
};

message::message(char *user_message)
 {
   strcpy(secret_message, user_message);
 }

void message::show_message(void)
 {
   cout << "The message is " << secret_message << endl;
 }

void main(void)
 {
   message greeting;
   message book("Success with C++");

   greeting.show_message();
   book.show_message();
 }
```

A Second Way to Initialize Class Members

As you have learned, constructor functions exist to help you initialize class members when the class is created. When you examine C++ programs, you might encounter a unique member initialization technique. Assume, for example, that you want the *counter* constructor to initialize the variable *count* to 0, as shown here:

```
counter::counter(void)
 {
    counter = 0;
    // Other statements
 }
```

As it turns out, C++ lets you initialize class member variables by placing the variable name and the desired value after a colon and before the function statements, as shown here:

```
counter::counter(void) : counter(0)
 {
    // Other statements
 }
```

Variable name and initial value

The following program, CON_INIT.CPP, uses this constructor initialization format to initialize three member variables to the values 1, 2, and 3:

```
#include <iostream.h>

class object {
  public:
    object::object(void);
    void show_object(void);
  private:
    int a;
    int b;
    int c;
};

object::object(void) : a(1), b(2), c(3) { };

void object::show_object(void)
 {
   cout << "a contains: " << a << endl;
   cout << "b contains: " << b << endl;
   cout << "c contains: " << c << endl;
 }

void main(void)
 {
   object numbers;

   numbers.show_object();
 }
```

Initialize the class members

When you compile and execute this program, your screen will display the following output:

```
C:\> CON_INIT  <ENTER>
a contains 1
b contains 2
c contains 3
```

Assigning One Object's Value to Another

Just as your program assign the values of one variable of type *int* to another, there will be times when you will need to assign the value of one object to another. As you will learn, C++ makes object assignment very easy. In fact, you simply use the assignment operator (=). For example, the following statement would assign the value of one *date* object to another:

```
work_day = today;
```

Assuming that the *date* object contains *month*, *day*, and *year* members, the assignment operator automatically takes care of assigning each member for you!. As a result, the previous statement is equivalent to the following statements:

```
work_day.month = today.month;
work_day.day = today.day;
work_day.year = today.year;
```

The following program, ASSIGN.CPP, uses the assignment operator to assign one *movie* object to another:

```
#include <iostream.h>
#include <string.h>

class movie {
 public:
  void show_movie(void);
  void initialize(char *name, char *first, char *second);
 private:
  char name[64];
  char first_star[64];
  char second_star[64];
};

void movie::show_movie(void)
 {
   cout << "Movie name: " << name << endl;
```

```
   cout << "Starring: " << first_star << " and " << second_star <<
           endl << endl;
 }

void movie::initialize(char *movie_name, char *first, char *second)
 {
   strcpy(name, movie_name);
   strcpy(first_star, first);
   strcpy(second_star, second);
 }

void main(void)
 {
   movie fugitive, sleepless;
   movie date_choice;

   fugitive.initialize("The Fugitive", "Harrison Ford",
     "Tommy Lee Jones");
   sleepless.initialize("Sleepless in Seattle", "Tom Hanks",
     "Meg Ryan");

   fugitive.show_movie();
   sleepless.show_movie();

   date_choice = sleepless;
   cout << "The date choice is: ";
   date_choice.show_movie();
 }
```

As you can see, the program assigns the value of the *sleepless* object to the *date_choice* object. When you compile and execute this program, your screen will display the following output:

```
C:\> ASSIGN  <ENTER>
Movie name: The Fugitive
Starring: Harrison Ford and Tommy Lee Jones

Movie name: Sleepless in Seattle
Starring: Tom Hanks and Meg Ryan

The date choice is: Movie name: Sleepless in Seattle
Starring: Tom Hanks and Meg Ryan
```

As you work with objects, the ability to quickly assign one object's member values to another in this way will be very convenient. In Chapter 8 you will learn how to overload C++ operators. Using operator overloading, your programs can test whether two objects are equal using the following syntax:

```
if (dates_choice == sleepless)
```

In this case, your operator overload directs the program to compare each member's value to determine if the two objects are equal.

Objects and Functions

Within your programs, you can use objects with functions much as you would use structures and functions. For example, you can pass an object to a function by value or by reference (if you need to change a member's value). Likewise, functions can return objects. The following program, CLASSFUN.CPP, passes the *message* object to two different functions. The first function uses call by value to display object's member variables. The second function uses call by reference to change member variables:

```
#include <iostream.h>
#include <string.h>

class message {
  public:
    message(char *user_message, char *owner);
    void show_message(void);
    char message_owner[64];
  private:
    char secret_message[64];
};

message::message(char *user_message, char *owner)
 {
   strcpy(secret_message, user_message);
   strcpy(message_owner, owner);
 }

void message::show_message(void)
 {
   cout << "The message owner is " << message_owner << endl;
   cout << "The message is " << secret_message << endl;
 }

void some_function(message note)
 {
    note.show_message();
 }

void change_owner(message *note)
 {
```

```
   strcpy(note->message_owner, "Fred");
 }

void main(void)
 {
   message book("Success with C++", "Kris");

   some_function(book);
   change_owner(&book);
   some_function(book);
 }
```

As you can see, the program passes the *book* object to *some_function*, which in turn, displays the object's member using the *show_message* function. In this case, the function cannot display the member fields itself because the *secret_message* is private. The only way the program can access the member variable is by using a member function. Next, by passing the *book* object by reference to the *change_owner* function, the function can change the *message_owner* member. As before, the function cannot change the *secret_message* member because the member is private.

Using Objects and Functions

When your programs work with objects and functions, you can treat the objects just as you would structures. For example, if a function simply needs to access class members, you can pass the object to the function by value. However, if the function needs to change a class member, you must pass the object to the function by reference. Keep in mind that within the function, the function can only directly access the public class members. To change a private class member, the function must use a class member function.

In Chapter 10 you will learn how to pass classes to functions using C++ references, which eliminate your need to use the indirection (->) operator within the function. Instead, your programs can access the class members using the dot (.) operator.

Understanding Class Members

In each of the previous programs, the classes have used simple member types, such as members of type *int*, *float*, and so on. As your classes become more complex, your members may be arrays, structures, or even other classes or pointers to classes. For example, the following program, NESTED.CPP, nests a pointer to the *date* class inside an employee class:

```
#include <iostream.h>
#include <string.h>

class date {
  public:
    date(int month, int day, int year);
    void show_date(void);
  private:
    int month;
    int day;
    int year;
};

class employee {
  public:
    employee(char *name, int age, int month, int day, int year);
    ~employee(void);
    void show_employee(void);
  private:
    char name[64];
    int age;
    date *hire_date;        // Nested class
};

date::date(int month, int day, int year)
 {
   date::month = month;
   date::day = day;
   date::year = year;
 }

void date::show_date(void)
 {
   cout << month << '/' << day << '/' << year << endl;
 }

employee::employee(char *name, int age, int month, int day,
  int year)
 {
   strcpy(employee::name, name);
   employee::age = age;
   hire_date = new date(month, day, year);
 }

employee::~employee(void)
 {
   delete hire_date;
 }
```

```
void employee::show_employee(void)
 {
   cout << "Name: " << name << endl;
   cout << "Age: " << age << endl;
   cout << "Hire date: ";
   hire_date->show_date();
 }

void main(void)
 {
   employee manager("Joe Smith", 33, 12, 25, 1994);

   manager.show_employee();
 }
```

If you don't yet understand the memory allocation and release that occur within the *employee* constructor and destructor, don't worry, Chapter 7 examines memory allocation in detail. For now, however, simply keep in mind that your class members can be arrays, structures, or even pointers to other classes.

Working with an Array of Classes

Just as there are times when your class may contain an array of values, there may be times your program uses an array to hold multiple objects. For example, the following program, ARRAY.CPP, uses an array to hold five *date* objects:

```
#include <iostream.h>
#include <string.h>

class date {
  public:
    date(int month, int day, int year);
    date(void);
    ~date(void);
    void show_date(void);
  private:
    int month;
    int day;
    int year;
};

date::date(int month, int day, int year)
 {
```

```
   date::month = month;
   date::day = day;
   date::year = year;
   cout << "In date constructor: ";
   show_date();
 }

date::date(void)
 {
   cout << "In date constructor with no date" << endl;
 }

date::~date(void)
 {
   cout << "In date destructor: ";
   show_date();
 }

void date::show_date(void)
 {
   cout << month << '/' << day << '/' << year << endl;
 }

void main(void)
 {
    date holidays[5];
    date christmas(12, 25, 94);
    date halloween(10, 31, 94);
    date fourth(7, 4, 94);
    date new_years(1, 1, 95);
    date birthday(9, 30, 94);

    holidays[0] = christmas;
    holidays[1] = halloween;
    holidays[2] = fourth;
    holidays[3] = new_years;
    holidays[4] = birthday;
 }
```

As you can see, the program initializes the array within *main*. When you use an array of objects, you need to understand that C++ calls the constructor and destructor functions for each array element. In this case, the constructor and destructor functions simply display a message letting you know that they have been called. When you compile and execute this program, your screen will display the following output:

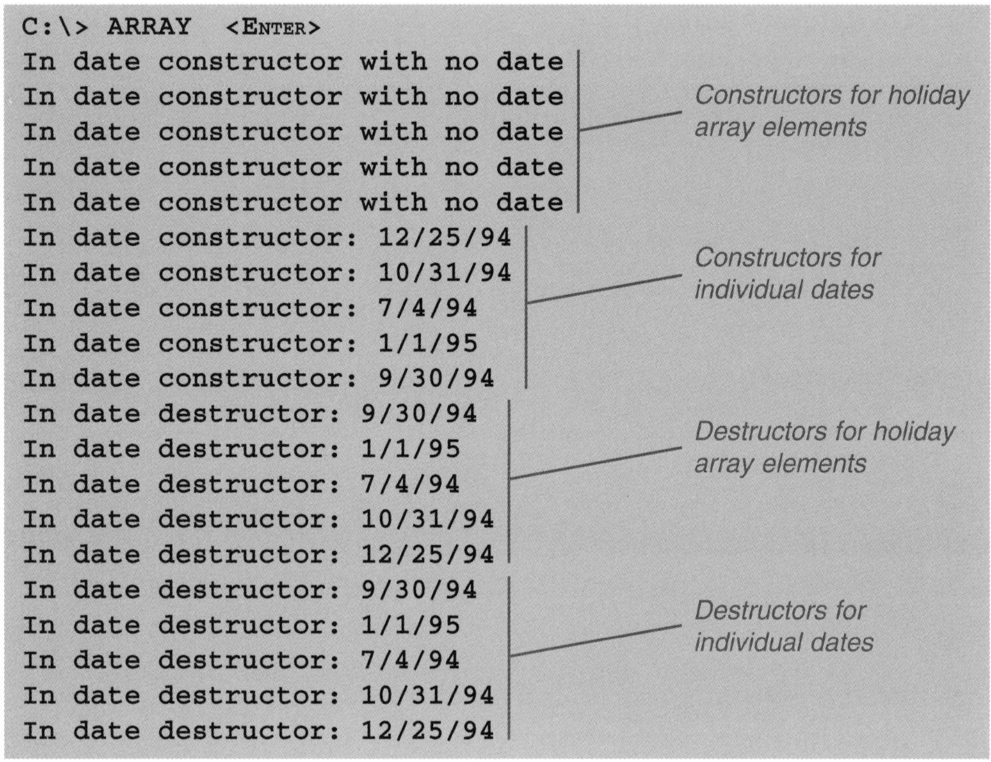

```
C:\> ARRAY  <ENTER>
In date constructor with no date
In date constructor with no date
In date constructor with no date
In date constructor with no date
In date constructor with no date
In date constructor: 12/25/94
In date constructor: 10/31/94
In date constructor: 7/4/94
In date constructor: 1/1/95
In date constructor: 9/30/94
In date destructor: 9/30/94
In date destructor: 1/1/95
In date destructor: 7/4/94
In date destructor: 10/31/94
In date destructor: 12/25/94
In date destructor: 9/30/94
In date destructor: 1/1/95
In date destructor: 7/4/94
In date destructor: 10/31/94
In date destructor: 12/25/94
```


Putting It All Together

This chapter has introduced many aspects of C++ classes. The chapters that follow will take detailed looks at the concepts and capabilities that make C++ so powerful. You will learn how to perform object-based file I/O, how to use inheritance, how to overload operators for specific classes, how templates simplify your object declarations, and much more. Before you continue, however, make sure that you have learned the following:

- ✓ An object represents a real-world entity (thing), may hold data (member variables) and has a specific set of operations (member functions) that are performed upon it.
- ✓ Conventional programming views programs as long lists of instructions that perform a specific task, whereas object-oriented programs look instead at the objects that make your program. If you think of all the functions a word processor, for example, performs, you can quickly become overwhelmed. However, if you view the word processor as a collection of distinct objects, the program becomes less intimidating.

- ✓ When you write an object (say a file object) that has certain characteristics (print, save, rename), you can reuse the code for that object in another section, or even another program, and save lots of time and effort.
- ✓ The main advantages of object use are ease of design and code reuse; increased reliability; ease of understanding; and increased abstraction, encapsulation, and information hiding.
- ✓ To create an object, you declare variables of the object type. To declare an object variable, you specify the class type, followed by the object's variable name
- ✓ The main advantages of object use are ease of design and code reuse; increased reliability; ease of understanding; and increased abstraction, encapsulation, and information hiding.
- ✓ An advantage of declaring member functions inline is that the entire class is consolidated at one location within your program code. Unfortunately, this also increases the size and complexity of your class definitions, and the code for inline functions is not shared among similar object types.
- ✓ To resolve conflicts between class members and parameters (local variables) of the same name, you use the global resolution operator (::) when you want to use the class member.
- ✓ A constructor is a function that automatically executes each time you create an object, eliminating the need for separate initialization functions, and a destructor is a function that automatically executes when an object is destroyed, usually freeing the memory allocated. Both have the same name as their class, do not return a value, and are not *void.* The destructor is preceded by a tilde (~).
- ✓ To assign the value of one object to another, simply use the assignment operator (*work_day.year = today.year;*).

Chapter 3
Getting Up to Speed with File I/O

In Chapter 1 you examined C++ I/O streams. As you learned, your compiler uses a header for the definitions of I/O stream classes, the class methods and variables. Using I/O stream manipulators and member functions, your programs performed a variety of I/O operations. This chapter examines C++ file I/O operations in detail. As you will learn your programs, using file streams, can perform I/O with insertion and extraction operators and member functions. By the time you complete this chapter, you will fully understand C++ file I/O operations, including:

- What you must specify when you open a file
- Which class types the header file FSTREAM.H defines
- How to open a file
- After you open a file, how you can perform output and input operations
- How to close a file
- How to perform formatted file output
- What an open mode specifiers is and how to control how the program opens the file
- How to test each operation's success, so that, should an operation fail, the programs can then detect and respond to the error
- What binary file operations are and what your programs need to read or write structures, arrays, or even floating-point values to files
- Sequential file operations and random file operations are
- How to position file pointers for random input and output operations

Understanding File I/O Operations

In Chapter 1, your programs performed extensive I/O operations to the I/O streams *cin* and *cout.* To use these I/O streams, your programs simply referenced the stream names. When you use these streams, C++ associates the streams to the screen and keyboard for you automatically, behind the scenes. When your programs read information from or write information to a file, however, they must specifically open the desired file, and you must specify whether you want to read from an input file or write to an output file.

To understand file streams better, you should examine the header file FSTREAM.H. Within the file you will find class definitions for *ifstream*, *ofstream*, and *fstream*. When your programs open files, you will create objects using these class types, based on the type of I/O operation you need to perform. For example, to perform file input operations, you will use the *ifstream* class. Likewise, for file output operations you use the *ofstream* class. Finally, in some cases your programs must read or write the same file. In such cases, you will use the *fstream* class.

Opening a File for Output

The simplest way to open a file is to create an object based on one of the file stream classes just discussed. For example, to open a file for output, you first declare an object of type *ofstream*, as shown here:

```
ofstream  output_file;
```

Output file stream — `ofstream`
File object name — `output_file`

Next, you can use the *open* member function to open the file, as shown here:

```
output_file.open("FILENAME.EXT");
```

open member function
Desired filename — `FILENAME.EXT`

In this case, the program will open a file named FILENAME.EXT for output. After you open a file output stream, you can use the insertion operator to write output to the file. For example, the following statement would output data to the file:

```
output_file << "This message is written to the file" << endl;
```

When your program no longer needs to use the file, the program should use the *close* member function to close the file as shown here:

```
output_file.close();
```

The following program, BOOKINFO.CPP, writes specifics about this book to a file named BOOKINFO.DAT:

```
#include <fstream.h>

void main(void)
 {
```

```
   ofstream output_file;

   output_file.open("BOOKINFO.DAT");  ——— Open the file for output

   output_file << "Title: Success with C++" << endl;     |
   output_file << "Author: Kris Jamsa" << endl;          |—— Write data
   output_file << "Publisher: Jamsa Press" << endl;      |   to the file
   output_file << "Price: $29.95" << endl;               |

   output_file.close();  ——— Close the file
 }
```

Opening a File for Output

To write output to a file, your program should create an object of type *ofstream*, which is defined within the header file FSTREAM.H. Next, your program must open the file stream using the *open* member function. Your program can then use the insertion operator to write data to the file. When your program has written its output, it should close the file using the *close* member function. The following program illustrates the steps involved to output data to a file:

```
#include <fstream.h>  ——— Include the header file FSTREAM.H

void main(void)  ——— Declare an object of type ofstream
 {
   ofstream budget;

   budget.open("BUDGET.DAT");  ——— Open the desired file

   budget << "Payroll Information" << endl;  |—— Perform the
   budget << "XYZ Corporation" << endl;      |    output operation

   budget.close();  ——— Close the file
 }
```

Using the Constructor Function to Open a File

As you have learned, your programs can open a specific file with the *open* member function. In addition to using the *open* function, your programs can use the class constructor function to open a specific file, as shown here:

```
ofstream output_file("FILENAME.EXT");
```

By using the constructor function in this way, you eliminate the **open** statement from your program. As a general rule, reducing the number of statements in your program normally improves your program's readability. As such, most programs will open files using the *ofstream* constructor function in this way.

Using Manipulators and Output Member Functions

When your programs perform file operations using file streams, you can use the output manipulators presented in Chapter 1. For example, the following program, HEXOCTDE.CPP, creates a file named HEXOCTDE.DAT that contains the decimal, octal, and hexadecimal representations of the values 1 through 255:

```
#include <fstream.h>
#include <iomanip.h>

void main(void)
 {
  int i;

  ofstream output("HEXOCTDE.DAT");

  output << "  Dec " << " Oct " << " Hex " << endl;
  for (i = 0; i <= 255; i++)
    output << dec << setw(5) << i << setw(5) << oct << i <<
              setw(5) << hex << i << endl;

  output.close();
 }
```

To use the manipulators, you must include the header file IOMANIP.H, as shown at the start of the previous program.

In addition to using the I/O stream manipulators presented in Chapter 1, your programs can also use the member functions that correspond to I/O streams. For example, the following program, ALPHABET.CPP, uses the *put* member function to write the letters of the alphabet to the file ALPHABET.DAT:

```
#include <fstream.h>

void main(void)
 {
   ofstream alphabet("ALPHABET.DAT");

   for (int letter = 'A'; letter <= 'Z'; letter++)
     alphabet.put((char)letter);
 }
```

In this case, the program uses the *put* member function to display values of type *int* in ASCII form.

The following program, ABC_INS.CPP, performs the identical processing, writing characters to the file with the insertion operator:

```
#include <fstream.h>

void main(void)
 {
   ofstream alphabet("ALPHABET.DAT");

   for (char letter = 'A'; letter <= 'Z'; letter++)
     alphabet << letter;
 }
```

Note that program uses variables of type *char*. If the program had instead used a variable of type *int*, the program would have written the numbers 65 though 90 to the file.

PERFORMING FORMATTED FILE OUTPUT OPERATIONS

If you are familiar with C, you know that you can perform formatted file output using the *fprintf* function. When you program in C++, you can use the manipulators presented in Chapter 1 to format output. For example, assume that you need to create a table similar to the following:

Name	Age	SSAN	Salary
Robert Jones	51	111-22-3333	$55000.00
Betty Smith	43	333-22-1111	$60000.00
Reggie Allen	30	111-11-0000	$9000.00

The following program, TABLE.CPP, uses the format manipulators to create the previous table:

```
#include <fstream.h>
#include <iomanip.h>

void main(void)
 {
   ofstream report("EMPLOYEE.RPT");

   struct {
     char name[64];
     int age;
     char ssan[64];
     float salary;
   } employees[]  =  {{"Robert Jones", 51, "111-22-3333", 55000.00},
                      {"Betty Smith", 43, "333-22-1111", 60000.00},
                      {"Reggie Allen", 30, "111-11-0000", 9000.00}};
```

```
   report << "Name\t\tAge\tSSAN\t\tSalary" << endl;

   for (int i = 0; i < 3; i++)
     {
       report << setiosflags(ios::left) << setw(16) <<
                 employees[i].name;
       report << setw(8) << employees[i].age << setw(16) <<
                 employees[i].ssan;
       report << setprecision(2) << setiosflags(ios::right |
                 ios::showpoint | ios::fixed);
       report << setw(8) << employees[i].salary << endl;
     }

   report.close();
}
```

Performing Formatted File Output

As your programs become more complex, you will eventually need to perform formatted output. Using the I/O stream manipulators presented in Chapter 1, such as *setw*, *setprecision*, and *setiosflags*, your programs can perform formatted file output.

Controlling How Output Files Are Opened

By default, when you open a file for output operations, an existing file with the same name one disk is overwritten. Depending on your program's purpose, there will be times when you will want the program to append information to the end of an existing file, or when you will want the file operation to fail should a file with the same name already exist on disk. To help you control how output files are opened, you can specify an open mode when you open a file. For example, the following statement opens the file BUDGET.DAT for append operations:

```
ofstream  output("BUDGET.DAT", ios::app);  // Opens the file for append operations
```

If the file BUDGET.DAT exists, the program will open the file, appending new output. If the file does not exist, the program will create the file. The following program, LOGFILE.CPP, for example, opens a file named LOGFILE.DAT for append operations. The program lets you place information into the file following a date and time entry. For example, if you want to keep track of the projects on which you work through out the day, you can invoke LOGFILE as shown here:

```
C:\> LOGFILE Formulate budget proposal   <ENTER>
C:\> LOGFILE Start research for new CD-ROM product  <ENTER>
```

Within the file LOGFILE.DAT, your entries would appear as follows:

```
C:\> TYPE LOGFILE.DAT  <ENTER>
11/09/93 17:07:38 Formulate budget proposal
11/09/93 17:07:50 Start research for new CD-ROM project
```

The following program implements LOGFILE.CPP:

```
#include <fstream.h>
#include <time.h>

void main(int argc, char **argv)
 {
   ofstream output_file("LOGFILE.DAT", ios::app);

   char time[9], date[9];

   if (argc > 1)
    {
      output_file << _strdate(date) << " " << _strtime(time);

      while (*++argv) {
        output_file << " " << *argv;
      } while (*argv);

      output_file << endl;

      output_file.close();
    }
 }
```

As you can see, the program opens the file using the *ios::app* append mode specifier. The program uses the *_strdate* and *_strtime* run-time library functions to obtain the date and time. The program then loops through the command line arguments, displaying each argument on the same line as the date and time. Finally, the program uses the *close* member function to close the file.

Special Characters and File I/O

In Chapter 1 you used special characters such as \n (newline), \t (tab), and \a (ASCII bell) with the *cout* output stream. When your programs perform file output operations, you can use each of the special characters presented in Chapter 1 within your file output operations. For example, the following program, HEX_TOO.CPP, changes the previous HEXOCTDE.CPP, program to create a hexadecimal, octal, and decimal table that uses the tab character (\t) for formatting:

```
#include <fstream.h>
#include <iomanip.h>

void main(void)
 {
  int i;

  ofstream output("HEXOCTDE.DAT");

  output << "\tDec\tOct\tHex" << endl;
  for (i = 0; i <= 255; i++)
    output << dec << '\t' << i << '\t' << oct << i << '\t' << hex <<
              i << endl;

  output.close();
 }
```

UNDERSTANDING OTHER FILE OPEN MODE SPECIFIERS

As you just learned, the *ios::app* mode specifier lets your program to open a file in append mode. As Table 3.1 shows, the *open* member function supports several different mode specifiers.

Open Mode	Purpose
ios::app	Opens an output file for append operations.
ios::ate	Opens a file open for input or output, placing the file pointer at the end of the file.
ios::in	Opens a file for input. This is the default setting for objects of type *ifstream.*
ios::out	Opens a file for output. This is the default setting for objects of type *ofstream.*
ios::nocreate	Opens an existing file. If the file does not exist, the open operation fails.
ios::noreplace	Creates a new file. If a file with the same name already exists, the open operation fails.
ios::trunc	Deletes an existing file, creating a new file.
ios::binary	Opens a file for binary read and write operations.

***Table 3.1** File open modes typically defined in a header file used for stream definitions.*

If you examine the contents of the header file used by your compiler for stream definitions, you should find an enumerated type, similar to the following, that defines the file open modes:

```
enum open_mode  {
  in    = 0x01,        // Opens a file for input
  out   = 0x02,        // Opens a file for output
  ate   = 0x04,        // Moves the file pointer to the end of the file
  app   = 0x08,        // Moves the file pointer of an output file to
                       // the end of the file
  trunc     = 0x10,    // Truncates an existing file
  nocreate = 0x20,     // Open an existing file or the operation fails
  noreplace= 0x40,     // Open a new file or fail if file exists
  binary    = 0x80     // Open a file in binary mode
 };
```

Controlling File Operations

When your programs perform file output, there will be times when you will need to write information to an existing file or times when you don't want an existing file's contents changed. In such cases, your programs can use mode specifiers within the file open operation. For example, the following statement opens a file for append operations:

```
ofstream output("FILENAME.EXT", ios::app);
```

In a similar way, the following statement uses the *ios::noreplace* flag to prevent an existing file from being overwritten:

```
ofstream output("FILENAME.EXT", ios::nopreplace);
```

Using the open mode specifiers, your programs can gain control over file open operations.

Opening Files for Input Operations

To open a file for input operations, your program normally creates an object of type *ifstream.* As is the case when you open file for output, your programs can open a file for input using the *open* function or you can use the *ifstream* constructor function. As a result, the following statements both open a file named BUDGET.DAT:

```
ifstream input_file;

input_file.open("BUDGET.DAT");
```

```
ifstream input_file("BUDGET.DAT");
```

After you open a file for input, your programs can read information using the extraction operator or member functions, as discussed next.

PERFORMING FILE INPUT OPERATIONS

After you open a file for input, you can read its contents using *ifstream* member functions or the extraction operator. When they read a file, your programs will normally start at the beginning of the file and read its contents until the end of file is encountered. To determine whether the end of a file has been reached, your programs can use *eof* member function within a *while* loop, as shown here:

```
while (! input_file.eof())
  {
    // Read and process the file
  }
```

The following program, SHOWFILE.CPP, opens the file specified as a command-line argument for input and then reads and displays its contents:

```
#include <fstream.h>

void main(int argc, char **argv)
 {
   ifstream input(argv[1]);

   if (input.fail())
     cerr << "Error opening the file: " << argv[1] << endl;
   else
    {
      while (! input.eof())
        cout.put((char)input.get());

      input.close();
    }
 }
```

*Note: The type cast, **(char)**, which is necessary in the above program to avoid an ambiguous call to the **put()** function, has been removed from the following examples in order to improve readability.*

As you can see, the program uses the following loop to read and display the file's contents a letter at a time:

```
while (! input.eof())
  cout.put(input.get());
```

The loop's statement actually combines the following two statements to read and output one character at a time:

```
letter = input.get();    // Read a character

cout.put(letter);        // Output the character
```

When the end of the file is encountered, the loop ends, and the program closes the file.

To display a file's contents, invoke the SHOWFILE program with the desired filename, as shown:

```
C:\> SHOWFILE  FILENAME.EXT  <ENTER>
```

If the file specified cannot be opened, the program detects the error using the *fail* member function:

```
if (input.fail())
  cerr << "Error opening the file: " << argv[1] << endl;
```

In a similar way, the following program, MOREFILE.CPP, reads and displays the file's contents one screenful at a time. Each time the program displays a screenful of information, the program pauses until the user presses any key:

```
#include <fstream.h>

void main(int argc, char **argv)
 {
   char line[128];

   long line_count = 0L;

   ifstream input(argv[1]);

   if (input.fail())
     cerr << "Error opening the file: " << argv[1] << endl;
   else
    {
      while (! input.eof())
        {
          input.getline(line, sizeof(line));
          cout << line << endl;

          if ((++line_count % 24) == 0)
            {
              cout << "--MOREFILE--";
              cin.get();
            }
        }
      input.close();
    }
 }
```

As you can see, the program opens the file specified by the first command-line argument for input operations. If an error occurs, the program displays an error message and ends. Otherwise, the program loops, reading the file's contents using the *getline* member function until the end of the file is encountered. As you can see, the program uses the *eof* member function to detect an end of file. Each time the program displays 24 lines of text, the program pauses until the user presses a key. The program uses the modulo operator (%) to determine when the program has displayed 24 lines. Each time the current line count divided by 24 has a remainder of 0, 24 lines have been displayed and the program pauses, prompting the user to press any key.

To display the contents of the file FILENAME.EXT one screenful at a time, you would invoke MOREFILE as shown here:

```
C:\> MOREFILE  <  FILENAME.EXT  <ENTER>
```

Opening a File for Input

To read input from a file, your program should create an object of type *ifstream*, which is defined within the header file FSTREAM.H. Next, your program must open the file stream using the *open* member function or the constructor function. Your program can then use the extraction operator to read data from the file. When your program has performed its input, it should close the file using the *close* member function. The following program illustrates the steps involved to read data from a file:

```
#include <fstream.h>                          Include the header
                                              file FSTREAM.H
void main(void)
 {
   char text[256];                            Declare an object
                                              of type ifstream
   ifstream budget("BUDGET.DAT") ;
                                              Open the desired file
   budget.getline(text, sizeof(text));        Perform the input operation

   budget.close();                            Close the file
 }
```

Testing File I/O Success

Two of the previous programs have used the *fail* member function to determine whether the program could successfully open a file for input, as shown here:

```
ifstream input(argv[1]);

if (input.fail())
  cerr << "Error opening the file: " << argv[1] << endl;
```

As you learned in Chapter 1, the *fail* member function returns the value 1 if an error occurred in the last file operation. In this case, the program only tested for errors on file open operations. As you learned in Chapter 1, however, you should test the success of each read and write operation. The following program, ASCICOPY.CPP, reads the contents of the first file specified in the command line, copying the file's contents from the first file to the second file on the command line.

```
#include <fstream.h>
#include <stdlib.h>

void main(int argc, char **argv)
 {
   ifstream source(argv[1]);

   char line[128];

   if (source.fail())
     cerr << "Error opening the file: " << argv[1] << endl;
   else
    {
      ofstream target(argv[2]);

      if (target.fail())
        cerr << "Error opening the file: " << argv[2] << endl;
      else
        {
          while (! source.eof())
            {
              source.getline(line, sizeof(line));

              if (source.good())
                {
                  target << line << endl;

                  if (target.fail())
                   {
                     cerr << "Error writing the file: " <<
                             argv[2] << endl;
                     exit(1);
                   }
                }
              else if (! source.eof())
                {
                  cerr << "Error reading the file: " <<
                          argv[1] << endl;
                  exit(1);
                }
            }
          source.close();
          target.close();
        }
    }
 }
```

As you can see, the program uses the *good* and *fail* member functions to test whether the files were successfully opened and the success of each file read and write operation. If an error occurs, the program displays an error message and uses the *exit* run-time library function to end the program. As you can see, the program first tests whether the read operation was successful. If the read operation was successful, the program writes the data to the target file.

As you can see, the program uses the *good* member function to test the success of a read operation. As it turns out, when a file read operation encounters the end of a file, the *fail* flag is set. If the program does not test for the end of the file when it tests for errors, the program might treat reaching the end of the file (a successful event) as an error. By testing with the *good* member function, the program eliminates this potential error.

Note: The ASCICOPY.CPP program will only copy ASCII text files, such as your C++ program source files. If you try to copy a binary file, such as an executable program, the copy operation will fail. To copy a binary file, you must open the file using the binary open mode, as discussed next.

The preceding programs have used the *fail* member function to determine the success and failure of different file I/O operations. However, as you read in Chapter 1, your programs can use the member functions listed in Table 3.2 to determine file I/O errors.

Member Function	Purpose
good	Returns 1if the previous operation was successful
eof	Returns 1 if the end of the file has been encountered
fail	Returns 1 if an error occurred
bad	Returns 1 if an invalid operation was performed

Table 3.2 File stream member functions for testing file errors.

As you learned in Chapter 1, your programs can test an I/O stream's success using the exclamation mark (!) operator. Thus, the following statements are identical:

```
if (input.fail())
```

```
if (! input)
```

In a similar way, the following statements both test if an I/O operation was successful:

```
if  (input.good())
```

```
if  (input)
```

Performing Binary File Operations

By default, file stream operations are performed in text mode. Depending on your program's purpose, there will be times when you need to perform binary file operations. For example, earlier in this chapter you created the program ASCICOPY.CPP, which copies one file's contents to another. As you learned, the program was unable to copy binary files such as an executable program. Here's why:

When a program reads a file in text mode, the program considers the ASCII value 26 (CTRL-Z) as the end of the file. If the program tries to read a binary file, it is very likely that the program may encounter this value midway through the file, causing the *eof* function to evaluate as true. To solve this problem, you need first to open the file in binary mode, as shown here:

```
ifstream input(argv[1], ios::binary);
```

Next, to perform the input and output operations, your programs must use *read* and *write* member functions.

```
input.read(buffer, sizeof(buffer));

output.write(buffer, sizeof(buffer));
```

For example, assume that your program needs to write 30 stock prices to a file. The following program, WRTSTOCK.CPP, writes the floating-point values to the file STOCKS.DAT using binary file operations:

```
#include <fstream.h>

void main(void)
 {
   int count;

   float price;

   ofstream stocks("STOCKS.DAT", ios::binary);

   if (stocks.fail())
     cerr << "Error opening the file STOCKS.DAT" << endl;
   else
     {
       for (count = 1; count <= 30; count++)
         {
           price = count * 100.0;

           stocks.write((char *) &price, sizeof(float));
         }

       stocks.close();
     }
 }
```

As you can see, the program invokes the *write* member function, passing to the function the address of the value to write to the file:

```
stocks.write((char *) &price, sizeof(float));
```

Data address

Size of data in bytes

If you try to display the contents of the file STOCKS.DAT using the TYPE command, the operation will fail, and your screen will display meaningless characters. Remember, the file STOCKS.DAT is a binary and not an ASCII file. To display the stock prices, you can use the program RDSTOCK.CPP, presented here:

```
#include <fstream.h>
#include <iomanip.h>

void main(void)
 {
   float price;

   ifstream stocks("STOCKS.DAT", ios::binary);

   while (! stocks.eof())
     {
       stocks.read((char *) &price, sizeof(float));

       cout << setprecision(2) << setiosflags(ios::showpoint |
               ios::fixed) << price << endl;
     }

   stocks.close();
 }
```

As you can see, the program loops, reading the floating-point values from the file until the end of the file has been encountered.

Earlier in this chapter you created the program ASCICOPY.CPP, which copies the contents of one ASCII file to another. The following program, BIN_COPY.CPP, opens the source and target files in binary mode, which lets the program copy text or binary files:

```
#include <fstream.h>
#include <stdlib.h>

void main(int argc, char **argv)
 {
   ifstream source(argv[1], ios::binary);
```

```
   char line[1];

   if (source.fail())
     cerr << "Error opening the file: " << argv[1] << endl;
   else
    {
      ofstream target(argv[2], ios::binary);

      if (target.fail())
        cerr << "Error opening the file: " << argv[2] << endl;
      else
        {
          while (! source.eof() && ! source.fail())
            {
              source.read(line, sizeof(line));

              if (source.good())
               {
                 target.write(line, sizeof(line));

                 if (target.fail())
                   {
                     cerr << "Error writing the file: " <<
                             argv[2] << endl;
                     exit(1);
                   }
               }
              else if (! source.eof())
                {
                  cerr << "Error reading the file: " <<
                          argv[1] << endl;
                  exit(1);
                }
            }
          source.close();
          target.close();
        }
    }
}
```

As you can see, the program opens both files for binary operations using the *ios::binary* mode specifier. The program then uses the *read* member function to read data from the input and the *write* member function to write data to the output file. In addition, the program uses the *fail* and *good* member functions to determine if I/O operations were successful. When the program encounters the end of the file, it closes both files.

Performing Binary File Operations

As the information your programs store in files becomes more complex, there will be times when your programs will need to read and write binary information (such as floating point data or structures). To perform a binary file operation, you must first open the file using the *ios::binary* mode specifier. For example, the following statement opens a file named OUTPUT.DAT for binary output operations:

```
ofstream  data("OUTPUT.DAT", ios::binary);
```

To perform binary input and output, your programs use the *read* and *write* member functions. To use these functions, you specify the starting address of the data buffer, as well as the number of bytes to input or output:

```
input_file.read(&data, sizeof(data));

output_file.write(&data, sizeof(data));
```

After the I/O operations are complete, your program should close the file using the *close* member function.

Be Aware of Binary File Insertion and Extraction Operations

As you just learned, to perform binary file input and output operations, your programs should use the *read* and *write* member functions. If your programs use the insertion and extraction operators to perform I/O to binary file, you may encounter unexpected errors. For example, consider the following program, BAD_OUT.CPP, which writes several floating-point values to the file BAD_DATA.DAT using the insertion operator:

```
#include <fstream.h>

void main(void)
 {
   ofstream output("BAD_DATA.DAT", ios::binary);

   output << 100.0 / 11.1;
   output << 22.0 / 7.0;
   output << 100.0 / 11.1;

   output.close();
 }
```

The following program, BAD_IN.CPP, in turn, reads the contents of the file BAD_DATA.DAT, displaying the values read and the values the file should have contained:

```
#include <fstream.h>

void main(void)
 {
   ifstream input("BAD_DATA.DAT", ios::binary);

   float value;

   input >>  value;
   cout << value << " should be " << 100.0 / 11.1 << endl;
   input >> value;
   cout << value << " should be " << 22.0 / 7.0 << endl;
   input >> value;
   cout << value << " should be " << 100.0 / 11.1 << endl;

   input.close();
 }
```

When you compile and execute this program, your screen will display output similar to that shown:

```
C:\> BAD_IN  <ENTER>
9.009001 should be 9.009001
0.142869 should be 3.14286
0.00901 should be 9.009001
```

As you can see, the values read from the file do not correspond to the values originally written to the file. Here's why. By default, when your programs perform stream output, the stream output functions convert values to their ASCII representations. As such, if your programs were to view the contents of the file BAD_DATA.DAT, using TYPE command, your screen would display the values, as shown here:

```
C:\> TYPE  BAD_DATA  <ENTER>
9.0090010.142869.009001
```

9.009001
3.14286
9.009001

When a program later reads the values from the file, the program tries to convert the ASCII values back to their floating-point form. Unfortunately, as you can see from the program's output, the conversion typically is not correct.

If you want to use the insertion and extraction operators with binary files, you must overload the operators to use the *read* and *write* functions previously discussed. Unfortunately, C++ will only let you overload the insertion and extraction operators for new data types your program defines. The following program, BIN_OPS.CPP, overloads the insertion operator for values of type *hidefloat.* By overloading the operations in this way, the program can successfully output, and later input the values from the file:

```
#include <fstream.h>

struct hidefloat { float data; };

ostream& operator <<(ostream& file, hidefloat value)
 {
   file.write((char *) &value.data, sizeof(float));
   return(file);
 }

void main(void)
 {
   ofstream output("BAD_DATA.DAT", ios::binary);

   hidefloat value;

   value.data = 100.0 / 11.1;
   output << value;

   value.data = 22.0 / 7.0;
   output << value;

   value.data = 100.0 / 11.1;
   output << value;

   output.close();
 }
```

Each time the C++ compiler encounters a value of type *hidefloat* used with the insertion operator and an output file stream, the program calls the operator function, which uses the *write* member function to write the binary value to the file.

To read the binary file, you can use the following program, READ_BIN.CPP, as shown here:

```
#include <fstream.h>

struct hidefloat { float data; };

ifstream& operator >>(ifstream& file, hidefloat *value)
 {
   file.read((char *) value, sizeof(float));
```

```
    return(file);
  }

void main(void)
  {
    ifstream input("BAD_DATA.DAT", ios::binary);

    hidefloat value;

    input >> &value;
    cout << value.data << " should be " << 100.0 / 11.1 << endl;
    input >> &value;
    cout << value.data << " should be " << 22.0 / 7.0 << endl;
    input >> &value;
    cout << value.data << " should be " << 100.0 / 11.1 << endl;

    input.close();
  }
```

In this case, when the program encounters a pointer to a variable of type *hidefloat* used within the extraction operator and an input file stream, the program calls the operator function. Because the function must change the value of a structure member, the structure address is passed to the function. As you can see, performing binary file operators using the insertion and extraction operators is possible, but can get pretty messy and difficult to understand.

Opening Files for Read and Write Operations

Each of the previous programs has opened files, either for input or output operations, but not both. When you create database programs or other file-based operations, there may be times when you will need to open the same file for both input and output operations. In such cases, your programs will create a file object of type *fstream*, as shown here:

```
fstream database("DATABASE.DAT", ios::in | ios::out);
```

When you open a file for input and output operations, your program keeps track of two file pointers—one for input operations and one for output. In many cases, the files you open for read and write operations are used for random access, as discussed next.

Random Access Files

Each of the programs presented throughout this chapter has performed *sequential* file operations, beginning at the start of the file and working toward the end of the file. *Random access* file operations, on the other hand, do not necessarily start at the beginning of the file. Instead, a program can move from one location in the file to another to perform an I/O operation. If you have opened the file for both read and write operations, your program can move the read file pointer to one location and the write file operation to another. To move a file pointer from one location in a file to another, your program can use the *seekg* and *seekp* member functions. The *seekg* function positions the file's input file pointer (*seekg* is an abbreviation for seek in preparation for a get operation). Likewise, the *seekp* function moves the file pointer for an output operation (*seekp* for put). The format of the *seekg* and *seekp* functions are as follows:

```
seekp(offset, from_position);

seekg(offset, from_position);
```

The *offset* parameter specifies a byte offset within the file. It can be a positive or negative value. The *from_position* parameter specifies the location within the file from which the offset is applied. Table 3.3 specifies enumerated values you can use to specify the *from_position* parameter.

Enumerated Value	File Position
ios::beg	From the beginning of the file
ios::cur	From the current file pointer position
ios::end	From the end of the file

Table 3.3 Enumerated values that specify random-file base positions.

The following statement, for example, moves the *put* (output) file pointer to the end of the file:

```
data_file.seekp(0, ios::end);
```

To understand random file operations better, create the program ABC.CPP, which creates the file LETTERS.DAT, which contains the letters A through H, followed by the letters O through Z:

```
#include <fstream.h>

void main(void)
 {
   ofstream output("LETTERS.DAT");

   for (char letter = 'A'; letter <= 'H'; letter++)
     output << letter;

   for (letter = 'O'; letter <= 'Z'; letter++)
     output << letter;

   output.close();
 }
```

Use the TYPE command to display the file's contents, as shown here:

```
C:\> TYPE  LETTERS.DAT  <ENTER>
ABCDEFGHOPQRSTUVWXYZ
```

Next, the following program, RANDOM.CPP, opens the file LETTERS.DAT for read and write operations. To begin, the program positions the write file pointer to the byte position that follows the letter H within the file. The program then writes the letters I through Z to the file. Next, the program positions the get file pointer to the start of the file and reads and displays the file's contents:

```
#include <fstream.h>

void main(void)
 {
   fstream letters("LETTERS.DAT", ios::in | ios::out);

   letters.seekp(8, ios::beg);

   for (char letter = 'I'; letter <= 'Z'; letter++)
     letters << letter;

   letters.seekg(0, ios::beg);

   while (! letters.eof())
     cout.put((char)letters.get());

   letters.close();
 }
```

As your programs make use of random files, there may be times when you need to determine the current position of the get and put file pointers. To obtain these values, your programs can use the *tellg* and *tellp* member functions shown here:

```
input_position = file_object.tellg();

output_position = file_object.tellp();
```

Revisiting File Open Modes

As you have learned, your programs can control how files are opened using file open mode specifiers. For example, your program can open a file in append mode using the *ios::app* specifier. The following program, ASCIAPPD.CPP, for example, appends the contents of the first file specified in the command line to the contents of the second file:

```
#include <fstream.h>
#include <stdlib.h>

void main(int argc, char **argv)
 {
   ifstream source(argv[1]);

   char line[128];

   if (source.fail())
     cerr << "Error opening the file: " << argv[1] << endl;
   else
    {
      ofstream target(argv[2], ios::app);

      if (target.fail())
        cerr << "Error opening the file: " << argv[2] << endl;
      else
        {
          while (! source.eof())
            {
              source.getline(line, sizeof(line));

              if (source.good())
                {
                  target << line << endl;

                  if (target.fail())
                   {
                     cerr << "Error writing the file: " <<
                             argv[2] << endl;
                     exit(1);
                   }
                }
              else if (! source.eof())
                {
                  cerr << "Error reading the file: " <<
                          argv[1] << endl;
                  exit(1);
                }
            }
          source.close();
          target.close();
        }
    }
 }
```

As you can see, the program opens the output file for append operations using the *ios::app* mode specifier. The program then performs standard read and write operations, using the *fail* and *good* member functions to verify each operation's success. To append the contents of the file TODAY.NTS to the file WEEKLY.NTS, invoke ASCIAPPD as follows:

```
C:\> ASCIAPPD  TODAY.NTS  WEEKLY.NTS  <ENTER>
```

Earlier in this chapter you created the file ASCICOPY.CPP, which copies the contents of one ASCII file to another. If the second file already exists, the program overwrites the existing file's contents. Depending on your program's purpose, there may be times when you don't want the program to overwrite an existing file in this way. To prevent a file from being overwritten in this way, your program can use *ios::noreplace* mode specifier, as shown here:

```
ofstream  output_file("FILENAME.EXT", ios::noreplace);
```

The following program, OVERWRIT.CPP, uses *ios::noreplace* mode specifier to prevent an existing file from being overwritten by a file copy operation.

```
#include <fstream.h>
#include <stdlib.h>

void main(int argc, char **argv)
 {
   ifstream source(argv[1], ios::binary);

   char line[1];

   if (source.fail())
     cerr << "Error opening the file: " << argv[1] << endl;
   else
    {
      ofstream target(argv[2], ios::binary | ios::noreplace);

      if (target.fail())
        cerr << "Error opening the file: " << argv[2] <<
                " or file exists" << endl;
      else
        {
          while (! source.eof() && ! source.fail())
            {
              source.read(line, sizeof(line));

              if (source.good())
               {
                 target.write(line, sizeof(line));

                 if (target.fail())
                   {
                     cerr << "Error writing the file: " <<
                             argv[2] << endl;
```

```
                    exit(1);
                  }
              }
            else if (! source.eof())
              {
                cerr << "Error reading the file: " <<
                        argv[1] << endl;
                exit(1);
              }

          }
        source.close();
        target.close();
      }
  }
}
```

As you can see, if the target file exists, the program displays an error message and ends. You might want to change this program to prompt the user, asking whether the existing file should be overwritten.

UNDERSTANDING RANDOM FILE ACCESS

Most programs perform sequential I/O, beginning at the start of the file and working to the end. Random file operations, on the other hand, let your programs perform read and write file operations from any location within your file. Before your program performs an I/O operation, the program moves the file pointer to desired location in the file using the *seekg* and *seekp* member functions. The *seekg* function moves the input (get) file pointer, while the *seekp* function moves the output (put) file pointer. Both functions specify the desired location using a byte offset from the start, end, or current file pointer position. After your program positions the file pointer, your program can perform the I/O operation using the *read* or *write* member functions.

PERFORMING PRINTER OUTPUT

Just as there are times when your programs must write their output to files, there may also be times when your programs need to perform printer output. In general, your programs can treat the printer much as they would any file, opening an output file using the device name PRN:

```
ofstream  printer("PRN");
```

For example, the following program, PRTFILE.CPP, prints the file specified by the first command-line argument:

```
#include <fstream.h>
#include <stdlib.h>

void main(int argc, char **argv)
 {
   char text[256];

   ofstream printer("PRN");

   ifstream file(argv[1]);

   if (file.fail())
     cerr << "Error opening the file " << argv[1] << endl;
   else
     {
       while (! file.eof())
         {
           file.getline(text, sizeof(text));

           if (file.good())
             {
               printer << text << endl;

               if (printer.fail())
                 {
                   cerr << "Error writing to printer" << endl;
                   exit(1);
                 }
             }
           else if (! file.eof())
             {
               cerr << "Error reading from file " <<
                       argv[1] << endl;
               exit(1);
             }
         }
     file.close();
     printer.close();
   }
 }
```

Putting It All Together

As your programs become more complex, they will regularly write information to and read information from files. As you have learned, C++ treats files very much like the I/O streams that were presented in Chapter 1. Before you continue with Chapter 4, make sure that you have learned the following:

- ✓ When you open a file, you will normally specify whether you are performing input or output operations.
- ✓ The header file FSTREAM.H defines the class types *ifstream*, *ofstream*, and *fstream*. The *ifstream* class corresponds to input files. The *ofstream* class is used for output files. Finally, the *fstream* class is used for files you open for read and write operations.
- ✓ To open a file, you can use the *open* member function or the class constructor function.
- ✓ After you open a file, you can use the insertion and extraction operators to perform output and input operations or you can perform I/O operations using member functions.
- ✓ After your program has finished using a file, it should close the file using the *close* member function.
- ✓ Using file stream manipulators such as *setw*, *setprecision*, and *setiosflags*, your programs can perform formatted file output. Likewise, you can write the special characters such as \a, \t, or even \n to the file.
- ✓ When you open a file for input or output, your programs can use open mode specifiers to control how the program opens the file. For example, using the *ios::app* mode specifier, your program can open an existing file in append mode.
- ✓ When your programs open files or perform file I/O operations, they should use member functions such as *fail* or *good* to test each operation's success. Should an operation fail, the programs can then detect and respond to the error.
- ✓ When your programs need to read or write structures, arrays, or even floating-point values to files, they need to perform binary file operations. To begin, your programs must open the file using the *ios::binary* mode. Next, they must perform I/O using *read* and *write* member functions.
- ✓ Sequential file operations begin at the start of a file and continue to the end of the file. Random file operations, on the other hand can occur at any location within a file. To position file pointers for random input operations your programs can use the *seekg* member function. Likewise, to position the file pointer for random file output, your programs can use the *seekp* function.

Chapter 4
Getting Up to Speed with Inheritance

In Chapter 2 you learned that, in the simplest sense, an object is a thing. As you define classes within your programs, you might find that classes often have similar characteristics. By taking advantage of such object relationships, you can significantly reduce the amount of code you must write. Whenever you reduce program code, you not only reduce your programming time, but you also improve your program's readability—because less code typically leads to less errors.

When you build classes based on relationships between objects, your programs take advantage of *inheritance*—a derived class can *inherit* properties from its base class. Normally, you will begin your design with a simple class, from which you will build more complex classes. For example, you might begin with an *engine* class from which you can build a *boat engine* class, a *car engine* class, or even a *motorcycle engine* class. This chapter examines C++ inheritance in detail. By the time you complete this chapter, you will learn

- What inheritance is and why it is beneficial
- How to use constructor functions with inheritance
- What the "science" of object-oriented programming is and what the "art" is
- What multiple inheritance is
- What multilevel inheritance is
- What a protected class member is and why you use one

What Inheritance Is

When you define classes within your programs, there will be many times when two or more classes share similar characteristics (members). Rather than duplicating members within each class, (and spending lots of time introducing lots of code that could have lots of errors and take lots of time to debug) you can define a base class that contains the common member functions. Next, you can build (derive) subsequent classes from the base class. When you define classes in this way, the derived classes inherit the characteristics of the base class.

LOOKING AT A SIMPLE EXAMPLE

Assume, for example, you are writing a program for a veterinarian who wants to keep records on the different types of dogs he treats and why. Specifically, the vet wants to learn how different problems affect dogs with spots versus dogs without spots. One way to approach this program would be to create two classes of dogs, one for those dogs with spots and one class for dogs without spots, as shown here:

```
class spotted_dogs {
  public:
    spotted_dogs(char *breed, int height, int weight, char *color,
       char *spot_color);
    void show_breed(void);
    void spot_info(void);
  private:
    char breed[64];
    int height;
    int weight;
    char color[64];
    char spot_color[64];
};

class unspotted_dogs {
  public:
    unspotted_dogs(char *breed, int height, int weight,
       char *color);
    void show_breed(void);
  private:
    char breed[64];
    int height;
    int weight;
    char color[64];
};
```

The following program, TWO_DOGS.CPP, uses these two classes to create spotted and unspotted dog objects:

```
#include <iostream.h>
#include <string.h>

class spotted_dogs {
  public:
    spotted_dogs(char *breed, int height, int weight, char *color,
       char *spot_color);
    void show_breed(void);
    void spot_info(void);
```

```
  private:
    char breed[64];
    int height;
    int weight;
    char color[64];
    char spot_color[64];
};

class unspotted_dogs {
  public:
    unspotted_dogs(char *breed, int height, int weight,
       char *color);
    void show_breed(void);
  private:
    char breed[64];
    int height;
    int weight;
    char color[64];
};

spotted_dogs::spotted_dogs(char *breed, int height, int weight,
   char *color, char *spot_color)
 {
   strcpy(spotted_dogs::breed, breed);
   spotted_dogs::height = height;
   spotted_dogs::weight = weight;
   strcpy(spotted_dogs::color, color);
   strcpy(spotted_dogs::spot_color, spot_color);
 }

void spotted_dogs::show_breed(void)
 {
   cout << "Breed: " << breed << endl;
   cout << "Height: " << height << " Weight: " << weight << endl;
   cout << "Color: " << color << endl;
   cout << "Spot color: " << spot_color << endl << endl;
 }

void spotted_dogs::spot_info(void)
 {
   cout << breed << " has " << spot_color << " spots" << endl <<
           endl;
 }

unspotted_dogs::unspotted_dogs(char *breed, int height, int weight,
   char *color)
 {
   strcpy(unspotted_dogs::breed, breed);
```

```
   unspotted_dogs::height = height;
   unspotted_dogs::weight = weight;
   strcpy(unspotted_dogs::color, color);
 }

void unspotted_dogs::show_breed(void)
 {
   cout << "Breed: " << breed << endl;
   cout << "Height: " << height << " Weight: " << weight << endl;
   cout << "Color: " << color << endl << endl;
 }

void main(void)
 {
   spotted_dogs happy("Dalmatian", 24, 60, "white",
     "black or brown (liver)");
   unspotted_dogs rover("Labrador Retriever", 24, 65,
     "black or yellow");

   happy.show_breed();
   happy.spot_info();

   rover.show_breed();
 }
```

As you can see, the program simply assigns values to the different member variables and then displays the values using the *show_breed* function. When you compile and execute this program, your screen will display the following output:

```
C:\> TWO_DOGS  <ENTER>
Breed: Dalmatian
Height: 24 Weight: 60
Color: white
Spot color: black or brown (liver)

Dalmatian has black or brown (liver) spots

Breed: Labrador Retriever
Height: 24 Weight: 65
Color: black or yellow
```

If you look at the two dog classes, you will find that they contain several common members. Using inheritance, you can create a class that contains the common members and then create two smaller classes that contain the members specific to spotted and unspotted dogs. To begin, create the *dogs* class, which contains the common members, as shown here:

```
class dogs {
  public:
    dogs(char *breed, int height, int weight, char *color);
    void show_breed(void);
  private:
    char breed[64];
    int height;
    int weight;
    char color[64];
};
```

Next, create two smaller classes that are based on the *dogs* class. In other words, two classes that *inherit* the characteristics (members) of the *dogs* class. The following statements, for example, create the classes using inheritance:

```
class spotted_dogs : public dogs {
  public:
    spotted_dogs(char *breed, int height, int weight, char *color,
       char *spot_color);
    void show_breed(void);
    void spot_info(void);
  private:
    char spot_color[64];
};

class unspotted_dogs : public dogs {
  public:
    unspotted_dogs(char *breed, int height, int weight,
       char *color);
};
```

Note the colon to the right of the class name that is followed by **public dogs**. The colon informs C++ that the class inherits the characteristics of the class that follows:

```
                                    Derived class
class spotted_dogs : public dogs {
                                    Base class
```

As you can see, the *spotted_dogs* class adds new member functions and a member variable. The *unspotted_dogs* class, however, does not add any new members. As it turns out, unspotted dogs in this program, don't require any other members than those provided by the *dogs* base class. The program could simply have used the *dogs* class each time it wanted to create an unspotted dog.

However, to improve the program's readability (to let the program work in terms of spotted and unspotted dogs, as opposed to spotted dogs and dogs), the program derived the *unspotted_dogs* class.

Understanding Class Inheritance

When you define classes within your programs, there will be many times when two or more classes share similar characteristics (members). Rather than duplicating members within each class, you can define a *base* class that contains the common member functions. Next, you can build (derive) subsequent classes from the base class. When you define classes in this way, the *derived* classes inherit the characteristics of the base class. Assume, for example, you create the following *vehicle* class:

```
class vehicle {
   public:
      vehicle(char *name, int wheels, int engine);
      void show_vehicle(void);
   private:
      char name[64];
      int wheels;
      int engine;
 };
```

Using inheritance, you can then declare a *motorcycle* class as follows:

```
class motorcycle : public vehicle {
   public:
      motorcycle(char *name, int wheels, int engine, int seats);
      void show_cycle(void);
   private:
      int seats;
 };
```

In a similar way, you can declare an *automobile* class as follows:

```
class automobile: public vehicle {
   public:
      automobile(char *name, int wheels, int engine, int doors);
      void show_auto(void);
   private:
      int doors;
 };
```

In this case, the *motorcycle* and *automobile* classes both inherit the characteristics defined within the *vehicle* class.

Using Constructor Functions with Inheritance

As you learned in Chapter 2, constructor functions let your programs initialize class member variables. When your programs use inheritance, you still use constructors to initialize classes. The only difference, however, is that the derived class constructor must invoke the base class constructor. The following function implements the *dogs* base class constructor function:

```
dogs::dogs(char *breed, int height, int weight, char *color)
 {
   strcpy(dogs::breed, breed);
   dogs::height = height;
   dogs::weight = weight;
   strcpy(dogs::color, color);
 }
```

The derived class constructor functions use a syntax similar to the class definition, with a colon followed by the base-class constructor function:


```
spotted_dogs::spotted_dogs(char *breed, int height, int weight,
   char *color, char *spot_color) : dogs (breed, height, weight,
   color)
 {
   strcpy(spotted_dogs::spot_color, spot_color);
 }

unspotted_dogs::unspotted_dogs(char *breed, int height, int weight,
   char *color) : dogs(breed, height, weight, color)
 {
    // Do nothing--base class constructor initialized members
 }
```

As you can see, the base class constructor invocation uses parameter names identical to those passed to the derived class function:


```
spotted_dogs::spotted_dogs(char *breed, int height, int weight,
   char *color, char *spot_color) : dogs (breed, height, weight,
   color)
 {
   strcpy(spotted_dogs::spot_color, spot_color);
 }

unspotted_dogs::unspotted_dogs(char *breed, int height, int weight,
   char *color) : dogs(breed, height, weight, color)
 {
    // Do nothing--base class constructor initialized members
 }
```

When your program invokes the *spotted_dogs* constructor, C++ will first automatically invoke the *dog* class constructor. As you will learn, the base class constructor function is always invoked before the derived class constructor. In this way, base class members are correctly initialized and memory for base class buffers correctly allocated before the derived class is referenced.

If you examine the constructor function for the *spotted_dogs* class, you will find that the function initializes the member variable *spot_color*. In the case of the *unspotted_dogs* constructor, however, the function has no values to assign (other than those handled by the base class constructor).

The following program, NEW_DOGS.CPP, uses inheritance to create the spotted and unspotted dog classes:

```
#include <iostream.h>
#include <string.h>

class dogs {
  public:
    dogs(char *breed, int height, int weight, char *color);
    void show_breed(void);
  private:
    char breed[64];
    int height;
    int weight;
    char color[64];
};

class spotted_dogs : public dogs {
  public:
    spotted_dogs(char *breed, int height, int weight, char *color,
       char *spot_color);
    void show_breed(void);
    void spot_info(void);
  private:
    char spot_color[64];
};

class unspotted_dogs : public dogs {
  public:
    unspotted_dogs(char *breed, int height, int weight,
       char *color);
};

dogs::dogs(char *breed, int height, int weight, char *color)
 {
   strcpy(dogs::breed, breed);
   dogs::height = height;
```

```
    dogs::weight = weight;
    strcpy(dogs::color, color);
  }

spotted_dogs::spotted_dogs(char *breed, int height, int weight,
    char *color, char *spot_color) : dogs (breed, height, weight,
    color)
  {
    strcpy(spotted_dogs::spot_color, spot_color);
  }

unspotted_dogs::unspotted_dogs(char *breed, int height, int weight,
    char *color) : dogs(breed, height, weight, color)
  {
     // Do nothing--base class constructor initialized members
  }

void dogs::show_breed(void)
  {
    cout << "Breed: " << breed << endl;
    cout << "Height: " << height << " Weight: " << weight << endl;
    cout << "Color: " << color << endl;
  }

void spotted_dogs::show_breed(void)
  {
    dogs::show_breed();
    cout << "Spot color: " << spot_color << endl << endl;
  }

void spotted_dogs::spot_info(void)
  {
    cout << "This breed has " << spot_color << " spots" << endl <<
            endl;
  }

void main(void)
  {
    spotted_dogs happy("Dalmatian", 24, 60, "white",
       "black or brown (liver)");
    unspotted_dogs rover("Labrador Retriever", 24, 65,
       "black or yellow");

    happy.show_breed();
    happy.spot_info();

    rover.show_breed();
  }
```

Because the *spotted_dogs* class contains the *spot_color* member, the class uses its own *show_breed* member function. Using the global resolution operator (::), the function first invokes the base-class *show_breed* function to display the member variables common to all dogs. Next, the function displays its member variable:

```
void spotted_dogs::show_breed(void)      Invoke the base class function
 {                                        Display spot_color member variable
   dogs::show_breed();
   cout << "Spot color: " << spot_color << endl << endl;
 }
```

When you compile and execute this program, your screen will display the following output:

```
C:\> NEW_DOGS  <ENTER>
Breed: Dalmatian
Height: 24 Weight: 60
Color: white
Spot color: black or brown (liver)
This breed has black or brown (liver) spots

Breed: Labrador Retriever
Height: 24 Weight: 65
Color: black or yellow
```

Note that the program's output has changed the following line of output:

```
Dalmatian has black or brown (liver) spots

This breed has black or brown (liver) spots
```

The program uses the *spot_info* function to display the message, like this:

```
void spotted_dogs::spot_info(void)
 {
   cout << "This breed has " << spot_color << " spots" << endl <<
             endl;
 }
```

In this case, the function cannot use the *dogs* class breed member that contains the actual breed name (Dalmatian), because the member is private to the *dogs* class. The only way a derived class can access base class private members is using a base class member function, such as *show_breed.* One way to solve this problem is to make the member variable *breed* a public member within the *dogs* class. Second, as you will learn later in this chapter, you can make the variable a *protected* class member, which only allows direct access to the variable by base or derived class objects.

Walking Through an Example

To help you better understand how and when constructor and destructor functions are invoked when you use inheritance, the following program, GENERIC.CPP, defines two classes named *base* and *derived*. Within each constructor and destructor, the program displays a message that identifies the current function:

```
#include <iostream.h>
#include <string.h>

class base {
  public:
    base(char *base_message);
    ~base(void);
  private:
    char base_message[64];
};

class derived : public base {
  public:
    derived(char *derived_message);
    ~derived(void);
  private:
    char derived_message[64];
};

base::base(char *message)
 {
   strcpy(base_message, message);
   cout << "In base class constructor: " << message << endl;
 }

base::~base(void)
 {
   cout << "In base class destructor: " << base_message << endl;
 }

derived::derived(char *message) : base("Hello, base")
 {
   strcpy(derived_message, message);
   cout << "In derived class constructor: " << message << endl;
 }

derived::~derived(void)
 {
   cout << "In derived class destructor: " << derived_message <<
           endl;
 }
```

```
void main(void)
 {
   derived object("Hello, world");
 }
```

When you compile and execute this program, your screen will display the following output:

```
C:\> GENERIC  <ENTER>
In base class constructor: Hello, base
In derived class constructor: Hello, world
In derived class destructor: Hello, world
In base class destructor: Hello, base
```

As you can see, when the program instantiates the derived object, the base class function is invoked first, followed then by the derived class constructor. When the object is destroyed, however, the opposite calling sequence is performed, with the program first invoking the derived class destructor function followed by base class destructor.

UNDERSTANDING THE PUBLIC KEYWORD

When you create a derived class, you specify the derived class name, followed by a colon and the base-class name, as shown here:

```
class derived : public base {
   // Members
 };
```

As you can see, the statement uses the *public* keyword. When you use the *public* keyword in this way, the base class *public* members are considered *public* within the derived class. Likewise, *protected* base-class members are treated as *protected* members within the derived class. Most of your programs will use the *public* keyword in this way. If your class definitions use the *private* keyword instead, base class *public* and *protected* members are treated as *private* members within the derived class.

LOOKING AT ANOTHER EXAMPLE

When you think about a disk drive, several attributes, such as storage capacity; disk geometry (number of sides, tracks, sectors, and so on); and transfer speeds quickly come to mind. As Figure 4.1 shows, hard disks and floppy disks each inherit these characteristics, while introducing new considerations, such as interface type (SCSI or IDE) or a write-protection mechanism.

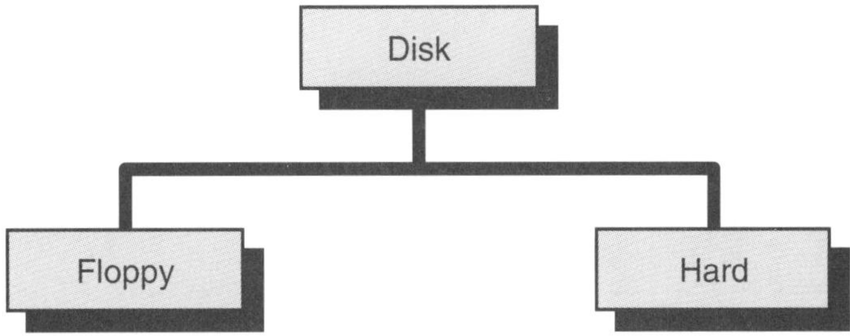

Figure 4.1 The relationship between disk types.

The following program, DISKCLAS.CPP, creates a base class named *disk*, as shown here:

```
class disk {
  public:
    disk(char *name, int sides, int tracks, int sectors_per_track,
      int bytes_per_sector);
    void show_disk(void);
  private:
    char name[64];
    int sides;
    int tracks;
    int sectors_per_track;
    int bytes_per_sector;
    long capacity;
};
```

Next, the program derives the *hard_disk* and *floppy_disk* classes, as follows:

```
class floppy_disk : public disk {
  public:
    floppy_disk(char *name, int sides, int tracks,
      int sectors_per_track, int bytes_per_sector, int state);
    void set_write_protect(int state);
    void show_floppy(void);
  private:
    int write_protect_state;
};

class hard_disk : public disk {
  public:
    hard_disk(char *name, int sides, int tracks,
      int sectors_per_track, int bytes_per_sector,
      char *controller_type);
    void show_hard_disk(void);
  private:
    char controller_type[64];
};
```

The following statements implement DISKCLAS.CPP:

```
#include <iostream.h>
#include <string.h>

class disk {
  public:
    disk(char *name, int sides, int tracks, int sectors_per_track,
      int bytes_per_sector);
    void show_disk(void);
  private:
    char name[64];
    int sides;
    int tracks;
    int sectors_per_track;
    int bytes_per_sector;
    long capacity;
};

class floppy_disk : public disk {
  public:
    floppy_disk(char *name, int sides, int tracks,
      int sectors_per_track, int bytes_per_sector, int state);
    void set_write_protect(int state);
    void show_floppy(void);
  private:
    int write_protect_state;
};

class hard_disk : public disk {
  public:
    hard_disk(char *name, int sides, int tracks,
      int sectors_per_track, int bytes_per_sector,
      char *controller_type);
    void show_hard_disk(void);
  private:
    char controller_type[64];
};

disk::disk(char *name, int sides, int tracks, int sectors_per_track,
   int bytes_per_sector)
 {
   strcpy(disk::name, name);
   disk::sides = sides;
   disk::tracks = tracks;
   disk::sectors_per_track = sectors_per_track;
   disk::bytes_per_sector = bytes_per_sector;
```

```
   capacity = (long) sides * (long) tracks;
   capacity *= (long) sectors_per_track * (long) bytes_per_sector;
 }

void disk::show_disk(void)
 {
   cout << "Disk name: " << name << endl;
   cout << "Sides: " << sides << " Tracks: " << tracks << endl;
   cout << "Sectors per track: " << sectors_per_track << endl;
   cout << "Bytes per sector: " << bytes_per_sector << endl;
   cout << "Capacity: " << capacity << " bytes" << endl;
 }

floppy_disk::floppy_disk(char *name, int sides, int tracks,
   int sectors_per_track, int bytes_per_sector, int state) :
   disk (name, sides, tracks, sectors_per_track, bytes_per_sector)
 {
   write_protect_state = state;
 }

void floppy_disk::show_floppy(void)
 {
   show_disk();
   cout << "Write-protect is: " << ((write_protect_state) ?
           "On": "Off") << endl << endl;
 }

hard_disk::hard_disk(char *name, int sides, int tracks,
   int sectors_per_track, int bytes_per_sector, char *controller) :
   disk(name, sides, tracks, sectors_per_track, bytes_per_sector)
 {
    strcpy(controller_type, controller);
 }

void hard_disk::show_hard_disk(void)
 {
    show_disk();
    cout << "Controller type: " << controller_type << endl << endl;
 }

void main(void)
 {
   hard_disk ide_drive("Hard disk", 4, 615, 80, 512, "IDE");
   floppy_disk high_density("Floppy disk", 2, 80, 18, 512, 1);

   ide_drive.show_hard_disk();
   high_density.show_floppy();
 }
```

When you compile and execute this program, your screen will display the following output:

```
C:\> DISKCLAS  <ENTER>
Disk name: Hard disk
Sides: 4 Tracks: 615
Sectors per track: 80
Bytes per sector: 512
Capacity: 100761600 bytes
Controller type: IDE

Disk name: Floppy disk
Sides: 2 Tracks: 80
Sectors per track: 18
Bytes per sector: 512
Capacity: 1474560 bytes
Write-protect is: On
```

A Last Example of Single-Level Inheritance

By now, you should be feeling more comfortable with the syntax for base and derived classes. The syntax is the "science" of object-oriented programming. The "art" of such programming begins when you must determine which attributes you should place in base classes and which attributes belong to derived classes. The best way to master the "art" of object-oriented design is through practice and refinement. So, let's walk through an example. Assume that you must create an employee database for a large company. The company has salaried managers, permanent hourly employees, and temporary hourly employees. Assume that for each employee type, your program must track the following information:

Salaried	Hourly Permanent	Hourly Temporary
name	name	name
home phone	home phone	home phone
office phone	office phone	office phone
salary level	wage	wage
bonus level		
reports to	reports to	reports to
assistant		

Your first "cut" at designing the base class is to select the common attributes, as shown here:

Salaried	Hourly Permanent	Hourly Temporary
name	name	name
home phone	home phone	home phone
office phone	office phone	office phone
salary level	wage	wage
bonus level		
reports to	reports to	reports to
assistant		

Using the common attributes, you can create the *employee* base class, as shown here:

```
class employee {
  public:
    employee(char *name, char *home_phone, char *office_phone,
       char *reports_to);
    void show_employee(void);
  private:
    char name[64];
    char home_phone[64];
    char office_phone[64];
    char reports_to[64];
};
```

Next, by removing the common attributes, your derived classes become the following:

```
class salaried : public employee {
  public:
    salaried(char *name, char *home_phone, char *office_phone,
       char *reports_to, float salary, float bonus_level,
       char *assistant);
    void show_salaried(void);
  private:
    float salary;
    float bonus_level;
    char assistant[64];
};

class hourly : public employee {
  public:
    hourly(char *name, char *home_phone, char *office_phone,
       char *reports_to, float wage);
    void show_hourly(void);
  private:
    float wage;
};
```

```
class temporary : public employee {
  public:
    temporary(char *name, char *home_phone, char *office_phone,
       char *reports_to, float wage);
    void show_temporary(void);
  private:
    float wage;
};
```

If you examine the *hourly* and *temporary* classes, you will find that the members are essentially identical. Here's where the art, programmer preference, and other such factors come into play.

Depending on how your program works with the objects, you might simply create a flag member variable within the *hourly* class that specifies whether an object corresponds to a permanent or temporary worker, as shown here:

```
enum worker_type { permanent, temporary };

class hourly : public employee {
  public:
    temporary(char *name, char *home_phone, char *office_phone,
       char *reports_to, float wage, worker_type flag);
    void show_temporary(void);
  private:
    float wage;
    worker_type flag;
};
```

Within the class member functions, your code can examine the flag to determine the correct type.

In some cases, however, there may be times when you want to restrict specific program operations to temporary employees and other operations to permanent employees. In such cases, however, the worker objects are no longer really the same—your program treats the objects differently. As such, your program should use two distinct class types. In this way, your program's readability will improve. For example, the following code fragments illustrate a function that restricts operations to temporary hourly workers:

```
float temporary::pay_overtime(void)
  {
       // Statements
  }
```

```
float hourly::pay_overtime(void)
   {
      if (flag == temporary)
         {
            // Statements
         }
   }
```

By simply examining the function header of the leftmost *pay_overtime* function, another programmer who is reading your code knows quickly that the function applies only to temporary worker objects. In the case of the rightmost function, the programmer must have access to the source code statements (the *if* statement in particular) to determine that the function only affects permanent objects.

The following program, WORKERS.CPP, uses the *employee*, *salaried*, *permanent*, and *temporary* classes:

```
#include <iostream.h>
#include <string.h>

class employee {
  public:
    employee(char *name, char *home_phone, char *office_phone,
       char *reports_to);
    void show_employee(void);
  private:
    char name[64];
    char home_phone[64];
    char office_phone[64];
    char reports_to[64];
};

class salaried : public employee {
  public:
    salaried(char *name, char *home_phone, char *office_phone,
       char *reports_to, float salary, float bonus_level,
       char *assistant);
    void show_salaried(void);
  private:
    float salary;
    float bonus_level;
    char assistant[64];
};

class hourly : public employee {
  public:
    hourly(char *name, char *home_phone, char *office_phone,
       char *reports_to, float wage);
    void show_hourly(void);
  private:
    float wage;
};
```

```
class temporary : public employee {
  public:
    temporary(char *name, char *home_phone, char *office_phone,
       char *reports_to, float wage);
    void show_temporary(void);
  private:
    float wage;
};

employee::employee(char *name, char *home_phone, char *office_phone,
   char *reports_to)
 {
   strcpy(employee::name, name);
   strcpy(employee::home_phone, home_phone);
   strcpy(employee::office_phone, office_phone);
   strcpy(employee::reports_to, reports_to);
 }

void employee::show_employee(void)
 {
   cout << "Name: " << name << endl;
   cout << "Home phone: " << home_phone << endl;
   cout << "Office phone: " << office_phone << endl;
   cout << "Reports to: " << reports_to << endl;
 }

salaried::salaried(char *name, char *home_phone, char *office_phone,
   char *reports_to, float salary, float bonus_level,
   char *assistant) : employee(name, home_phone, office_phone,
   reports_to)
 {
   salaried::salary = salary;
   salaried::bonus_level = bonus_level;
   strcpy(salaried::assistant, assistant);
 }

void salaried::show_salaried(void)
 {
    show_employee();
    cout << "Salary: $" << salary << endl;
    cout << "Bonus level: $" << bonus_level << endl;
    cout << "Assistant: " << assistant << endl;
 }

hourly::hourly(char *name, char *home_phone, char *office_phone,
   char *reports_to, float wage) : employee(name, home_phone,
   office_phone, reports_to)
 {
    hourly::wage = wage;
 }
```

```
void hourly::show_hourly(void)
 {
    show_employee();
    cout << "Wage: $" << wage << endl;
 }

temporary::temporary(char *name, char *home_phone,
   char *office_phone, char *reports_to, float wage) :
   employee(name, home_phone, office_phone, reports_to)
 {
    temporary::wage = wage;
 }

void temporary::show_temporary(void)
 {
    show_employee();
    cout << "Wage: $" << wage << endl;
 }

void main(void)
 {
   salaried top_boss("Joe Smith", "555-1111", "555-1112",
      "Mark Jones", 30000.0, 10000.0, "Alicia Jones");

   hourly typist("David Kline", "555-2222", "555-2223",
      "John Martin", 4.50);

   temporary receptionist("Mary Scott", "555-3333", "555-3334",
      "Doris Davis", 4.00);

   top_boss.show_salaried();

   cout << endl << endl;

   typist.show_hourly();

   cout << endl << endl;

   receptionist.show_temporary();
 }
```

When you compile and execute this program, your screen will display the following output:

```
C:\> WORKERS  <ENTER>
Name: Joe Smith
Home phone: 555-1111
Office phone: 555-1112
Reports to: Mark Jones
```

```
Salary: $30000
Bonus level: $10000
Assistant: Alicia Jones

Name: David Kline
Home phone: 555-2222
Office phone: 555-2223
Reports to: John Martin
Wage: $4.5

Name: Mary Scott
Home phone: 555-3333
Office phone: 555-3334
Reports to: Doris Davis
Wage: $4
```

PROTOTYPE, REVISE, AND THEN FINALIZE

Object-oriented programming is an art, as well as a science. After you have written one or two programs, the science of object-oriented programming becomes fairly straightforward. The art of program design is assigning the correct class member to base and derived classes.

As a rule, consider your first class design and member assignments as a prototype (a first cut). As you code, continually review and update your member assignments. In most cases, by regularly spending time reviewing your object use, you will eliminate a considerable amount of code rewriting you must perform at a later time because your original design was not quite right.

In general, if you find yourself passing parameters to functions that contain additional information about an object, you need to rework your design. In such cases, stop and fix your design. If you instead "kludge" your code, you open the door for errors and increase your program's difficulty of understanding.

UNDERSTANDING MULTIPLE INHERITANCE

When you design your classes, there may be times when you have classes that use the characteristics of two or more base classes. Multiple inheritance is the use of two or more base classes to derive a class. For example, assume that you declared the following *book* and *disk* classes:

```
class book {
  public:
    book(char *title, char *author, int pages);
    void show_book(void);
  private:
    char title[64];
    char author[64];
    int pages;
};

class disk {
  public:
    disk(float capacity);
    void show_disk(void);
  private:
    float capacity;
};

class bundle : public book, public disk {
  public:
    bundle(char *title, char *author, int pages, float capacity,
       float price);
    void show_bundle(void);
  private:
    float price;
};
```

Next, you can create a class named *bundle* that is a book and disk combination, similar to this product:

```
class bundle : public book, public disk {
  public:
    bundle(char *title, char *author, int pages, float capacity,
       float price);
    void show_bundle(void);
  private:
    float price;
};
```

In this case, *bundle* is the derived class, and the *disk* and *book* are the base classes:

```
class bundle : public book, public disk {
```


When a class is derived from two or more classes, you separate the base classes using commas, as shown. When you declare the derived class constructor function, you specify the base class constructor in a similar way:

Derived class constructor

```
bundle::bundle(char *title, char *author, int pages, float capacity,
float price) : book(title, author, pages) , disk(capacity)
 {
   bundle::price = price;
 }
```

Base class constructors

In this case, C++ will first invoke the *book* constructor, followed by the *disk* function and finally the *bundle* function.

The following program, MULT_INH.CPP, illustrates multiple inheritance, creating the *bundle* class. In general, the program simply invokes the constructor and destructor functions, which in turn, display messages so you can view the execution flow:

```
#include <iostream.h>
#include <string.h>

class book {
  public:
    book(char *title, char *author, int pages);
    void show_book(void);
  private:
    char title[64];
    char author[64];
    int pages;
};

class disk {
  public:
    disk(float capacity);
    void show_disk(void);
  private:
    float capacity;
};

class bundle : public book, public disk {
  public:
    bundle(char *title, char *author, int pages, float capacity,
       float price);
    void show_bundle(void);
  private:
    float price;
};

book::book(char *title, char *author, int pages)
 {
   strcpy(book::title, title);
   strcpy(book::author, author);
   book::pages = pages;
 }
```

```
void book::show_book(void)
 {
   cout << "Title: " << title << endl;
   cout << "Author: " << author << endl;
   cout << "Pages: " << pages << endl;
 }

disk::disk(float capacity)
 {
   disk::capacity = capacity;
 }

void disk::show_disk(void)
 {
   cout << "Capacity: " << capacity << "Mb" << endl;
 }

bundle::bundle(char *title, char *author, int pages, float capacity,
   float price) : book(title, author, pages) , disk(capacity)
 {
   bundle::price = price;
 }

void bundle::show_bundle(void)
 {
   show_book();
   show_disk();
   cout << "Price: $" << price << endl;
 }

void main(void)
 {
   bundle this_book("Jamsa's 1001 C/C++ Tips", "Jamsa", 896,
      1.44, 39.95);

     this_book.show_bundle();
 }
```

When you compile and execute this program, your screen will display the following output:

```
C:\> MULT_INH  <ENTER>
Title: Jamsa's 1001 C/C++ Tips
Author: Jamsa
Pages: 896
Capacity: 1.44Mb
Price: $39.95
```

As you can see, the program invokes the *book*, *disk*, and *bundle* class constructor functions in order.

Understanding Multiple Inheritance

Multiple inheritance is the use of two or more base classes to derive a new class. When you derive a class using two or more base classes, you specify the derived class name, followed by the base classes, as shown here:

```
class derived : public base1, public base2;
  {
     // members
  }
```

Note the use of the *public* keyword that precedes each base class. The *public* keyword lets derived classes treat base class *public* and *protected* members as derived class *public* and *protected* members. When you define the derived class constructor, you specify the base class constructors, as shown here:

```
derived::derived(int a, int b): base1(a), base2(b)
  {
     // Statements
  }
```

In this case, when your program invokes the *derived* class constructor, C++ will first invoke the *base1* class constructor, followed by the *base2* constructor.

Understanding Multilevel Inheritance

As you have learned, multiple inheritance is the use of two or more base classes to derive a new class. *Multilevel inheritance*, on the other hand, occurs when you derive a class from a base class that is actually derived from another class. For example, Figure 4.2 illustrates the *manager* class, which is based on the *worker* class, which in turn, is based on the *person* class.

To create these classes, you begin with the *person* class, shown here:

```
class person {
  public:
    person(char *name, int age);
    void show_person(void);
  private:
    char name[64];
    int age;
};
```

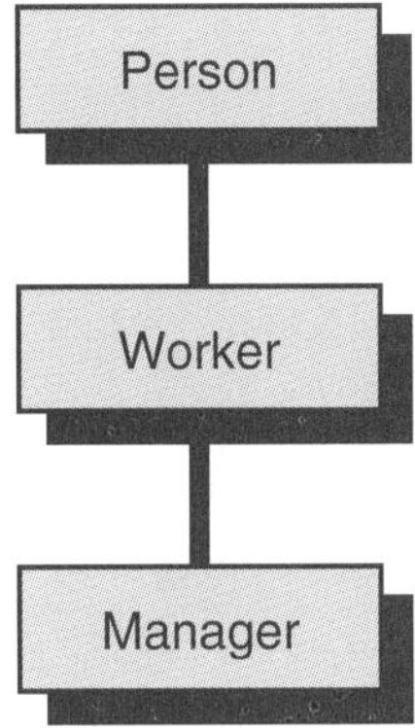

Figure 4.2 A multilevel inheritance.

Next, you define the *worker* class:

```
class worker : public person {
  public:
    worker(char *name, int age, char *phone, float wage);
    void show_worker(void);
  private:
    char phone[64];
    float wage;
};
```

Finally, you derive the *manager* class as, shown here:

```
class manager : public worker {
  public:
    manager(char *name, int age, char *phone, float wage,
       char *office);
    void show_manager(void);
  private:
    char office[64];
};
```

The following program, MULTILVL.CPP, illustrates the use of multilevel inheritance:

```
#include <iostream.h>
#include <string.h>

class person {
  public:
    person(char *name, int age);
```

```
    void show_person(void);
  private:
    char name[64];
    int age;
};

class worker : public person {
  public:
    worker(char *name, int age, char *phone, float wage);
    void show_worker(void);
  private:
    char phone[64];
    float wage;
};

class manager : public worker {
  public:
    manager(char *name, int age, char *phone, float wage,
       char *office);
    void show_manager(void);
  private:
    char office[64];
};

person::person(char *name, int age)
 {
   strcpy(person::name, name);
   person::age = age;
 }

void person::show_person(void)
 {
   cout << endl << "Name: " << name << endl;
   cout << "Age: " << age << endl;
 }
worker::worker(char *name, int age, char *phone, float wage) :
   person(name, age)
 {
   strcpy(worker::phone, phone);
   worker::wage = wage;
 }

void worker::show_worker(void)
 {
   show_person();
   cout << "Phone: " << phone << endl;
 }
```

```
manager::manager(char *name, int age, char *phone, float wage,
   char *office) : worker(name, age, phone, wage)
 {
   strcpy(manager::office, office);
 }

void manager::show_manager(void)
 {
   show_worker();
   cout << "Office: " << office << endl;
 }

void main(void)
 {
   worker security("Ken Smith", 43, "555-1212", 4.50);

   manager boss("Betty Louis", 30, "555-2121", 12.50, "Room 3B");

   security.show_worker();

   boss.show_manager();
 }
```

When you compile and execute this program, your screen will display the following output:

```
C:\> MULTILVL  <ENTER>
Name: Ken Smith
Age: 43
Phone: 555-1212

Name: Betty Louis
Age: 30
Phone: 555-2121
Office: Room 3B
```

Understanding Protected Members

As you learned in Chapter 2, you can declare class member functions as *public* or *private*. When you declare a member as *public*, the member is accessible throughout your program (when the object is in scope—see Chapter 9). If you declare a member as *private*, however, the member can only be accessed using class member functions. In the programs shown in this chapter, derived classes have only accessed base class public members. For example, the following program, INPUBLIC.CPP, illustrates how a derived class accesses base class public members. In this case, the program can access the base class public member *base_number* but cannot access the private member *base_message*:

```
#include <iostream.h>
#include <string.h>

class base {
  public:
    base(char *base_message, int number);
    int base_number;
  private:
    char base_message[64];
};

class derived : public base {
  public:
    derived(char *derived_message, int number);
  private:
    char derived_message[64];
};

base::base(char *message, int number)
 {
   strcpy(base_message, message);
   base_number = number;
 }

derived::derived(char *message, int number) : base("Base message",
   number)
 {
   strcpy(derived_message, message);
 }

void main(void)
 {
   derived object("Hello, world", 1001 );

   cout << "The base number is " << object.base_number << endl;
 }
```

When you compile and execute this program, your screen will display the following output:

```
C:\> INPUBLIC  <ENTER>
The base number is 1001
```

Experiment with this program by changing it to reference the member *base_message*, instead of *base_number*, within *main*. Because the private member is not accessible outside of the class, even derived objects cannot access the member.

Depending on your program's purpose, there may be times when you will want to grant derived class objects with direct access to base class members, while still protecting those members from the rest of program. In such cases, your programs can use protected members. A *protected* class member can be directly accessed by derived classes, but cannot be accessed otherwise. The following program, PROTECT.CPP, illustrate the use of protected class members:

```
#include <iostream.h>
#include <string.h>

class base {
  public:
    base(char *base_message, int number);
  protected:
    int base_number;
  private:
    char base_message[64];
};

class derived : public base {
  public:
    derived(char *derived_message, int number);
    void show_number(void);
  private:
    char derived_message[64];
};

base::base(char *message, int number)
 {
   strcpy(base_message, message);
   base_number = number;
 }

derived::derived(char *message, int number) : base("Base message",
   number)
 {
   strcpy(derived_message, message);
 }

void derived::show_number(void)
 {
   cout << "The base-class number is " << base_number << endl;
 }

void main(void)
 {
   derived object("Hello, world", 1001 );

   object.show_number();
 }
```

When you compile and execute this program, your screen will display the following output:

```
C:\> PROTECT  <ENTER>
The base-class number is 1001
```

Take time to experiment with this program. For example, try adding the following statements to *main*:

```
void main(void)
 {
   derived object("Hello, world", 1001 );

   object.show_number();

   cout << "The base-class number is " << base_number << endl;
 }
```

Because the program cannot access the protected class members, the compiler will generate syntax errors.

Understanding Protected Class Members

When you derive one class from another, the derived class cannot access the base class private members. Depending on your programs, there may be times when you want to give derived classes special access to the base-class members. In such cases, you can use protected-class members, which are accessible by derived classes but not the remainder of the program. For example, given the following class definition, derived classes can access the members *filename* and *size*, but a derived class not the private member *some_value:*

```
class base {
    public:
        base(char name[64], int value);
        void show_base(void);
   protected:
        char filename[64];
        long size;
   private:
        int some_value;
};
```

Putting It All Together

Inheritance is the use of base class to derive a second class. Multiple inheritance is the use of two or more base classes to derive a class. As you have learned in this lesson, C++ fully supports single- and multiple inheritance. By taking advantage of inheritance, you can eliminate program code by exploiting relationships between objects. Inheritance is a key concept used in object-oriented programming and design. Before you continue with Chapter 5, make sure that you have learned the following:

- ✓ Inheritance is when a derived class shares (inherits) similar characteristics (members) with its base class. This saves you a lot of time and code.
- ✓ When your programs use inheritance, you still use constructors to initialize classes, but the derived-class constructor must invoke the base-class constructor. The derived-class constructor functions use a syntax similar to the class definition, with a colon followed by the base-class constructor function.
- ✓ The syntax is the "science" of object-oriented programming. The "art" of such programming begins when you must determine which attributes you should place in base classes and which attributes belong to derived classes.
- ✓ When you design your classes, there may be times when you have classes that use the characteristics of two or more base classes. This is multiple inheritance.
- ✓ When a class is derived from two or more classes, you separate the base classes using commas.
- ✓ Multilevel inheritance occurs when you derive a class from a base class that is actually derived from another class.
- ✓ A protected class member can be directly accessed by derived classes but cannot be accessed otherwise. Use it to give derived members direct access to base class members, while still protecting them from the rest of the program.

Chapter 5
Getting Up to Speed with Function and Operator Overloading

When you create classes within your C++ programs, you create your own data types. In the simplest sense, a *type* defines a set of values the data can store and a set of operations your programs can perform on the data. For example, a variable of type *int* can store whole numbers in the range of –32,768 through 32,767. Your programs can perform addition, subtraction, multiplication, division, and several bitwise operations on the variable.

When you create a class, there may be times when it is very meaningful to express specific operations using operators. For example, assume that your program is using a date class variable to store a day, month, and year. If your program wants to add 30 days to the date, or subtract 15 days from the date, the plus and minus operators can produce quite readable code as shown here:

```
invoice_date = order_date + 30;

first_notice = invoice_date - 15;
```

Keep in mind, however, that the date class member variables contain day, month, and year fields. For the plus and minus operators to make sense, your programs must define the operations the program should perform when it encounters these operators with date class variables. In other words, your program will perform one set of operations (probably addition and subtraction) when it encounters the plus and minus operators used with variables of type *int*, *float*, and so on, and a second set of operations when it encounters the operators used with variables of the date class. *Operator overloading* is the process of assigning two or more operations to the same operator. Using operator overloading, your program code can become very natural and easy to understand. This chapter examines operator overloading and function overloading in detail. By the time you finish this chapter, you will find that operator overloading is very easy and powerful and that you have learned the following:

- What is function overloading
- When two different functions have the same name, how C++ determines which overloaded function to invoke
- How does function overloading improve your program's readability

- How default parameters make life easier
- What to do when using parameters other than the default
- How to create a function library
- What is operator overloading
- How the C++ compiler determines the desired operation
- How to overload an operator
- Which operators the C++ compiler will let you overload
- How to use an overloaded operator
- How to provide an overloaded operator with access to the class member structures

UNDERSTANDING FUNCTION OVERLOADING

Before you examine operator overloading, it is important that you have a good understanding of function overloading. As you will learn, the concepts are quite similar and both are implemented by the C++ compiler. *Function overloading* is the process of defining two or more functions, with the same name, that differ only by return type and parameters—either the number of parameters, or the type. When the C++ compiler compiles your program, the compiler will determine which function to invoke, based on how your program uses the function. For example, the following program, OVERLOAD.CPP, creates two functions named *show_message*. The first function definition does not support parameters, it simply displays a default message. The second definition lets your program pass a character string message to the function:

```
#include <iostream.h>

void show_message(void)
 {
   cout << "Success with C++!" << endl;
 }

void show_message(char *message)
 {
   cout << message;
 }

void main(void)
 {
   show_message("My favorite book is: ");
   show_message();
 }
```

When you compile and execute this program, your screen will display the following output:

```
C:\> OVERLOAD  <ENTER>
My favorite book is: Success with C++!
```

As you can see, the program's first function invokes the definition of *show_message* that supports the first character-string parameter, whereas the second invocation uses the function definition that displays the default message. When you compile and execute this program, the C++ compiler determines which function to invoke, based on the parameter use.

UNDERSTANDING FUNCTION OVERLOADING

Function overloading is the process of defining two or more functions, with the same name, within your programs. The functions differ only by the number of parameters they support or the parameter type. When you compile your program, the C++ compiler determines which function to invoke, based on the function parameters. In this way, your programs always invoke the correct function automatically.

Note: Although function overloading can be very powerful and a very convenient tool, too much of a good thing can also decrease your program's readability. Thus, if you find yourself defining several different versions of the same function, evaluate your use of function overloading to ensure that your program is still very readable.

LOOKING AT A FEW MORE EXAMPLES

As you have learned the C++ compiler determines, during compilation, which function it should invoke, based on the parameters you pass to the function. Consider, for example, the following program, INTARRAY.CPP, which uses the function *sum_values* to return the sum of the values contained in an array of type *int*:

```
#include <iostream.h>

long sum_array(int *array, int num_elements)
 {
   long sum = 0L;

   for (int i = 0; i < num_elements; i++)
     sum += array[i];

   return(sum);
 }
```

```
void main(void)
 {
   int array[5] = {1, 2, 3, 4, 5};

   cout << "The values sum to " << sum_array(array, 5) << endl;
 }
```

When you compile and execute this program, your screen will display the following:

```
C:\> INTARRAY  <ENTER>
The values sum to 15
```

Next, assume that program now needs to sum the values in an array of type *float*, as well, as shown here:

```
float float_array[5] = {1.1, 2.2., 3.3, 4.4, 5.5};
```

If you were using C programming, your program would have to create two functions, with unique names, for each array type, as shown in the following program, C_ARRAYS.C:

```
#include <stdio.h>

float sum_float_array(float *array, int num_elements)
 {
   float sum = 0.0;
   int i;

   for (i = 0; i < num_elements; i++)
     sum += array[i];

   return(sum);
 }

long sum_int_array(int *array, int num_elements)
 {
   long sum = 0L;
   int i;

   for (i = 0; i < num_elements; i++)
     sum += array[i];

   return(sum);
 }

void main(void)
 {
   int int_array[5] = {1, 2, 3, 4, 5};
```

```
   float float_array[5] = {1.1, 2.2, 3.3, 4.4, 5.5};

   printf("Values in int array: %ld\n",
          sum_int_array(int_array, 5));
   printf("Values in float array: %f\n",
          sum_float_array(float_array, 5));
 }
```

As you can see, the program defines the functions *sum_int_array* and *sum_float_array* to add up the sum of the values of the arrays of type *int* and *float*. Although the program is successful, having to create unique function names for each type can become cumbersome and can, at times, actually decrease your program's readability, due to the long function names. Using C++ function overloading, however, your program can use one function name, *sum_array*, and pass to the function arrays of each type. The compiler, in turn, will determine which function to invoke. The following program, SUMARRAY.CPP, for example, does just that:

```
#include <iostream.h>

float sum_array(float *array, int num_elements)
 {
   float sum = 0.0;

   for (int i = 0; i < num_elements; i++)
     sum += array[i];

   return(sum);
 }

long sum_array(int *array, int num_elements)
 {
   long sum = 0L;

   for (int i = 0; i < num_elements; i++)
     sum += array[i];

   return(sum);
 }

void main(void)
 {
   int int_array[5] = {1, 2, 3, 4, 5};
   float float_array[5] = {1.1, 2.2, 3.3, 4.4, 5.5};

   cout << "Values in int array: " << sum_array(int_array, 5) <<
          endl;
   cout << "Values in float array: " << sum_array(float_array, 5) <<
          endl;
 }
```

As you can see, the program uses the function *sum_array* for arrays of type *int* and *float.* It is important to note that the program still must define two functions, one for each type, but the program is free to use the same function name for each array type.

In previous program, the C++ compiler determined which *sum_array* function to invoke, based on the type of the array parameter. In the case of the following program, GETLINE.CPP, the compiler will determine which *getline* function to invoke, based on the number of parameters. In Chapter 1 you learned that the *getline* member function lets the *cin* input stream read a line of text from the keyboard or standard input device:

```
cin.getline(line, sizeof(line));
```

When you use *getline,* you can also specify a character at which you want input operations to end. For example, the following function call reads a line of text or up to, but not including, first occurrence of the letter X:

```
cin.getline(line, sizeof(line), 'X');
```

The following program, GETLINE.CPP, uses function overloading to create two functions that support these two operations:

```
#include <iostream.h>

void getline(char *line, int size)
 {
   char letter;

   for (int i = 0; i < size; i++)
    if ((letter = cin.get()) == '\n')
      break;
    else
      line[i] = letter;

    line[i] = NULL;
 }

void getline(char *line, int size, char terminator)
 {
   char letter;

   for (int i = 0; i < size; i++)
    if ((letter = cin.get()) == '\n')
      break;
    else if (letter == terminator)
      break;
    else
```

```
        line[i] = letter;

      line[i] = NULL;
   }

void main(void)
 {
   char text[256];

   cout << "Type in a line of text: ";
   getline(text, sizeof(text));
   cout << "You typed: " << text << endl;

   cout << "Type text followed by X: ";
   getline(text, sizeof(text), 'X');
   cout << "You typed: " << text << endl;
 }
```

As you can see, the program defines two different *getline* functions. During compilation, the C++ compiler determines the correct function to invoke. In this case, the program simply defined a function named *getline.* The function does not affect *cin*'s *getline* member function because of scoping rules discussed in Chapter 9.

Finally, the following program, SHOWDATE.CPP, creates several functions named *show_date.* The first function displays the current system date. The second displays the date specified in the character string date, and the third displays the date contained in a structure:

```
#include <iostream.h>
#include <time.h>

void show_date(void)
 {
   time_t current_datetime;

   time(&current_datetime);

   cout << "Current date: " << ctime(&current_datetime);
 }

void show_date(char *date)
 {
   cout << "String date: " << date << endl;
 }

struct Date {
  int month;
  int day;
```

```
   int year;
  };

void show_date(struct Date date)
  {
    cout << "Structure date: ";

    switch (date.month) {
      case  1: cout << "January ";
               break;
      case  2: cout << "February ";
               break;
      case  3: cout << "March ";
               break;
      case  4: cout << "April ";
               break;
      case  5: cout << "May ";
               break;
      case  6: cout << "June ";
               break;
      case  7: cout << "July ";
               break;
      case  8: cout << "August ";
               break;
      case  9: cout << "September ";
               break;
      case 10: cout << "October ";
               break;
      case 11: cout << "November ";
               break;
      case 12: cout << "December ";
               break;
    };

    cout << date.day << ", " << date.year << endl;
  }

void main(void)
  {
    struct Date date = {9, 30, 1994};
    char datestr[9];

    show_date();  // Show default

    show_date(_strdate(datestr));

    show_date(date);
  }
```

As you can see, program uses three different functions named *show_date*. Depending on the parameters the program passes to the function, the C++ compiler determines which function to invoke. When you compile and execute this program, your screen will display the following output:

```
C:\> SHOWDATE  <ENTER>
Current date: Wed Nov 24 19:30:03 1993
String date: 11/24/93
Structure date: September 30, 1994
```

Note: For simplicity, the previous program used a ***case*** *statement to display the character string month names that correspond to the value contained in the field* ***date.month****. If you change the program slightly, you can use an array of pointers to character strings to display the month string, as shown here:*

```
void show_date(struct Date date)
 {
   char *months[] = { "January", "February", "March", "April",
                      "May", "June", "July", "August", "September",
                      "October", "November", "December" };

   cout << "Structure date: ";

   cout << months[date.month] << " " << date.day << ", " <<
           date.year << endl;
 }
```

As you can see, by defining the array of character strings in this way, you reduce the number of statements within the function, which in turn, improves the function's readability.

Using Default Parameters

In addition to letting your programs overload functions, as just discussed, C++ also lets your functions specify *default parameter values*. In this way, if the program invokes a specific function and omits one or more parameter values, the function will use the default values. To understand better how default parameters work, consider the following program, DEF_PAR.CPP, which defines the function *show_values*. As you will find, the function supports three parameters. If your program invokes the function and does not specify values for each parameter, the function will use its default values as necessary:

```
#include <iostream.h>

void show_values(int a = 1, int b = 2, int c = 3)
 {
```

```
    cout << a << ' ' << b << ' ' << c << endl;
  }

void main(void)
  {
    show_values();
    show_values(1001);
    show_values(1001, 2002);
    show_values(1001, 2002, 3003);
  }
```

As you can see, the program invokes the function four times, using four different parameter combinations. When you compile and execute this program, your screen will display the following output:

```
C:\> DEF_PAR   <ENTER>
1 2 3
1001 2 3
1001 2002 3
1001 2002 3003
```

As you can see, when the program does not specify a specific parameter value; the function uses the parameter's default.

When your program omits a parameter from a function that supports default parameters, your program must omit values for all the parameters that follow. For example, in the previous program, your program could not specify a value for parameter *a*, omit the value for parameter *b*, and then specify a value for parameter *c*, as shown here:

```
show_values(1001, , 3003);
```
Syntax error for omitting a middle parameter

In this case, if your program omits the value for parameter *b*, your program must also omit the value for parameter *c*.

Earlier in this chapter you created two versions of the *getline* function. As you may recall, the first function read a line of text from the keyboard up to, but not including, a carriage return. The second function let your program specify a termination character. The following program, DEF_LINE.CPP, changes your previous program to use a default parameter value for the termination character. In this way, your program is able to achieve the same purpose using only one function:

```
#include <iostream.h>

void getline(char *line, int size, char terminator = '\n')
 {
   char letter;

   for (int i = 0; i < size; i++)
    if ((letter = cin.get()) == terminator)
      break;
    else
      line[i] = letter;

    line[i] = NULL;
 }

void main(void)
 {
   char text[256];

   cout << "Type in a line of text: ";
   getline(text, sizeof(text));
   cout << "You typed: " << text << endl;

   cout << "Type text followed by X: ";
   getline(text, sizeof(text), 'X');
   cout << "You typed: " << text << endl;
 }
```

As you can see, the program now only uses one *getline* function. If your program invokes *getline* without specifying a termination character, *getline* uses the newline character ('\n') by default. However, if your program specifies a termination character as a parameter, the program will read characters until the buffer is full or the termination character is encountered. In this way, the program will read past a newline character. Thus, your programs can use *getline* to read characters from the keyboard that include newline characters.

It's interesting to note that if you examine the *istream* class definition in the header file that your compiler uses for stream-related functions, you will find a function prototype for the *getline* member function similar to the following:

```
istream _FAR & _Cdecl getline(unsigned char _FAR *, int, char = '\n');
```

As you can see, the function specifies the newline character as the default value for the terminator parameter.

Understanding Default Parameters

When you create functions, there may be times when most programs will use the same values for specific parameters. To simplify the function's use, C++ lets your programs specify default parameter values. To specify a default value, you simply place the desired value within the function header preceded by an equal sign. For example, the following *getline* function specifies the newline character as a default parameter value:

```
void getline(char *text, int size, char terminator = '\n')
```

If the program invokes *getline* with only two parameters, *getline* will use the default parameter value:

```
getline(line, sizeof(line));
```

If the program specifies a termination character, the default value is overridden:

```
getline(line, sizeof(line), 'X');
```

Depending on the function's use, a function may provide several default parameter values. For example, the following *get_tax* function uses two default parameter values:

```
float get_tax(float amount, float sales_tax = 0.06,
              float state_tax = 0.03);
```

In this case, the program can omit values for the *sales_tax* and *state_tax*. When a program omits the value for a parameter, the program must also omit values for all parameters that follow. In this case, if the program omits the value for the *sales_tax* parameter, it must also omit the value for *state_tax* parameter.

How to Create Your Own Function Libraries

As the number of functions you create increases, you will want to create your own *function libraries*, with which your programs can link to your functions. To make the functions easy to use, you should create a header file that contains the prototypes for each function. If your functions support default parameters, you will specify the default values within the prototype file.

Understanding Operator Overloading

Operator overloading is the process of assigning two or more operations to the same operator. Depending on how the operator is used, the C++ compiler will determine the actual operation to be performed. To understand operator overloading better, let's first examine a program that creates a *stack* class, with which you can *push* values on to the stack for storage and later *pop* from the stack. The *stack* class takes the following form:

```
class stack {
public:
  stack(int size);
  int push(int value);
  int pop(void);
  int is_empty(void) { return(isempty); };
  int is_full(void) { return(isfull); };
private:
  int *storage;    // Stack data buffer
  int elements;    // Number of values in the stack
  int isempty;     // True when stack is empty
  int isfull;      // True when stack is full
  int stack_size; // Number of values the stack can store
};
```

The following program, STACK.CPP, creates a stack object capable of holding 64 values. The program then uses pushes values on to the stack until the stack is full. Next, the program pops the values one at a time from the stack:

```
#include <iostream.h>

class stack {
public:
  stack(int size);
  int push(int value);
  int pop(void);
  int is_empty(void) { return(isempty); };
  int is_full(void) { return(isfull); };
private:
  int *storage;                // Stack data buffer
  int elements;                // Number of values in the stack
  int isempty;                 // True when stack is empty
  int isfull;                  // True when stack is full
  int stack_size;              // Number of values the stack can store
};
```

```
stack::stack(int size)
 {
   storage = new int[size];  // Allocate memory for the stack
   elements = 0;
   isempty = 1;
   isfull = 0;
   stack_size = size;
 }

int stack::pop(void)
 {
   if (is_empty())
     return(0);
   else
     {
       if (--elements == 0)
         isempty = 1;

       isfull = 0;

       return(storage[elements]);
     }
 }

int stack::push(int value)
 {
   if (is_full())
     return(0);
   else
     {
       isempty = 0;
       storage[elements++] = value;

       if (elements == stack_size)
         isfull = 1;

       return(value);
    }
 }

void main(void)
 {
   stack fifo(64);

   int i;

   for (i = 0; ! fifo.is_full(); i++)
     fifo.push(i);

   while (! fifo.is_empty())
     cout << fifo.pop() << endl;
 }
```

As you can see, the program uses the *push* and *pop* member functions to place items on to and later to remove items from the stack. To make your program easier to read, you might want to overload the plus and double-minus operators for the *stack* class. For example, your program would use the plus operator to push and item on to the stack and the double-minus operator to pop an item from the stack:

```
pushed_value = fifo + 54;
fifo = --fifo;
```

When you overload an operator, you specify a function that your program executes whenever the C++ compiler encounters the operator used in a specific way. For example, when the C++ compiler encounters the plus operator with the objects of the *stack* class, the compiler will insert code that invokes your function, as opposed to performing addition. To define the operator function, you define a function much as you always do, except that you include the *operator* keyword. The following function, for example, overloads the plus operator:

```
int stack::operator +(int value)
 {
   if (is_full())
     return(0);
   else
     {
       isempty = 0;
       storage[elements++] = value;

       if (elements == stack_size)
         isfull = 1;

       return(value);
     }
 }
```


In a similar way, the following function overloads the double-minus operator:

```
int stack::operator --(void)
 {
   if (is_empty())
     return(0);
   else
     {
       if (--elements == 0)
         isempty = 1;

       isfull = 0;
```

```
       return(storage[elements]);
     }
 }
```

When you define operators for a class, you need to include the operators within the class definition, as shown here:

```
class stack {
public:
  stack(int size);
  int operator +(int value);
  int operator --(void);
  int is_empty(void) { return(isempty); };
  int is_full(void) { return(isfull); };
private:
  int *storage;    // Stack data buffer
  int elements;    // Number of values in the stack
  int isempty;     // True when stack is empty
  int isfull;      // True when stack is full
  int stack_size; // Number of values the stack can store
};
```

Public class operators

The following program, STACKOVR.CPP, uses the plus and double-minus operators to place values onto and later remove values from the stack:

```
#include <iostream.h>

class stack {
public:
  stack(int size);
  int operator +(int value);
  int operator --(void);
  int is_empty(void) { return(isempty); };
  int is_full(void) { return(isfull); };
private:
  int *storage;                // Stack data buffer
  int elements;                // Number of values in the stack
  int isempty;                 // True when stack is empty
  int isfull;                  // True when stack is full
  int stack_size;              // Number of values the stack can store
};


stack::stack(int size)
 {
   storage = new int[size];  // Allocate memory for the stack
   elements = 0;
```

```
    isempty = 1;
    isfull = 0;
    stack_size = size;
  }

int stack::operator --(void)
  {
    if (is_empty())
      return(0);
    else
      {
        if (--elements == 0)
          isempty = 1;

        isfull = 0;

        return(storage[elements]);
      }
  }

int stack::operator +(int value)
  {
    if (is_full())
      return(0);
    else
      {
        isempty = 0;
        storage[elements++] = value;

        if (elements == stack_size)
          isfull = 1;

        return(value);
      }
  }

void main(void)
  {
    stack fifo(64);

    int i;

    for (i = 0; ! fifo.is_full(); i++)
      fifo + i;

    while (! fifo.is_empty())
      cout << --fifo << endl;
  }
```

As you can see, the program uses the following statement to push items on to the stack:

```
fifo + i;
```

Likewise, the program uses this statement to display the value of an item popped from the stack:

```
cout << --fifo << endl;
```

Understanding Operator Overloading

Operator overloading is the process of assigning two or more operations to the same operator. By overloading specific operators, your programs can express class operations in a more natural way. For example, your programs might use the plus operator for addition, to add days to a date structure, or to append one string to another, as shown here:

```
value = some_value + 100;

expiration_date = sales_date + 30;       // date class

new_string = "Success " + "with C++!";   // string class
```

To overload an operator, you define a function in your program the C++ compiler invokes whenever it sees data types that match those you for which you have defined the operation. The function definition is very similar to a normal function, except you must include the *operator* keyword within the function header.

Rules for Operator Overloading

When you overload an operator, you essentially specify two data types for which you want the C++ compiler to treat a specific operator differently. Thus, you can only use operators in ways the operator would normally be used within your program. For example, you cannot use a unary operator such as the decrement operator to perform an operation on two data values:

```
result = a -- b;    // Syntax error
```

In general, C++ will let your programs overload all operators except those listed in Table 5.1.

Operator	Purpose	Example
.	Class or structure member operator	cin.get();
.*	Pointer to member operator	object.*member
::	Global resolution operator	class_name::member
?:	Conditional expression operator	c = (a > b) ? a: b;

Table 15.1 *C++ operators your programs cannot overload.*

OVERLOADING I/O OPERATORS

In the previous program you overloaded the plus and double-minus operators for use with stack objects. Depending on how your program uses a class, there may be times when you want to overload the insertion (<<) and extraction (>>) operators. Consider, for example, the following program, BOOKONE.CPP, that uses the *book* class to store information about a specific book:

```
#include <iostream.h>
#include <iomanip.h>
#include <string.h>

class book {
public:
  book(char *title, char *author, char *publisher, float price);
  void show_book(void);
private:
  char title[64];
  char author[64];
  char publisher[64];
  float price;
};

book::book(char *title, char *author, char *publisher, float price)
 {
   strcpy(book::title, title);
   strcpy(book::author, author);
   strcpy(book::publisher, publisher);
   book::price = price;
 }

void book::show_book(void)
 {
```

```
   cout << "Title: " << title << endl;
   cout << "Author: " << author << endl;
   cout << "Publisher: " << publisher << endl;
   cout << setprecision(2) << "Price: " << price << endl;
 }

void main(void)
 {
   book computer_book("Success with C++", "Kris Jamsa",
                      "Jamsa Press", 29.95);

   computer_book.show_book();
 }
```

As you can see, the program uses the *show_book* member function to display information about the book. Within *show_book*, the function uses the insertion operator with *cout*. In this case, the program can eliminate the *show_book* member function by overloading the extraction operator (<<) for use with *book* objects. In this way, your program can display information about the book using the extraction operator as follows:

```
cout << computer_book;
```

To overload an operator, your program must define a function that executes each time the operator is used for the corresponding class. The following statements, for example, overload the extraction operator for use by *book* objects:

```
ostream& operator <<(ostream&stream, book bookinfo)
 {
   cout << "Title: " << bookinfo.title << endl;
   cout << "Author: " << bookinfo.author << endl;
   cout << "Publisher: " << bookinfo.publisher << endl;
   cout << setprecision(2) << "Price: " << bookinfo.price << endl;
   return(stream);
 }
```

As you can see, much of the operator definition is similar to the *show_book* function previously used in that different fields of the *book* object are written to *cout*.

The most confusing part of the definition, by far, is the header statement:

```
ostream& operator <<(ostream&stream, book bookinfo)
```

The key to understanding this statement is to remember that when you overload an operator, you specify a function your program executes when the operator is encountered. In this case, the function returns a reference (&) to a *ostream* object. The parameters for the operation are an *ostream* object (probably *cout*) and a *book* object:

```
ostream& operator <<(ostream& stream, book bookinfo)
```

Function return type

Function parameters

The best way to understand the function's parameters is to think about the values that appear on the left and right side of the operator:

```
cout << computer_book;
```

ostream object

book object

As you can see, after the function inserts the fields into the output stream, the function uses the *return* statement to return the updated stream:

```
return(stream);
```

If you do not feel comfortable with I/O stream references, don't worry. Chapter 10 discusses C++ references in detail.

The following program, BOOKTWO.CPP, uses the overloaded operator to display information about the corresponding book object:

```
#include <iostream.h>
#include <iomanip.h>
#include <string.h>

class book {
public:
  book(char *title, char *author, char *publisher, float price);
  friend ostream& operator <<(ostream& stream, book bookinfo);
private:
  char title[64];
  char author[64];
  char publisher[64];
  float price;
};

book::book(char *title, char *author, char *publisher, float price)
 {
   strcpy(book::title, title);
   strcpy(book::author, author);
   strcpy(book::publisher, publisher);
   book::price = price;
 }

ostream& operator <<(ostream&stream, book bookinfo)
 {
   cout << "Title: " << bookinfo.title << endl;
   cout << "Author: " << bookinfo.author << endl;
   cout << "Publisher: " << bookinfo.publisher << endl;
```

```
    cout << setprecision(2) << "Price: " << bookinfo.price << endl;
    return(stream);
  }

void main(void)
  {
    book computer_book("Success with C++", "Kris Jamsa",
      "Jamsa Press", 29.95);

    cout << "Book Information" << endl;
    cout << computer_book;
  }
```

As you can see, the program displays information about the *book* object using the insertion operator. Note that the program also uses the insertion operator to write a message to *cout* immediately before displaying the object's members:

```
cout << "Book Information" << endl;
cout << computer_book;
```

Note also that you could even combine these two lines:

```
cout << "Book Information" << endl << computer_book;
```

Keep in mind that the overloaded operator is only used for *book* objects. Thus, the first statement uses the standard insertion operator while the second uses the overloaded operator. In this way, the overloaded operator is very similar to an overloaded function, as just discussed. Also note that within the class definition, the program defines the overloaded operator as a *friend*:

```
class book {
public:
  book(char *title, char *author, char *publisher, float price);
  friend ostream& operator <<(ostream& stream, book bookinfo);
private:
  char title[64];
  char author[64];
  char publisher[64];
  float price;
};
```

Declaring the operator as a **friend**

By declaring the insertion operator as a *friend* in this way, the class grants the operator function access to the private class members.

Looking at a Few More Examples

The more your programs take advantage of operator overloading, the more you will gain an appreciation of its true power and convenience. Therefore, this section examines several programs that overload operators for different types of classes. Take time to experiment with these programs. As you will find, operator overloading is actually very easy when you have done it once or twice.

The following program, DATE_OPS.CPP, overloads the insertion and extraction operators letting your program perform input and output operators using the *Date* structure:

```
#include <iostream.h>
#include <string.h>

class Date {
  public:
    Date(int month, int day, int year);
    friend ostream& operator <<(ostream& stream, Date date);
    friend istream& operator >>(istream& stream, Date *date);
  private:
    int month;
    int day;
    int year;
};

Date::Date(int month, int day, int year)
 {
   Date::month = month;
   Date::day = day;
   Date::year = year;
 }

ostream& operator <<(ostream& stream, Date date)
 {
   stream << date.month << '/' << date.day << '/' << date.year <<
             endl;
   return(stream);
 }

istream& operator >>(istream& stream, Date *date)
 {
   stream >> date->month;
   stream >> date->day;
   stream >> date->year;
```

```
    return(stream);
  }

void main(void)
  {
    Date christmas(12, 25, 94);
    Date birthday(9, 30, 94);

    cout << "Christmas is " << christmas;

    cout << "Type in your birthday mm dd yy: ";
    cin >> &birthday;
    cout << "You typed: " << birthday;
  }
```

As you can see, within the *Date* class, the overloaded insertion and extraction operators are declared as *friends*, giving the operator functions access to the private member variables:

```
class Date {
  public:
    Date(int month, int day, int year);
    friend ostream& operator <<(ostream& stream, Date date);
    friend istream& operator >>(istream& stream, Date *date);
  private:
    int month;
    int day;
    int year;
};
```

Declaring the operator functions as ***friends***

The overloaded operator functions work return a reference to a stream, receiving the stream and the class as a parameter:

```
ostream& operator <<(ostream& stream, Date date)
  {
    stream << date.month << '/' << date.day << '/' <<
              date.year << endl;
    return(stream);
  }
istream& operator >>(istream& stream, Date *date)
  {
    stream >> date->month;
    stream >> date->day;
    stream >> date->year;

    return(stream);
  }
```

Returns a stream reference — *Stream parameter* — *Date structure* — *Returns a stream reference* — *Stream parameter* — *Pointer to a date structure*

Because the overloaded extraction operator assigns values to class variables, the function must work with a pointer to the class. When your programs work with classes or structures that contain multiple values, such as a date, there may be times when your programs need to test two classes or structures for equality. The following program, TEST_OPS.CPP, overloads the equal (==) and not equal (!=) operators for use with classes of type *Date.* Using these operators, your program's can quickly determine if two classes contain the same or different values:

```
#include <iostream.h>
#include <string.h>

class Date {
  public:
    Date(int month, int day, int year);
    friend int operator ==(Date date_one, Date date_two);
    friend int operator !=(Date date_one, Date date_two);
  private:
    int month;
    int day;
    int year;
};

Date::Date(int month, int day, int year)
 {
   Date::month = month;
   Date::day = day;
   Date::year = year;
 }

int operator ==(Date date_one, Date date_two)
 {
   if (date_one.day != date_two.day)
     return(0);
   else if (date_one.month != date_two.month)
     return(0);
   else if (date_one.year != date_two.year)
     return(0);
   return(1);
 }

int operator !=(Date date_one, Date date_two)
 {
   if (date_one.day != date_two.day)
     return(1);
   else if (date_one.month != date_two.month)
     return(1);
   else if (date_one.year != date_two.year)
     return(1);
   return(0);
 }
```

```
void main(void)
 {
   Date christmas(12, 25, 94);
   Date santas_day(12, 25, 94);
   Date birthday(9, 30, 94);

   if (christmas == santas_day)
     cout << "Christmas and Santa's day are the same" << endl;

   if (christmas != birthday)
     cout << "My birthday is not Christmas" << endl;
 }
```

In this case, by overloading the equal-to and not-equal-to operators, your program becomes more meaningful.

The alternative code to test two *Date* classes for equality would be the following:

```
if ((christmas.day) == birthday.day) &&
   (christmas.month == birthday.month) &&
   (christmas.year == birthday.year))
  cout << "My birthday is on Christmas!" << endl;
```

In this case, not only does the program code become more difficult to understand, the additional statements increase the possibility of a program error. As you examine programs throughout the remainder of this book, you will find several programs that overload operators to improve the program's readability and, in turn, programmer understanding.

Putting It All Together

Operator overloading is the assignment of two or more operations to the same operator. Function overloading assigns two or more operations to the same function. This chapter examined both in detail. Before you continue with Chapter 6, make sure that you have learned the following:

- ✓ Function overloading is the process of defining two or more functions with the same name, which differ only by return type and parameters.
- ✓ During compilation, the C++ will determine which overloaded function to invoke, based on your the required return type or the types of the parameters specified.
- ✓ Function overloading lets you improve your program's readability by letting you use similarly named functions for the same operations, which differ only by the type of data with which they work.

- ✓ To increase your function ease of use, the C++ compiler supports default parameters. If, when your program invokes a function, your program does not specify a value for each parameter, the C++ compiler will substitute the default value.
- ✓ When your program omits a default parameter, your program must also omit the parameters that follow. In other words, your program can't specify a value for parameter one, use the default for parameter two, and then specify a value for parameter three.
- ✓ To create a function library, create a header file that contains the prototypes for each function. If your functions support default parameters, specify the default values within the prototype file.
- ✓ Operator overloading is the assignment of two or more operations to the same operator. During compilation, the C++ compiler determines the desired operation, based on how the operator is used.
- ✓ To overload an operator, your program simply specifies a function that the compiler invokes when it encounters the use of the operator.
- ✓ The C++ compiler will let you overload most operators, with the exception of the following:

Operator	Name
.	Class member operator
.*	Pointer to class member operator
::	Global resolution operator
?:	Conditional assignment operator

- ✓ When your programs overload an operator, your program must use the operator in a manner consistent with the operator's normal use.
- ✓ When you overload an operator for a class, you will normally declare the operator within the class as a *friend*, to provide the operator with access to the class member structures.

Chapter 6
Getting Up to Speed with Templates

In Chapter 5 you learned how overloading functions and operators can make your programs easier to understand by letting you use more meaningful function names. For example, assume your program needs to calculate the average value in arrays of type *int* and *float*. By overloading the function name *average_value*, your program can use two functions with the same name, one for integer values and one for floating-point values. If other programmers read your program, they will find the function name *average_value* easier to understand than function names such as *f_average_value* and *i_average_value*, which would have been required in C. Unfortunately, although the ability to use the same function name is convenient, you must still write the code for each function. In most cases, the only difference between such functions is the data types with which the functions work.

This chapter examines C++ templates, which let you define the "template" or "blueprint" for function definitions. As you will learn, using templates, your programs can direct the compiler to create function code for different variable types automatically. For example, your program might create an *average_value* template. Using the template, your program can quickly create functions for arrays of type *int*, *float*, and so on. In addition to examining function templates, this chapter examines class templates, which let you quickly define classes whose member differ only by type.

By the time you finish this chapter, you will have learned

- What a template is and how it is useful
- That C++ supports function and class templates.
- How to create a function template
- How to create later a function that returns or supports parameters of a specific type
- How the compiler assigns types, if the function template supports multiple parameter types
- How to create a class template
- How to create objects using a class template
- How the compiler assigns types, if the class template supports multiple parameter types

- How the compiler performs type substitutions, if one class template uses a second template

Creating Your First Function Template

A *function template* is a blueprint for functions used by the C++ compiler to construct functions for the variable types you specify. For example, the following statements create a template for the function *average_value*:

```
template<class T> T average_value(T *array, int num_elements)
 {
   T sum = 0;

   for (int i = 0; i < num_elements; i++)
     sum += array[i];

   return (sum / num_elements);
 }
```

Before you examine the template's function code, examine the first line very closely:

```
template<class T> T average_value(T *array, int num_elements)
```

The *template* keyword informs the C++ compiler that the statements that follow define a template. As you just read, function templates let your programs specify the statements for functions that differ only by type. The *<class T>* that follows the *template* keyword lets you specify the symbol that is used to represent the function type or the type of the function parameters. In this case, the template uses the symbol T. The remainder of the line specifies the function's return value and parameter types, much like a normal function declaration.

Assume, for example, that you were to substitute the type *float* for each occurrence of *T*. The function header would become the following:

```
float average_value(float *array, int num_elements)
```

Likewise, if you substitute *T* with the type *int*, the function header becomes the following:

```
int average_value(int *array, int num_elements)
```

Within the function, note that the statement that uses the *T* symbol to declare the variable *sum*:

```
T sum = 0;
```

When the C++ compiler substitutes the correct type name for *T* within the function header, the compiler will also substitute the type for the symbol specified within the function code itself. For the compiler to know the desired function types, you can specify function prototypes, following the template definitions similar to those shown here:

```
int average_value(int *, int);

float average_value(float *, int);
```

In this case, the C++ compiler will create functions for the type *int* and *float*, automatically, during compilation. As you can see here, the C++ compiler uses the first parameter's type to determine the type it substitutes for *T*:

```
int average_value(int *, int);

    template<class T> T average_value(T *array, int num_elements)
     {
       T sum = 0;

       for (int i = 0; i < num_elements; i++)
         sum += array[i];

       return (sum / num_elements);
     }

        int average_value(int *array, int num_elements)
         {
           int sum = 0;

          for (int i = 0; i < num_elements; i++)
            sum += array[i];

          return (sum / num_elements);
         }
```

In addition to using the prototypes, your program can simply use the function, passing to the function parameters whose types determine the corresponding function types. The following program, TEMP_AVG.CPP, uses the *average_value* template:

```
#include <iostream.h>

template<class T> T average_value(T *array, int num_elements)
 {
   T sum = 0;

   for (int i = 0; i < num_elements; i++)
     sum += array[i];
```

```
   return (sum / num_elements);
 }

int average_value(int *, int);

float average_value(float *, int);

void main(void)
 {
   int values[] = { 1, 2, 3, 4, 5 };
   float prices[] = { 1.1, 2.2, 3.3, 4.4, 5.5 };

   cout << "Average of integer values is " <<
           average_value(values, 5) << endl;
   cout << "Average of floating-point values is " <<
           average_value(prices, 5) << endl;
 }
```

When you compile and execute this program, your screen will display the following output:

```
C:\> TEMP_AVG  <ENTER>
Average of integer values is 3
Average of floating-point values is 3.3
```

Take time to experiment with this program, first removing the function prototypes. When you compile the program a second time, the C++ compiler will determine the correct types for the template based on the parameters passed to function. Second, you might want to add the following array declaration to the program:

```
long distances[] = { 1000000L, 2000000L, 3000000L };
```

To determine the array's average value, use the following statement:

```
cout << "Average of long values is " <<
      average_value(distances, 3) << endl;
```

Note: The ***average_value*** *for the type* ***int*** *works in the previous program because the sum of the values doeo not overflow the* ***int*** *variable sum. If you change the program to use the following array, however, the function will return an errant result:*

```
int values[] = {1000, 5000, 10000, 15000, 20000};
```

To solve the overflow error, the function needs to use to use the *long:*

```
long sum = 0;
```

Unfortunately, hard-coding the *long* variable declaration within the function result causes problems for other data types, such as an array of type *float*. Later in this chapter, you will learn how to specify multiple parameter types within your templates, for scenarios just like this.

Understanding Function Templates

A function template specifies a blueprint for functions automatically created by the compiler during compilation. Function templates are ideal for functions that differ only by type. To create a function template, use the *template* keyword, as shown here:

```
template<class T> T max_value(T *array, int num_elements)
 {
   T max = array[0];

   for (int i = 0; i < num_elements; i++)
     if (max < array[i])
      max = array[i];

   return(max);
 }
```

In this case, the statements create a template for functions named *max_value*. The characters *<class T>* specify a symbol (in this case, *T*), the compiler will substitute with the correct type during compilation. To tell the compiler the desired type, your program can specify function prototypes similar to those shown here:

```
float max_value(float *, int);

int max_value(int *, int);
```

During compilation, the compiler will substitute the first parameter type for *T*, creating overloaded functions for the desired type. Function templates have the advantage that programmers who examine your program can quickly determine the different ways the template is used. If your program does not specify function prototypes, the compiler will determine which functions to create, based on the function's use, within the program.

The following program, MIN_MAX.CPP, creates and uses templates for the functions *max_value* and *min_value*:

```
#include <iostream.h>

template<class T> T max_value(T *array, int num_elements)
 {
   T max = array[0];

   for (int i = 0; i < num_elements; i++)
     if (max < array[i])
      max = array[i];

   return(max);
 }

template<class T> T min_value(T *array, int num_elements)
 {
   T min = array[0];

   for (int i = 0; i < num_elements; i++)
     if (min > array[i])
      min = array[i];

   return(min);
 }

float max_value(float *, int);

int max_value(int *, int);

float min_value(float *, int);

int min_value(int *, int);

void main(void)
 {
   int values[] = {5, 1, 6, 12, 7};

   float prices[] = { 1.1, 3.3, 4.4, 2.2, 5.5 };

   cout << "Max of integer values is " << max_value(values, 5) <<
           endl;
   cout << "Max of floating-point values is " <<
           max_value(prices, 5) << endl;

   cout << "Min of integer values is " << min_value(values, 5) <<
           endl;
   cout << "Min of floating-point values is " <<
           min_value(prices, 5) << endl;
 }
```

When you compile and execute this program, your screen will display the following output:

```
C:\> MIN_MAX  <ENTER>
Max of integer values is 12
Max of floating-point values is 5.5
Min of integer values is 1
Min of floating-point values is 1.1
```

Making Your Templates Less Confusing

As you have learned, the *template* keyword lets your programs define blueprints for function definitions. When programmers first encounter templates, the template declaration can be confusing. For example, the following statement starts a definition for a template for the function *max_value*:

```
template<class T> T max_value(T *array, int num_elements)
```

Depending on the template's complexity, you might want to use two lines to present the template, as shown here:

```
template<class T>
T max_value(T *array, int num_elements)
 {
   T min = array[0];

   for (int i = 0; i < num_elements; i++)
     if (min > array[i])
      min = array[i];

   return(min);
 }
```

As you can see, once the reader gets past the first line of the template, the definition looks much more like that of a standard function definition.

Templates That Use Multiple Types

You have learned that when the C++ compiler encounters a function prototype for a template or an invocation of a function defined by a template, the C++ compiler creates a function substituting the type specified by the function's first parameter. Each of the templates previously examined has used only one type symbol. In many cases, there are times when your functions require different parameter types. As you will find, the same is true for functions defined by templates. Assume, for example, your program needs to compare the sum of a values in an array to a specified limit value. Assuming that you are working with integer values, the function *sum_and_compare* might take the following form:

```
int sum_and_compare(int *array, long value, int num_elements)
 {
    long sum = 0;

   for (int i = 0; i < num_elements; i++)
      sum += array[i];

   return((sum > value) ? 1: 0);
 }
```

If you are summing values in a floating-point array, however, your function would appear as follows:

```
int sum_and_compare(float *array, float value, int num_elements)
 {
    float sum = 0;

   for (int i = 0; i < num_elements; i++)
      sum += array[i];

   return((sum > value) ? 1: 0);
 }
```

As you can see, the functions use different types for the array, as well as the local variable *sum*.

To create a template for the *sum_and_compare* function, the template must support two types. The following template creates the blueprint for such a function:

```
template<class T1, class T2>
int sum_and_compare(T1 *array, T2 value, int num_elements)
 {
   T2 sum = 0;

   for (int i = 0; i < num_elements; i++)
     sum += array[i];

   return((sum > value) ? 1: 0);
 }
```

In this case, the C++ will use the first two parameters specified in a function prototype or function invocation to determine the template types. Assuming your program uses a function prototype, the C++ compiler will substitute the types, as shown here:

```
int sum_and_compare(int *array, long value, int num_elements);

    int sum_and_compare(T1 *array, T2 value, int num_elements)
     {
       T2 sum = 0;

       for (int i = 0; i < num_elements; i++)
         sum += array[i];

       return((sum > value) ? 1: 0);
     }

        int sum_and_compare(int *array, long value, int num_elements)
         {
          long sum = 0;

          for (int i = 0; i < num_elements; i++)
            sum += array[i];

          return((sum > value) ? 1: 0);
         }
```

As you can see, the compiler users the first parameter's type for the symbol *T1* and the second parameter's type for the symbol *T2.* The following program, USE_MULT.CPP, uses the template to create functions that support arrays of type *int* and *float:*

```
#include <iostream.h>

template<class T1, class T2>
int sum_and_compare(T1 *array, T2 value, int num_elements)
 {
   T2 sum = 0;

   for (int i = 0; i < num_elements; i++)
     sum += array[i];

   return((sum > value) ? 1: 0);
 }

int sum_and_compare(int *array, long value, int num_elements);

int sum_and_compare(float *array, float value, int num_elements);
```

```
void main(void)
 {
   int values[] = { 1000, 20000, 30000, 4000, 500 };
   float prices[] = { 1.1, 2.2, 3.3, 4.4, 5.5 };

   if (sum_and_compare(values, 32767L, 5))
     cout << "Values will overflow an int value" << endl;

   if (sum_and_compare(prices, 25.5, 5))
     cout << "Values exceed 25.5" << endl;
   else
     cout << "Values are less than 25.5" << endl;
 }
```

TEMPLATES THAT SUPPORT MULTIPLE TYPES

When you create function templates, there may be times when the various functions use two or more types that differ. In such cases, your template definition must specify symbols for each type following type *template* keyword, as shown here:

```
template<class T1, class T2>
```

In this case, the C++ will assign the types of the function's first two parameters to the symbols *T1* and *T2*, later substituting the types throughout the function as required.

WHERE TO PLACE YOUR TEMPLATES

When you use templates within your programs, you might want to place the actual templates within a header file that you later include within your program. In this way, you reduce the number of statements within your program's source file, possibly making the program easier to read and understand. If a programmer needs to examine templates, the programmer can open the template header file. Within your program, however, you should use function prototypes to help programmers who are reading your program better understand the template's use.

CREATING CLASS TEMPLATES

Just as there are times when functions differ only by types, the same is often true for classes. For example, in Chapter 5 you created the following *stack* class, which lets your programs store and retrieve values of type *int*:

```
class stack {
public:
  stack(int size);
  int push(int value);
  int pop(void);
  int is_empty(void) { return(isempty); };
  int is_full(void) { return(isfull); };
private:
  int *storage;    // Stack data buffer
  int elements;    // Number of values in the stack
  int isempty;     // True when stack is empty
  int isfull;      // True when stack is full
  int stack_size; // Number of values the stack can store
};
```

Next, assume that your program's requirements change and you now need to store values of type *int* and *float*. Rather than create two different classes, your programs can create a class template, creating a stack object of type *int* and a different object for type *float*.

To create a class template, you begin with the *template* keyword, followed by the open brackets and class symbols. Next, within the class definition, you use the class symbols, as shown here:

```
template<class T>
class stack {
public:
  stack(int size);
  T push(T value);
  T pop(void);
  int is_empty(void) { return(isempty); };
  int is_full(void) { return(isfull); };
private:
  T *storage;      // Stack data buffer
  int elements;    // Number of values in the stack
  int isempty;     // True when stack is empty
  int isfull;      // True when stack is full
  int stack_size; // Number of values the stack can store
};
```


Next, if the class defines out-of-line member functions, you must precede each member function with the template keyword and type symbols. For example, the *push* and *pop* member functions become the following:

```
template<class T>
T stack<T>::pop(void)
 {
```

```
    if (is_empty())
      return(0);
    else
      {
        if (--elements == 0)
          isempty = 1;

        isfull = 0;

        return(storage[elements]);
      }
  }

template<class T>
T stack<T>::push(T value)
  {
    if (is_full())
      return(0);
    else
      {
        isempty = 0;
        storage[elements++] = value;

        if (elements == stack_size)
          isfull = 1;

        return(value);
     }
  }
```

To create a *stack* object within your program, your program uses the class name and type within *main*, as shown here:

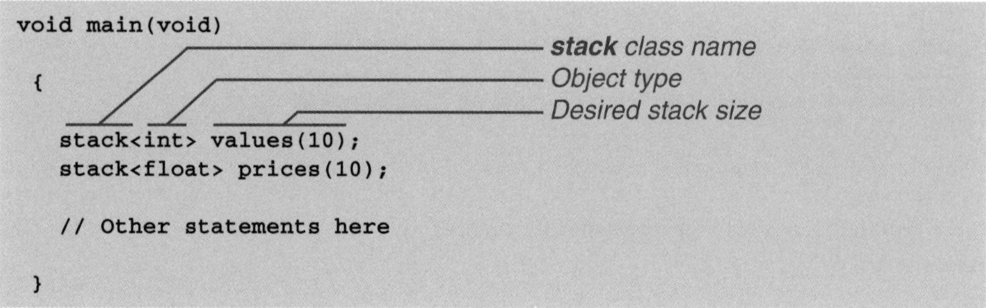


```
void main(void)
  {
    stack<int> values(10);
    stack<float> prices(10);

    // Other statements here
  }
```

The following program, STACKEXP.CPP, creates and uses two objects of type stack. One object holds values of type *int* and one holds values of type *float*:

```
#include <iostream.h>
#include <iomanip.h>

template<class T>
class stack {
public:
  stack(int size);
  T push(T value);
  T pop(void);
  int is_empty(void) { return(isempty); };
  int is_full(void) { return(isfull); };
private:
  T *storage;                // Stack data buffer
  int elements;              // Number of values in the stack
  int isempty;               // True when stack is empty
  int isfull;                // True when stack is full
  int stack_size;            // Number of values the stack can store
};

template<class T>
stack<T>::stack(int size)
 {
   storage = new T[size];    // Allocate memory for the stack
   elements = 0;
   isempty = 1;
   isfull = 0;
   stack_size = size;
 }

template<class T>
T stack<T>::pop(void)
 {
   if (is_empty())
     return(0);
   else
     {
       if (--elements == 0)
         isempty = 1;

       isfull = 0;

       return(storage[elements]);
     }
 }

template<class T>
T stack<T>::push(T value)
 {
```

```
    if (is_full())
      return(0);
    else
      {
        isempty = 0;
        storage[elements++] = value;

        if (elements == stack_size)
          isfull = 1;

        return(value);
      }
  }

void main(void)
  {
    stack<int> values(10);
    stack<float> prices(15);

    for (int i = 0; ! values.is_full(); i++)
      values.push(i);

    while (! values.is_empty())
      cout << values.pop() << endl;

    for (i = 0; ! prices.is_full(); i++)
      prices.push(i * 100.0);

    while (! prices.is_empty())
      cout << setiosflags(ios::showpoint) << prices.pop() << endl;
  }
```

In this case, the program places ten values into the integer stack and 15 values into the floating-point stack. When you compile and execute this program, your screen will display values each stack contains.

Looking at a Second Example

The following program, LINKLIST.CPP, creates a simple *LinkList* class whose members are similar to the following:

```
struct Node {
  int value;
  Node *next;
  Node *previous;
};
```

```
class LinkList {
 public:
   LinkList(void);
   void show_list(void);
   Node *append_value(int);
 private:
   Node *first;
   Node *end;
};
```

As you can see, the class tracks the first node and last node within the doubly linked list. The class uses the *show_list* function to display the list's contents and the *append_value* function to assign values to the end of the list.

The following statements implement the entire LINKLIST.CPP program:

```
#include <iostream.h>

struct Node {
 int value;
 Node *next;
 Node *previous;
};

class LinkList {
 public:
   LinkList(void);
   void show_list(void);
   Node *append_value(int);
 private:
   Node *first;
   Node *end;
};

LinkList::LinkList(void)
 {
   first = NULL;
   end = NULL;
 }

void LinkList::show_list(void)
 {
   Node *node;

   node = first;
```

```
   while (node)
     {
       cout << node->value << endl;
       node = node->next;
     }
 }

Node *LinkList::append_value(int value)
 {
   Node *ptr = end;

   end = new Node;

   if (first == NULL)
     first = end;
   else
     ptr->next = end;

   if (end)
     {
       end->next = NULL;
       end->previous = ptr;
       end->value = value;
     }

   return(end);
 }

void main(void)
 {
   LinkList list;

   for (int i = 0; i < 10; i++)
     list.append_value(i);

   list.show_list();

   for (i = 10; i < 20; i++)
     list.append_value(i);

   list.show_list();
 }
```

In this case, the linked list supports only values of type *int*. Using a class template, however, you can quickly change the program to support values of type *int* and *float*. The following program, LINKTEMP.CPP, uses a template to create two such lists:

```
#include <iostream.h>
#include <iomanip.h>

template<class T>
struct Node {
 T value;
 Node *next;
 Node *previous;
};

template<class T1>
class LinkList {
 public:
   LinkList(void);
   void show_list(void);
   Node<T1> *append_value(T1);
 private:
   Node<T1> *first;
   Node<T1> *end;
};

template<class T1> LinkList<T1>::LinkList(void)
 {
   first = NULL;
   end = NULL;
 }

template<class T1> void LinkList<T1>::show_list(void)
 {
   Node<T1> *node;

   node = first;

   while (node)
     {
       cout << node->value << endl;
       node = node->next;
     }
 }

template<class T1>
Node<T1> *LinkList<T1>::append_value(T1 value)
 {
   Node<T1> *ptr = end;

   end = new Node<T1>;

   if (first == NULL)
     first = end;
```

```
    else
      ptr->next = end;

    if (end)
      {
        end->next = NULL;
        end->previous = ptr;
        end->value = value;
      }

    return(end);
  }

void main(void)
  {
    LinkList<int> list;
    LinkList<float> values;

    for (int i = 0; i < 10; i++)
      list.append_value(i);

    list.show_list();

    cout << setiosflags(ios::showpoint);

    for (i = 1; i < 20; i++)
      values.append_value(i * 100.0);

    values.show_list();
  }
```

To begin, the program uses a nodes that contain a value, and pointers to the previous and next nodes as shown in Figure 6.1.

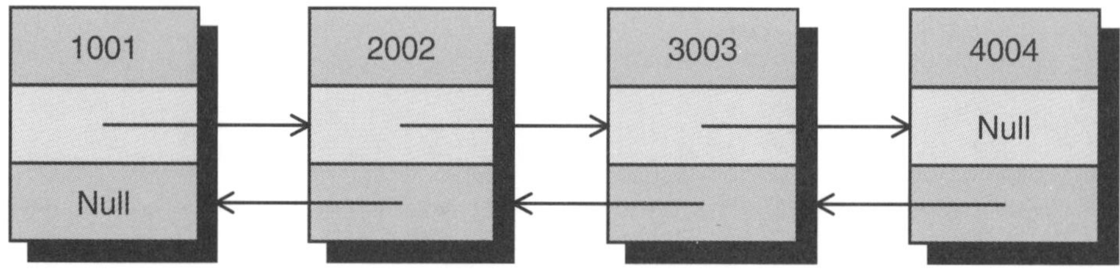

Figure 6.1 The node structure used within the linked list.

To allow the node structure to hold values of different types, such as *int* or *float*, the program uses a template, as shown here:

```
template<class T>
struct Node {
 T value;
 Node *next;
 Node *previous;
};
```

Next, the program uses a class template, which defines the operations on a linked list. Using the template, the class can be used to create linked-list objects of type *int*, *float*, and so on:

```
template<class T1>
class LinkList {
 public:
   LinkList(void);
   void show_list(void);
   Node<T1> *append_value(T1);
 private:
   Node<T1> *first;
   Node<T1> *end;
};
```

The program can builds two linked-list objects, one that contains values of type *int* and one that contains values of type *float* using the following statements:

```
LinkList<int> list;

LinkList<float> values;
```

When the C++ compiler encounters the object definitions, it first substitutes the type names for the *T1* symbol within the class. Within the class, the compiler in turn creates node structures for the correct type, assigning the type names that have been used for *T1* to *T*. In the case of the integer linked list, the substitutions become the following:

```
LinkList<int> list;

     template<class T1>
     class LinkList {
      public:
        LinkList(void);
        void show_list(void);
        Node<T1> *append_value(T1);
      private:
        Node<T1> *first;
        Node<T1> *end;
     };
```

```
class LinkList {
 public:
   LinkList(void);
   void show_list(void);
   Node *append_value(int);
 private:
   Node<int> *first;
   Node<int> *end;
};

     template<class T>
     struct Node {
      T value;
      Node *next;
      Node *previous;
     };

          struct Node {
           int value;
           Node *next;
           Node *previous;
          };
```

As you can see, the compiler approaches such templates in a step-by-step fashion. As you use complex templates within your programs, try performing similar substitutions on your own statements, and template use should become easier to understand.

Putting It All Together

C++ templates allow the compiler to replicate functions and classes automatically whose parameters or members differ only by type. Using the compiler to replicate functions or classes that you know work, you decrease the amount of code you must write, as well as your chances of introducing errors. This chapter has examined templates in detail. Before you continue with Chapter 7, make sure that you have learned the following:

- ✓ A template provides a blueprint for a function or class that the C++ compiler automatically replicates using the types you specify. Templates are ideal for similar functions or classes whose parameters or members differ only by type.
- ✓ C++ supports function and class templates.

- ✓ To create a function template, use the *template* keyword, followed by the *class* keyword and type symbols within open and closed brackets, such as *template<class T1>*. The remainder of your function declaration is unchanged, except that you use the *T1* symbol in place of a type name, such as *int* or *float*.
- ✓ To later create a function of that returns or supports parameters of a specific type, include a function prototype or simply use the function. During compilation, the C++ compiler will determine the types it must support, based on the parameter types passed to the function.
- ✓ If the function template supports multiple parameter types, the compiler will assign types as specified within a function prototype or from left to right, based on the parameters passed to the function.
- ✓ To create a class template, precede your class definition with a the *template* keyword and class symbols, as just discussed.
- ✓ To create objects using a class template, specify the class name, followed by the desired type within brackets, such as *ClassName<int> ObjectName.*
- ✓ If the class template supports multiple parameter types, the compiler will assign types as specified in the object declaration, from left to right. For example, the following declaration uses the type *int* for the template's first type symbol and *float* for the second symbol: *ClassName<int, float> ObjectName.*
- ✓ If one class template uses a second template, the compiler will perform type substitutions one class at a time, beginning with the first class referenced.

Chapter 7
Getting Up to Speed with Memory Allocation

When your programs work with large amounts of information, such as 50 class test scores, 100 employee records, or even a long character string, they can store the information in arrays, or they can allocate the memory dynamically as the memory is required. The advantages of allocating the memory dynamically are that your program can allocate an amount of memory that more accurately meets the program's requirements, and the program can allocate when the memory is required, later freeing the memory to make it available for other use.

In C, programmers make extensive use of run-time library functions such as *alloc*, *calloc*, and *malloc* to allocate memory dynamically during the program's execution. When the program no longer requires the memory, C programs release the memory for reuse with the *free* function. Although C++ programs can dynamically allocate memory using these run-time library functions, C++ programs normally allocate memory using the *new* and *delete* operators. This chapter examines *new* and *delete* in detail. You will learn not only how to allocate memory to contain values of type *int*, *float*, and structures, but also how to allocate memory for C++ classes. When you finish this chapter, you will understand

- How your C++ programs allocate memory
- What happens if the *new* operator cannot successfully allocate memory
- How your programs can specify a function that automatically executes when a memory request cannot be satisfied
- How your C++ programs release previously allocated memory
- How to initialize a memory location with a specified value
- How to allocate memory for an array of values
- How to override the *new* or *delete* operators

Looking at a Simple Memory Allocation Example

The following program, SORT_TEN.CPP, defines an array capable of storing ten integer values. The program then fills the array with ten random values, passing the array to the function *bubble_sort* for sorting. The program then displays the sorted values:

```
#include <iostream.h>
#include <stdlib.h>

void bubble_sort(int *array, int num_elements)
 {
  for (int i = 0; i < num_elements; i++)
    for (int j = 0; j < num_elements; j++)
      if (array[i] < array[j])
        {
          int temp = array[i];
          array[i] = array[j];
          array[j] = temp;
        }
 }

void main(void)
 {
   int array[10];

   for (int i = 0; i < 10; i++)
     array[i] = random(SIZE);          // Values from 0 through SIZE

   bubble_sort(array, 10);

   for (i = 0; i < 10; i++)
     cout << array[i] << endl;
 }
```

Note: If your compiler does not use the ***random()*** *function, the* ***rand()*** *function should be available. While not exactly the same as the* ***random()*** *function shown here,* ***rand()*** *performs a similar function.*

When you compile and execute this program, your screen will display the ten sorted values. When the number of values with which your program must work is fixed, such as ten integer values, your programs can use an array similar to the one used in the program just shown. However, keep in mind that if the program only uses the array at the start or end of the program, there may be a considerable amount of time when the array unnecessarily consumes memory. In such cases, you should dynamically allocate memory for the array as your needs require.

Dynamically allocating memory also reduces the number of changes you must make to a program as the program's requirements change. Assume, for example, that the previous program must now sort and display 20 integer values. To change the program, you must change each occurrence of the number 10 to 20 and then recompile the program.

One way to reduce the number of such changes is to define your array and loops in terms of a constant, as shown in the following program, SORT_CON.CPP:

```
#define SIZE 20

void main(void)
 {
   int array[SIZE];

   for (int i = 0; i < SIZE; i++)
     array[i] = random(SIZE);        // Values from 0 through SIZE

   bubble_sort(array, SIZE);

   for (i = 0; i < SIZE; i++)
     cout << array[i] << endl;
 }
```

Note: This program does not display the code for the ***bubble_sort*** *function previously shown. However, the code does exist on the book's companion disk file SORT_CON.CPP.*

Then, should your array size change again in the future, the only program statement you need to change is the size definition:

```
#define SIZE 20
```

In many cases, however, you will not know your storage requirements until the program executes. Assume, for example, that the user will specify how many values the array will hold. If you are using arrays, your program must allocate the largest possible array size, using only those elements the user requires. The following program, BIGARRAY.CPP, does exactly that:

```
#define SIZE 30000

void main(void)
 {
   int array[SIZE];
   int size;

   cout << "Type in the number of values to sort (less than " <<
           SIZE << "): ";
   cin >> size;

   if (size <= SIZE)
    {
      for (int i = 0; i < size; i++)
        array[i] = random(SIZE);    // Values from 0 through SIZE

      bubble_sort(array, size);
```

```
        for (i = 0; i < size; i++)
          cout << array[i] << endl;
      }
    else
      cerr << "Array size must be less than " << SIZE << endl;
  }
```

Note: This program does not display the code for the ***bubble_sort*** *function previously shown. However, the code does exist on the book's companion disk file BIGARRAY.CPP.*

In this case, the program declares an array capable of storing 30,000 values. If the user needs fewer values, part of the array is unused (wasted). As you will find, a much better solution is to allocate the memory dynamically.

Note: The previous program used 30,000 for the array size. This size was not chosen at random. Many PC-based compilers still restrict (non-huge) arrays to 64Kb in size because the compiler stores the array in a 64Kb segment. 30,000 elements × 2 bytes/element = 60Kb, which leaves a little heap space free for other uses.

The following program, C_MALLOC.CPP, dynamically allocates memory for the array using the C run-time library *malloc* function. By allocating the memory dynamically, the program can allocate an array whose size matches the user's requirements:

```
#include <malloc.h>

#define SIZE 30000

void main(void)
 {
   int *array;
   int size;

   cout << "Type in the number of values to sort (less than " <<
           SIZE << "): ";
   cin >> size;

   if (size <= SIZE)
    {
      if ((array = (int *) malloc(size * sizeof(int))) == NULL)
        cerr << "Error allocating memory" << endl;
      else
        {
          for (int i = 0; i < size; i++)
            array[i] = random(SIZE);  // Values from 0 thru SIZE

          bubble_sort(array, size);
```

```
        for (i = 0; i < size; i++)
          cout << array[i] << endl;

        free(array);
      }
  }
  else
    cerr << "Array size must be less than " << SIZE << endl;
}
```

Note: This program does not display the code for the ***bubble_sort*** *function previously shown. However, the code does exist on the book's companion disk file C_MALLOC.CPP.*

The prototype for the *malloc* function resides in the header file MALLOC.H. The *malloc* function returns a pointer to the allocated memory region or the NULL value if it could not satisfy the memory request:

```
if ((array = (int *) malloc(size * sizeof(int))) == NULL)
  cout << "Error allocating memory" << endl;
```

As you can see, the program invokes *malloc* with the number of bytes required—which in this case, is the number of elements (*size*) multiplied by the size of each element (*sizeof(int)*). When the program has finished with the allocated memory, it releases the memory for reuse using the *free* run-time library function. By default, the *malloc* function returns a *void* pointer. The *(int *)* that precedes the function invocation casts the *void* pointer to a pointer of type *int*.

This program also restricts the array size to less than 30,000 or less. As was the case with arrays, many DOS-based compilers restrict the amount of dynamic memory your programs can allocate to a 64Kb segment. Later in this chapter, you will learn how to determine the amount of memory your programs can dynamically allocate.

Working with Dynamic Memory

As you know, arrays let your programs store related pieces of information of the same type. For example, one array might hold 50 student test scores, and another array might hold 100 employee salaries. Although arrays are very convenient for grouping data, arrays can introduce the need for many changes to your programs when the number of elements your arrays hold needs to change. In addition, if your program only uses the arrays at specific times, the arrays can consume considerable memory, even when they are not in use. As an alternative, your programs can allocate memory dynamically, as the program's need require. In this way, the program can allocate the amount of memory it needs, when the program needs the memory. When the program has finished with the memory, the program should release the memory for reuse. As you will learn, the C++ *new* operator lets your programs allocate memory dynamically. When your program no longer needs the memory, the program can release the memory using the *delete* operator.

Dynamic Memory Allocation in C++

To allocate memory dynamically in C++, your programs use the *new* and *delete* operators, which are very similar to the *malloc* and *free* run-time library functions just discussed. To dynamically allocate an array of 100 *int* values, for example, you use *new*, as shown here:

```
int *array = new int[100];
```

As is the case with the *malloc* function, if the *new* operator is unable to allocate the memory requested, it normally assigns the NULL value to the pointer. Within your program, you can test for the NULL pointer assignment as follows:

```
if (array == NULL)
   cerr << "Unable to allocate memory" << endl;
```

Note: As you will learn later in this chapter, some compilers do not assign the NULL value when ***new*** *cannot allocate the requested memory. Instead, some compilers immediately end your program (by raising an uncaught exception, as discussed in Chapter 14). However, as you will learn, C++ lets you specify your own function, which executes when a memory request cannot be satisfied. In this way, your programs can handle the insufficient memory error in their own way.*

When your program no longer needs the memory, you release the memory, as shown here:

```
delete array;
```

The following program, NEW_TEN.CPP, uses the *new* operator to allocate an array of ten *int* values. The program then assigns values to the array, sorts the array's contents, and then displays the array. When the array is no longer needed, the array program uses the *delete* operator to release the corresponding memory:

```
void main(void)
 {
   int *array = new int[10];

   if (array == NULL)
     cerr << "Error allocating memory" << endl;
```

```
   else
     {
       for (int i = 0; i < 10; i++)
         array[i] = random(30000);    // Values from 0 thru 30,000

       bubble_sort(array, 10);

       for (i = 0; i < 10; i++)
         cout << array[i] << endl;

       delete array;
     }
 }
```

Note: This program does not display the code for the ***bubble_sort*** *function previously shown. However, the code does exist on the book's companion disk file NEW_TEN.CPP.*

As you can see, if the *new* operator successfully allocates the memory, the program treats the dynamic memory no differently than a standard array. The following program, NEW_ASK.CPP, asks the user for the amount of memory required. The program then allocates an array using the *new* operator:

```
#define SIZE 30000

void main(void)
 {
   int *array;
   int size;

   cout << "Type in the number of values to sort (less than " <<
           SIZE << "): ";
   cin >> size;

   if (size <= SIZE)
    {
      if ((array = new int[size]) == NULL)
        cerr << "Error allocating memory" << endl;
      else
        {
          for (int i = 0; i < size; i++)
            array[i] = random(SIZE);    // Values from 0 thru SIZE

          bubble_sort(array, size);

          for (i = 0; i < size; i++)
            cout << array[i] << endl;
```

```
            delete array;
          }
      }
    else
      cerr << "Array size must be less than " << SIZE << endl;
  }
```

Note: This program does not display the code for the ***bubble_sort*** *function previously shown. However, the code does exist on the book's companion disk file NEW_ASK.CPP.*

If the *new* operator cannot allocate the requested memory, it assigns the NULL value to the pointer.

As you can see, the program uses the *new* operator to allocate the desired memory within an *if* statement:

```
      if ((array = new int[size]) == NULL)
        cerr << "Error allocating memory" << endl;
```

Allocating Memory Dynamically Using the new *Operator*

The C++ *new* operator lets your programs allocate memory dynamically. To use *new* your program must specify the number of elements required. The *new* operator, in turn, will determine the required number of bytes, based on the data type your program is allocating. For an element of type, *int*, for example, the *new* operator allocates two bytes. Likewise, for a *float*, *new* will allocate four bytes. If the *new* operator is successful, it returns a pointer to the allocated memory. If *new* cannot satisfy the memory request, *new* returns the NULL value. The following statement, for example, uses *new* to allocate a 50-element array of type *int*:

```
int *array = new int[50];
```

Element type — `int`
Pointer to the allocated memory — `*array`
Number of elements — `50`
Type of element being allocated — `new`

In a similar way, this statement allocates an array of 100 floating-point values:

```
float *salaries = new float[100];
```

After your programs allocate memory using the *new* operator, you should test the pointer value assigned to ensure that the operation was successful. If *new* cannot allocate the requested memory, it will assign the NULL value to the pointer:

```
if (salaries == NULL)
  cerr << "Error allocating memory" << endl;
```

When your program no longer requires the memory, it should release the memory for reuse with the *delete* operator as shown here:

```
delete array;
delete salary;
```

The previous program used the *new* operator to allocate memory to hold an array of type *int.* Using *new* to allocate memory to hold other types of information is very easy. The following program, SUMFLOAT.CPP, uses *new* to allocate an array to hold 15 floating-point values. The program then assigns random values to the array, displaying the values and their sum:

```
#include <iostream.h>
#include <iomanip.h>
#include <stdlib.h>

#define SIZE 15

void main(void)
 {
   float *array = new float[SIZE];
   float sum = 0.0;

   if (array == NULL)
     cerr << "Error allocating memory" << endl;
   else
     {
       for (int i = 0; i < SIZE; i++)
         {
           array[i] = rand() / 1000.0;
           sum += array[i];
           cout << setw(6) << setprecision(2) <<
                   setiosflags(ios::fixed || ios::right) <<
                   array[i] << endl;
         }

       cout << "Array sum is " << sum << endl;
       delete array;
     }
 }
```

As you can see, the program allocates the memory using the *new* operator and later releases the memory using *delete.*

Note: If you do not release allocated memory using ***delete****, the memory is automatically released when the program ends. However, keep in mind that one of your reasons for using dynamic memory is to allocate memory as needed, releasing it as soon as the memory is no longer required. By releasing memory as soon as the memory is no longer required, the memory is available for other use.*

WORKING WITH POINTER VARIABLES

The previous examples have used *new* to allocate memory to hold an array. Because C++ treats the array name as a pointer, your programs do not have to worry about pointer variables and pointer redirection. If your program allocates memory for use other than an array, your program must use pointers to access the memory. For example, the following program, USE_PTRS.CPP, allocates memory for values of type *int* and *float*. The program then assigns values to and displays the values of the memory locations referenced by the pointers:

```
#include <iostream.h>

void main(void)
 {
   int *int_pointer;
   float *float_pointer;

   if ((int_pointer = new int) == NULL)
     cerr << "Error allocating memory for int" << endl;
   else
     {
       *int_pointer = 1001;
       cout << "The value assigned to memory location " <<
               int_pointer << " is " << *int_pointer << endl;
     }

   if ((float_pointer = new float) == NULL)
     cerr << "Error allocating memory for float" << endl;
   else
     {
       *float_pointer = 11.22;
       cout << "The value assigned to memory location " <<
               float_pointer << " is " << *float_pointer << endl;
     }
 }
```

As you can see, the program uses the indirection operator (*) when working with the value stored at a memory location pointed to by a pointer. Notice the following statement:

```
cout << "The value assigned to memory location " << float_pointer <<
        " is " << *float_pointer << endl;
```

Because the first reference to *float_pointer* is not preceded by an asterisk, the program displays *float_pointer's* value, the memory address. The second reference to *float_pointer* is preceded by an asterisk and, as a result, the program displays the value contained in the memory location pointed to by *float_pointer*. When you compile and execute this program, your screen will display output similar to the following:

```
C:\> USE_PTRS  <ENTER>
The value assigned to memory location 0x14c0 is 1001
The value assigned to memory location 0x14c8 is 11.22
```

When you compile and run this program, the memory locations displayed might differ on your system, depending on your operating system, device drivers, memory-resident programs, and so on. As you can see, the program displays the pointer value (the address) and the value contained in the memory location. Figure 7.1 illustrates how the pointers reference memory locations, which, in turn, contain values.

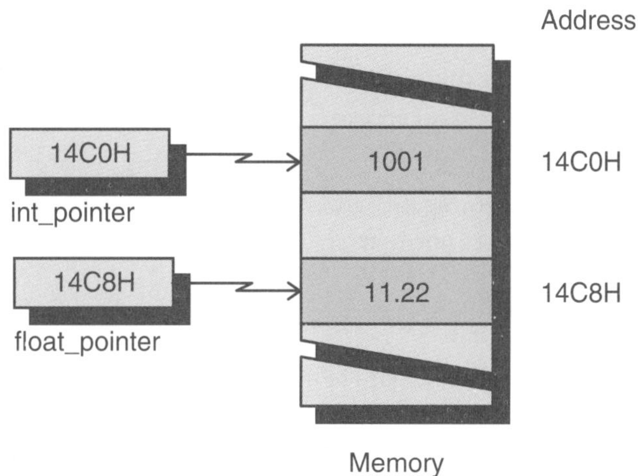

Figure 7.1 A pointer contains the memory address of a value or the starting address of a range of values.

Note that the previous program declared the pointer variables as follows:

```
int   *int_pointer;
float  *float_pointer;
```

When you examine C and C++ programs, you may encounter pointer declarations that place the asterisk immediately after the type name, as shown here:

```
int*  int_pointer;
float*  float_pointer;
```

Likewise, you may encounter declarations that float the asterisk between the type and variable name:

```
int   *   int_pointer;
float   * float_pointer;
```

No matter where the programmer places the asterisk, all three positions create identical pointer variables. For consistency, the programs presented in this book all place the asterisk immediately before the variable name.

Initializing a Value Using new

When you allocate simple values, such as a value of type *int* or *float*, there may be times when you want to assign a value to the memory location immediately. For example, consider the following statements, which allocate an *int* pointer and then assign the memory location the value 1001:

```
int *int_ptr = new int;

if (int_ptr)
  *int_ptr = 1001;
```

As it turns, the *new* operator lets you specify an initial value when you allocate memory by placing the value within parentheses, as shown here:

```
int *int_ptr = new int(1001);
```

If *new* successfully allocates the memory, it will perform the initialization. If the memory cannot be allocated, the initialization is ignored. The following program, NEW_INIT.CPP, uses *new* to allocate space for and then to initialize values of type *int* and *float*:

```
#include <iostream.h>

void main(void)
 {
   int *int_pointer = new int(1001);
   float *float_pointer = new float(3.12345);

   cout << *int_pointer << endl;
   cout << *float_pointer << endl;
 }
```

Understanding Pointer Arithmetic

Many C and C++ programmers use pointers instead of array operations to improve their program's performance. Consider, for example, the following functions, each of which displays the values in an array of type *float*:

```
void show_values(float array[], int size)
  {
      for (int i = 0; i < size; i++)
         cout << array[i] << endl;
  }
```

```
void show_values(float *array, int size)
  {
      for (int i = 0; i < size; i++)
         cout << *array++;
  }
```

The function on the left displays the values using an array and array indexing. The function on the right, on the other hand, uses a pointer to display the values. If you place these two functions in different programs and generate assembly language listings, you will find that the compiler inserts more instructions to manipulate the array of values than are required by the pointer. As a result, the pointer implementation has fewer instructions and executes faster.

Within your programs, a pointer normally points to a value of a specific type. The only exception to this rule are *void* pointers, which are typeless. The reason pointers are typed is to ensure that the compiler knows how many bytes to advance the pointer in memory (by how much to increment the pointer) when the user uses the pointer to traverse a list of values as previously shown. For example, if you use a pointer to traverse a character string, the compiler will increment the pointer by one byte each time your program increments the pointer using an expression such as *string++*. If your program uses a pointer to an array of integer values, the compiler will increment the pointer by two bytes, so that the pointer will then point to the next integer value. Likewise, for a floating-point list, the compiler will increment the pointer by four bytes. If pointers were not typed, the compiler could not perform such operations.

Treating Pointers as Arrays

Many C++ programs treat arrays as pointers. For example, the following program SHOW_STR.CPP, passes a character string array to the function *show_string*, which in turn displays the string a character at a time using a pointer:

```
#include <iostream.h>

void show_string(char *string)
 {
   while (*string)
     cout.put(*string++);
 }
```

```
void main(void)
 {
   char book[] = "Success with C++\n";

   show_string(book);
 }
```

As you examine C and C++ programs, you may periodically encounter code that mixes pointer and array-like operations. For example, the following statements assign the value 3 to the fourth element (offset from 0) in an array of integer values:

```
void some_function(int *array, int size)
 {
   array[3] = 3;

   // Other statements
 }
```

As you can see, the function receives a pointer to an integer value. The function then treats that pointer as the base of an array. It is important to note that any pointer, at any time, can be treated as the base of an array.

The following program, PTRARRAY.CPP, performs just the opposite operations as the previous program. In this case, the function *show_string* receives a pointer to a string and then treats the pointer as the base of an array:

```
#include <iostream.h>

void show_string(char string[])
 {
   for (int i = 0; string[i]; i++)
     cout.put(string[i]);
 }

void main(void)
 {
   char *book = "Hi, Hello, world!\n";

   show_string(book + 4);
 }
```

Note that the program passes to the function, the address of the string plus four (skipping the characters "Hi, "). If you compile and execute this program, your screen will display the following output:

```
C:\> PTRARRAY  <ENTER>
Hello, world!
```

As you can see, any pointer can be treated as the base of an array at any time.

Using Pointers with Function Parameters

One of the most common pointer operations your program will perform is to change parameters within a function. By default, when your programs invoke a function, C and C++ make copies of the parameter's value, placing the copied values on to the stack. Because the function receives a copy of the parameter value, the function cannot change the actual parameter in any way. The following program, NOCHANGE.CPP, passes three parameters to the function *one_two_three* which in turn, assigns the values 1, 2, and 3 to the parameters. Because the function does not have access to the actual parameters, but rather to copies of the parameter values, the parameters remain unchanged when the function ends:

```
#include <iostream.h>

void one_two_three(int a, int b, int c)
 {
   cout << "Values passed to the function: " << a << ' ' << b <<
           ' ' << c << endl;
   a = 1;
   b = 2;
   c = 3;
   cout << "Values within the function: " << a << ' ' << b <<
           ' ' << c << endl;
 }

void main(void)
 {
   int one = 0, two = 0, three = 0;
   one_two_three(one, two, three);
   cout << "Values in main: " << one << ' ' << two << ' ' <<
           three << endl;
 }
```

When you compile and execute this program, your screen will display the following output:

```
C:\> NOCHANGE  <ENTER>
Values passed to the function: 0 0 0
Values within the function: 1 2 3
Values in main: 0 0 0
```

As you can see, the actual parameter values where not changed by the function. To change the parameter values, your program must use pointers. To begin, you must use pointer variables within the function *one_two_three*, as shown here:

```
void one_two_three(int *a, int *b, int *c)
 {
   cout << "Values passed to the function: " << *a << ' ' <<
           *b << ' ' << *c << endl;
   *a = 1;
   *b = 2;
   *c = 3;
   cout << "Values within the function: " << *a << ' ' << *b <<
           ' ' << *c << endl;
 }
```

As you can see, the function's parameters are pointers to values of type *int.* Next, when you invoke the function, you must pass the address of each variable using the address operator (&), as shown here:

```
one_two_three(&one, &two, &three);
```

By passing the address of the variables to the function, the function works with the actual parameter values instead of value copies. In this way, changes the function makes to the function remain after the function ends. The following program, PAR_CHG.CPP, uses pointers to change parameter values within the function *one_two_three*:

```
#include <iostream.h>

void one_two_three(int *a, int *b, int *c)
 {
   cout << "Values passed to the function: " << *a << ' ' <<
           *b << ' ' << *c << endl;
   *a = 1;
   *b = 2;
   *c = 3;
   cout << "Values within the function: " << *a << ' ' << *b <<
           ' ' << *c << endl;
 }

void main(void)
 {
   int one = 0, two = 0, three = 0;

   one_two_three(&one, &two, &three);

   cout << "Values in main: " << one << ' ' << two << ' ' <<
           three << endl;
 }
```

When you compile and execute this program, your screen will display the following output:

```
C:\> PAR_CHG  <ENTER>
Values passed to the function: 0 0 0
Values within the function: 1 2 3
Values in main: 1 2 3
```

As you can see, the values passed to the function remain changed after the function ends. In Chapter 10 you will examine C++ references, which provide a second way to change parameter values within a function.

Using Pointers with Structures and Classes

Just as your programs can use pointers to variables of type *int*, *float*, and *char*, or to arrays of the same, your programs can also use pointers to structures and classes. As you know, when you work with a structure or pointer, you use the dot (.) operator to reference specific members. For example, the following statements assign the date December 25, 1994 to a structure of type *Date:*

```
struct Date {
   int month;
   int day;
   int year;
} xmas;

xmas.month = 12;
xmas.day = 25;
xmas.year = 1994;
```

When your programs work with pointers to structures and classes, they can access members in one of two ways. First, your programs can use the indirection operator and the pointer within parentheses. For example, the following function, *assign_xmas* assigns the date to a structure pointed to by the variable *date_ptr*:

```
void assign_xmas(struct Date *date_ptr)
   {
       (*date_ptr).month = 12;
       (*date_ptr).day = 25;
       (*date_ptr).year = 1994;
   }
```

Because this pointer syntax can be confusing to new programmers and because programmers periodically forget the parentheses, C and C++ let your programs access members of structure pointed to by a pointer as follows:

```
void assign_xmas(struct Date *date_ptr)
  {
      date_ptr->month = 12;
      date_ptr->day = 25;
      date_ptr->year = 1994;
  }
```

When your programs work with classes, they can use these same two formats to access class members.

Pointers Are Not References

In Chapter 10 you will learn that a C++ *reference* is an alias or second name your programs can use for a variable. In general, references exist to simplify functions that change parameter values by eliminating the need to perform pointer operations. For example, the following program, SWAP_PTR.CPP, uses pointers to exchange the values contained in the variables *a* and *b:*

```
#include <iostream.h>

void swap_values(int *first, int *second)
 {
   int temp = *first;
   *first = *second;
   *second = temp;
 }

void main(void)
 {
   int a = 1;
   int b = 1001;

   swap_values(&a, &b);

   cout << "Values after swap a: " << a << " b: " << b << endl;
 }
```

In a similar way, the following program SWAP_REF.CPP, uses references to exchange the values:

```
#include <iostream.h>

void swap_values(int& first, int& second)
 {
   int temp = first;
   first = second;
   second = temp;
 }
```

```
void main(void)
 {
   int a = 1;
   int b = 1001;

   int& a_alias = a;     // Declare the references
   int& b_alias = b;

   swap_values(a_alias, b_alias);

   cout << "Values after swap a: " << a << " b: " << b << endl;
 }
```

As you can see, the references eliminate the need for pointer operations within the function. However, references also add to program complexity by introducing additional variables for the programmer to track and understand. Chapter 10 examines references in detail. For now, simply keep in mind that a reference is not a pointer.

Be Aware of Pointers and Local Variables

As your programs become more complex, there may be times when your programs allocate memory from within functions. It is important that you keep in mind that when you allocate memory from within a function, the memory remains allocated, even after the function ends. Consider, for example, the following program, LOCALPTR.CPP, which allocates 1,000 bytes of memory within the function *bad_pointer*:

```
#include <iostream.h>

void bad_pointer(void)
 {
   char *ptr = new char[1000];          // Allocate the memory

   // Perform some operation
 }

void main(void)
 {
   // Invoke function
   bad_pointer();

   // Perform some operation

   // Invoke the function a second time
   bad_pointer();
 }
```

Each time the program invokes *bad_pointer*, the function allocates the memory, assigning the corresponding pointer the local variable *ptr*. Unfortunately, the function does not free the memory when it is no longer needed. Because the memory is pointed to by a local function variable, the program has no way to release the memory after the function ends. As a result, the memory is allocated, but there is no way for the program to access it. If your program allocates temporary memory within a function, make sure it releases the memory before the function ends. In some cases, as discussed next, you will want the memory to remain allocated after the function ends.

Working with Functions That Return Pointers

Depending on your function's purpose, there may be times when you want memory allocated within a function to remain in effect after the function ends. For example, the following program, STR_DUP.CPP, uses the *string_duplicate* function, which allocates memory to hold the number of characters contained in a character string parameter, copies the string to the memory, and then returns a pointer to the start of the new string. If the function cannot successfully duplicate the string, the function returns NULL:

```
#include <iostream.h>
#include <string.h>

char *string_duplicate(char *source)
 {
   char *target = new char[strlen(source)];

   if (target)
     for (int i = 0; target[i] = source[i]; i++)
      ;

   return(target);
 }

void main(void)
 {
   char *new_string;

   new_string = string_duplicate("Success with C++!");

   cout << new_string << endl;
 }
```

Because the program needs to access the memory buffer allocated by the function after the function ends, the function does not release the memory using *delete*.

Understanding the Free Space

When your programs allocate memory dynamically, the memory is allocated from a reserved pool of memory called the *free space* or *heap*. As Figure 7.2 shows, the *free space* normally resides above the program's data area and beneath the program's stack space.

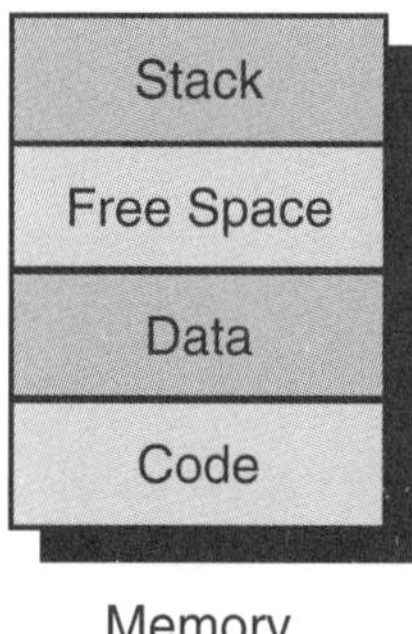

***Figure** 7.2 The free space resides above the program's data area and beneath the program's stack space.*

Depending on your operating system and compiler memory model (for PC-based compilers), the amount of free space available for your program use will differ. Chapter 15 takes a detailed look at the free space (which is often called the heap). You will learn what happens behind the scenes when you allocate and later release memory. For now, however, remember that your programs do not have an unlimited amount of available heap space. Depending on your program's memory requirements, it is possible for your program to consume all of the available free space.

Handling Out-of-Memory Conditions

As you have learned, when the *new* operator cannot allocate a sufficient amount of memory to satisfy your request, it assigns the value NULL to the corresponding pointer variable. The following program, TAKE_ALL.CPP, uses the *new* operator within a loop to allocate memory from the free space in 10Kb blocks until the no more memory is available. The program then displays a message stating how much memory it successfully allocated:

```
#include <iostream.h>

void main(void)
 {
```

```
   char *buffer;
   long sum = 0L;

   do {
     buffer = new char[10000];
     if (buffer)
      {
        cout << "Allocated 10,000 bytes" << endl;
        sum += 10000;
      }
   } while (buffer);

   cout << "The amount of memory allocated was " << sum <<
           " bytes" << endl;
}
```

Compile and execute this program. In most cases, the *new* operator will assign NULL to the pointer as previously discussed. Some compilers, however, will end the program when the memory request cannot be satisfied, as shown here:

```
C:\> TAKE_ALL  <ENTER>
Allocated 10,000 bytes
Allocated 10,000 bytes
Allocated 10,000 bytes
Allocated 10,000 bytes
Allocated 10,000 bytes
Abnormal program termination
```

To understand why the program abruptly ended in this way, you need to know that C++ lets you specify a function that you want to execute when a memory request cannot be satisfied. For such cases, C++ supports the *set_new_handler* function, which lets you specify a program-defined function that you want to execute when a memory request cannot be satisfied. The prototype for the *set_new_handler* function resides in the header file NEW.H.

The following program, SET_NEW.CPP, uses the *set_new_handler* to invoke the function *message_and_exit* when a memory request cannot be satisfied. When the *message_and_exit* function is invoked, the function displays a message to the *cerr* stream and then exits the program:

```
#include <iostream.h>
#include <stdlib.h>
#include <new.h>

void message_and_exit(void)
 {
```

```
    cerr << "\a\aNo more memory!" << endl;
    exit(1);
 }

void main(void)
 {
    char *buffer;
    long sum = 0L;

    set_new_handler(message_and_exit);

    do {
      buffer = new char[10000];
      if (buffer)
        {
          cout << "Allocated 10,000 bytes" << endl;
          sum += 10000;
        }
    } while (buffer);

    cout << "The amount of memory allocated was " << sum <<
             " bytes" << endl;
 }
```

*Note: The exact name and syntax used by your compiler for the **set_new_handler** function may differ from that which is shown here.*

In most cases, however, you will not want a special function invoked at all when a memory request cannot be satisfied, but rather, you will simply want *new* to return NULL. In such cases, you can invoke the *set_new_handler* function with the NULL parameter to disable the function. The following program, USE_NULL.CPP, uses disables the out of memory handler using NULL with *set_new_handler*.

```
#include <iostream.h>
#include <stdlib.h>
#include <new.h>

void main(void)
 {
    char *buffer;
    long sum = 0L;

    set_new_handler(NULL);

    do {
      buffer = new char[10000];
```

```
      if (buffer)
        {
          cout << "Allocated 10,000 bytes" << endl;
          sum += 10000;
        }
    } while (buffer);

    cout << "The amount of memory allocated was " << sum <<
            " bytes" << endl;
  }
```

As you will learn in the next section, the best way for your programs to truly control memory allocation operations is to override the *new* and *delete* operators.

Specifying a Function to Handle Insufficient Memory Errors

Normally, when the *new* operator cannot satisfy a memory request, *new* assigns the NULL value to the corresponding pointer. In some cases (such as when you test a program), you might want your program to end, possibly displaying an error message when a memory request cannot be satisfied. By ending the program in this way, you may be able to locate a memory allocation operation within your program whose result is not being tested for NULL. To specify a function that you want to run when a memory request cannot be satisfied, you can use the *set_new_handler* function. The header file NEW.H provides the function prototype:

```
set_new_handler(* new_handler());
```

To disable the invocation of the special handler function, invoke the function with the NULL value, as shown here:

```
set_new_handler(NULL);
```

Overloading new and delete

In Chapter 5 you learned how to overload operators within your programs. Because *new* and *delete* are C++ operators, you can overload them as well. As you will learn in Chapter 15, C++ does not perform garbage collection to try to recover (group) unused free space to create a large enough section of memory to satisfy a memory allocation request. For example, in Figure 7.3, the free space contains allocated and available memory. As you can see, there are 500 bytes of available memory.

Unfortunately, the largest block of available memory is 250 bytes. If your program needs to allocate 300 bytes, the allocation will fail.

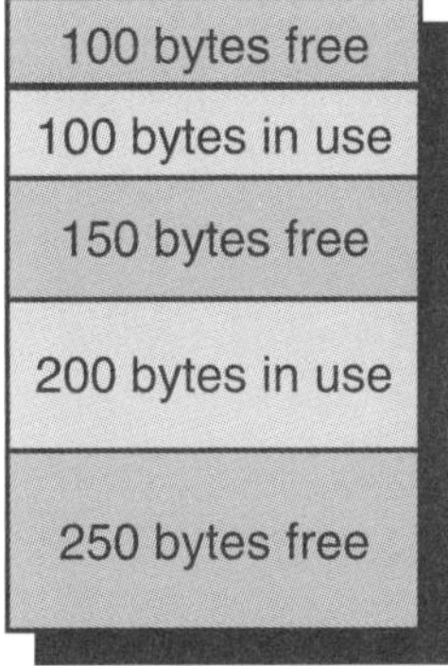

Figure 7.3 *Fragmented locations within the free space can prevent memory allocation.*

Garbage collection is a technique used to group the available memory into a large block. Using garbage collection techniques, the available free space can be grouped, as shown in Figure 7.4.

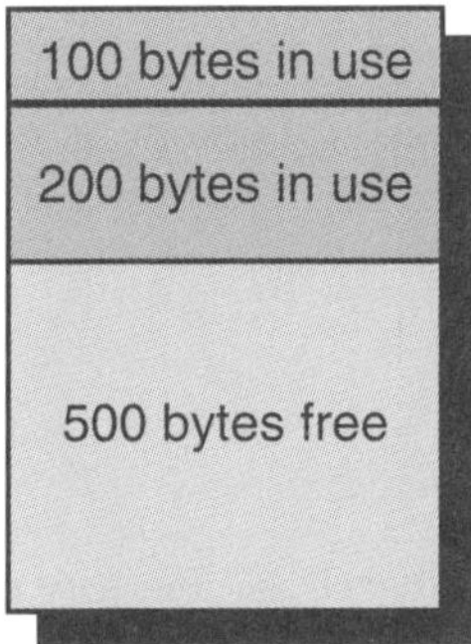

Figure 7.4 *Grouping available free space.*

To perform garbage collection, allocated and available blocks of memory are moved to create a large block of available memory. C++ itself cannot perform garbage collection because C++ does not know how your program may be using pointers to different memory regions. However, it is possible for your program to perform such operations because it can keep knowledge of the pointer use. One way to implement garbage collection is to overload the *new* or *delete* operators with functions that periodically perform such operations.

Unfortunately, the steps you must perform to implement an efficient and useful garbage collection are more than we can discuss in this section. However, as you will find, overloading the *new* and *delete* operators is very easy. To overload the *new* and *delete* operators, you declare functions similar to the following:

```
void *operator new(size_t size)
 {
   // Statements
 }

void *operator new[](size_t size)
 {
   // Statements
 }

static void operator delete(void *pointer)
 {
   // Statements
 }
```

As you can see, most compilers provide two definitions for the *new* operator, one that allocates memory for simple data types such as pointers to values of type *int* or *float*, and one that allocates memory for arrays. Normally, within *new*, you will allocate memory using the *malloc* function, as shown here:

```
void *operator new(size_t size)
 {
   // Statements

   return(malloc(size));
 }
```

Likewise, within *delete*, you will normally release memory using the *free* function:

```
static void operator delete(void *pointer)
 {
   // Statements

   free(pointer);
 }
```

Overriding and the *new* and *delete* operators might require a little experimentation, depending on your compiler. To begin, the following program, LIM_1000.CPP, overloads the *new* operator so that it will not support memory allocations larger than 1000 bytes. Should the program invoke *new* with a value larger than 1000, *new* immediately returns NULL:

```
#include <iostream.h>
#include <alloc.h>

void *operator new[](size_t size)
 {
   if (size >= 1000)
     return(0);

   return(malloc(size));
 }

void main(void)
 {
   char *string = new char[1000];
   float *salaries = new float[200];
   int *ages = new int[250];

   if (string)
     cout << "string[1000] was allocated" << endl;
   else
     cout << "Error allocating string[1000]" << endl;

   if (salaries)
     cout << "salaries[200] was allocated" << endl;
   else
     cout << "Error allocating salaries[200]" << endl;

   if (ages)
     cout << "ages[250] was allocated" << endl;
   else
     cout << "Error allocating ages[250]" << endl;
 }
```

*Note: Your compiler might use **malloc.h** instead of the header file **alloc.h**.*

In this case, the program overrides the *new[]* operator. As you can see, the program tries to allocate memory for several different arrays, whose memory requirements are 1000, 800 (4 bytes per float * 200), and 500 (2 bytes per int * 250). When you compile and execute this program, your screen will display the following output:

```
C:\> LIM_1000  <ENTER>
Error allocating string[1000]
salaries[200] was allocated
ages[250] was allocated
```

Normally, your programs will not override the global *new* and *delete* operators. Instead, your programs will override the operators for a specific class type. The following program, OVER_NEW.CPP, for example, overloads the *new* operator for use with the *Date* class to assign a default date of January 1, 1994 to the date buffer. Depending on your program's requirements, you might perform similar processing assigning instead, the current date to the buffer:

```
#include <iostream.h>
#include <alloc.h>

class Date {
  public:
    void *operator new(size_t size);
    int month;
    int day;
    int year;
};

class DateClass {
  public:
    DateClass(int month, int day, int year);
    void show_date(void);
  private:
    Date *buffer;
};

DateClass::DateClass(int month, int day, int year)
 {
   buffer = new Date;

   cout << "Default date: ";
   show_date();

   buffer->month = month;
   buffer->day = day;
   buffer->year = year;
 }

void *Date::operator new(size_t size)
 {
   Date *ptr = (Date *) malloc(size);

   if (ptr)
    {
      ptr->month = 1;
      ptr->day = 1;
      ptr->year = 1994;
    }
```

```
   return((void *) ptr);
 }

void DateClass::show_date(void)
 {
   cout << buffer->month << '/' << buffer->day << '/' <<
           buffer->year << endl;
 }

void main(void)
 {
   DateClass birthday(9, 30, 94);

   cout << "Birthday date: ";
   birthday.show_date();
 }
```

Note: Your compiler may use malloc.h instead of the header file alloc.h.

When you compile and execute this program, your screen will display the following output:

```
C:\> OVER_NEW  <ENTER>
Default date: 1/1/1994
Birthday date: 9/30/94
```

As you can see, by overloading the *new* or *delete* operators, your programs can gain considerable control over memory allocation operations.

Putting It All Together

As you have learned, allocating memory dynamically as your programs require it has several advantages. To begin, during execution your programs can more accurately determine their memory needs. In addition, dynamically allocating memory instead of using arrays reduces the number of changes you must make to your programs as your program's memory requirements change. Finally, by allocating memory when it is required and then releasing the memory as soon as it is no longer needed, your programs allow the memory to be used for other purposes. In Chapter 8 you will learn how to use virtual functions within your programs. Before you continue with Chapter 8, make sure that you have learned the following:

- ✓ In C, programs use run-time library functions such as *malloc* or *calloc* to allocate memory and the *free* routine to release the memory when it is no longer required. In C++, your programs allocate memory using the *new* operator and later release the memory using the *delete* operator.

- ✓ If the *new* operator cannot successfully allocate memory, *new* will normally assign the NULL value to the corresponding pointer. Some compilers, however, may invoke a function that in turn, ends the program's execution.
- ✓ Using the *set_new_handler* function, your programs can specify a function that automatically executes when a memory request cannot be satisfied. Depending on your program's requirements, this function might try to free up memory so the request can be repeated. If you invoke the *set_new_handler* function with NULL, no out-of-memory handler function executes.
- ✓ When your program no longer needs previously allocated memory, your program should release the memory using the *delete* operator. When your program ends, any previously allocated memory is automatically released.
- ✓ To allocate a memory for a simple value, such as value of type *int* or *float*, use the *new* operator as follows:

```
int *int_pointer = new int;

float *float_pointer = new float;
```

- ✓ If you include a value within parentheses in a *new* statement, *new* will initialize the memory location with the specified value, providing the memory request was satisfied, for example:

```
int *int_pointer = new int(1001);
```

- ✓ To allocate memory for an array of values using *new*, specify the desired number of elements within brackets, as shown here:

```
int *int_array = new int[50];
```

- ✓ Depending on your program's requirements, there may be times when you need to override the *new* or *delete* operators. Normally, your programs will not override the global operators, but rather, the operators used by a specific class.

Chapter 8
Getting Up to Speed with Virtual Functions and Polymorphism

It's hard to pick up a book or C++ magazine article that does not discuss *polymorphism.* Unfortunately, most discussions make polymorphism and the use of C++ virtual functions seem difficult. As you will learn in this chapter, however, the most difficult part of polymorphism is the term itself. Once you get past the term, the concepts are very easy. So, let's get past the term right now. To begin, *poly* simply means many. Likewise, *morphic* means forms. When you combine the two terms you get *many forms.* In short, a polymorphic object is an object that is capable of having two or more forms. For example, assume you have a telephone object. To place a phone call, you would use the *dial* member. As you know, a phone can use either a touch tone or rotary dial. In other words, phones can have one of two *forms.* Depending on which form is used, the *telephone* object would use a different *dial* member function. This chapter examines what polymorphism is and what it is not. You will learn

- What polymorphism is and what it's good for
- How C++ supports polymorphism
- What a virtual function is and how it is denoted
- How to replace a virtual function with your own function
- Which conditions are necessary for polymorphism to occur
- What a pure virtual function is

In Chapter 13 you will take a more detailed look at what polymorphism means to the C++ compiler.

Understanding Virtual Functions

C++ implements polymorphism using *virtual functions.* In the simplest sense, a virtual function is a class member function that is designed to work with *virtually* any base and derived class members (type as yet unknown), each of which can choose to use the virtual function or a function of its own, thus saving you the trouble of having to write several different functions when one will do. You can think of a virtual function as something like a "variable function," an operable class member function that is designed to be replaced later by an as yet unknown derived member function. By defining the function as *virtual*, your program can create objects with their own member functions, which they use instead of the original virtual function, as well as objects that use the default function.

A virtual function's declaration is preceded by the *virtual* keyword. For example, the following *telephone* base class defines the *dial* member function as *virtual* so that it can work with *rotary* and *touch_tone telephones*:

```
class telephone {
  public:
    telephone(char *number, int volume);
    virtual int dial(char *outgoing_number);
  protected:
    char phone_number[32];
    int volume;
};
```

The *virtual* keyword

The following derived classes, *rotary* and *touch_tone* are based on the *telephone* class:

```
class rotary: public telephone {
  public:
    rotary(char *number, int volume) : telephone(number,
      volume) { };
    int dial(char *outgoing_number);
};

class touch_tone: public telephone {
  public:
    touch_tone(char *number, int volume) : telephone(number,
      volume) { };
    int dial(char *outgoing_number);
};
```

As you can see, both classes define a *dial* member function. The following program, TELEPHON.CPP, uses these two classes and their individual *dial* functions:

```
#include <iostream.h>
#include <string.h>

class telephone {
  public:
    telephone(char *number, int volume);
    virtual int dial(char *outgoing_number);
  protected:
    char phone_number[32];
    int volume;
};
```

```
telephone::telephone(char *number, int volume)
 {
   strcpy(telephone::phone_number, number);
   telephone::volume = volume;
 }

int telephone::dial(char *outgoing_number)
 {
   cout << "Use a rotary or touch-tone phone to call: " <<
           outgoing_number;

   cout << " Volume: " << volume << endl;
   return(1);
 }

class touch_tone: public telephone {
  public:
    touch_tone(char *number, int volume) : telephone(number,
      volume) { };
    int dial(char *outgoing_number);
};

int touch_tone::dial(char *outgoing_number)
 {
   cout << "Beep beep beep with touch tone: " << outgoing_number;
   cout << " Volume: " << volume << endl;

   return(1);
 }

class rotary: public telephone {
  public:
    rotary(char *number, int volume) : telephone(number,
      volume) { };
    int dial(char *outgoing_number);
};

int rotary::dial(char *outgoing_number)
 {
   cout << "Click click click with rotary: " << outgoing_number;
   cout << " Volume: " << volume << endl;

   return(1);
 }

void main(void)
 {
    touch_tone office("363-1111", 5);
    rotary home("555-1234", 2);

    home.dial("222-3333");
    office.dial("333-4444");
 }
```

As you can see, the program declares *rotary* and *touch_tone* phone objects and then uses the objects to place a phone call. When you compile and execute this program, your screen will display the following output:

```
C:\> TELEPHON  <ENTER>
Click click click with rotary: 222-3333 Volume: 2
Beep beep beep with touch tone: 333-4444 Volume: 5
```

In this case, the program uses virtual functions, but the program does not use polymorphism. In other words, the objects used in this program do not use more than one form—each object is either a rotary or touch-tone phone, but not both.

UNDERSTANDING VIRTUAL FUNCTIONS

C++ polymorphism is based on *virtual functions.* In the simplest sense, a virtual function is a class member function for which your programs can create their own as yet unknown members, using their own function or the virtual function, saving you the trouble of writing a different function for each member class, kind of like a variable that class members can substitute their own functions for.

To declare a virtual function, precede it with the *virtual* keyword. For example, the following *computer* class uses a virtual *processor* member function:

```
class computer {
    public:
      computer(int processor_type);
      virtual processor(unsigned *instructions);
      void load_program(char *program_name);
   private:
       int processor_type;
       int memory_size;
};
```

In this way, your program can derive PC and Mac classes, each of which use a specific processor member function.

The previous program used virtual functions but did not perform polymorphism. The following program, POLY.CPP, changes *main* to use a pointer to an object of type *telephone* named *cellular.* Throughout the program's execution, the pointer points to an object of type *rotary* and one of type *touch_tone.* In this way, the pointer references two different types of objects during the program's execution:

```
void main(void)
 {
    touch_tone office("363-1111", 5);
    rotary home("555-1234", 2);

    telephone *cellular;

    home.dial("222-3333");
    office.dial("333-4444");

    cellular = &home;
    cellular->dial("555-1234");

    cellular = &office;
    cellular->dial("555-5678");
 }
```

Note: To save book pages, this program code does not contain the class definitions and member functions. However, the source file POLY.CPP on this book's companion disk contains the complete program code.

As you can see, this program assigns the address of the two different object types to the *cellular* pointer variable. When you compile and execute this program, your screen will display the following output:

```
Click click click with rotary: 222-3333 Volume: 2
Beep beep beep with touch tone: 333-4444 Volume: 5
Click click click with rotary: 555-1234 Volume: 2
Beep beep beep with touch tone: 555-5678 Volume: 5
```

As the program assigns a different object type to the *cellular* pointer, the program invokes a different function for the *dial* member function. In other words, this program performs polymorphism—the *cellular* phone object takes on different forms.

Experiment with the previous program, using a *telephone* object, as opposed to an object pointer. The following program, NOPOLY.CPP, assigns *rotary* and *touch_tone* objects to the cellular object. As you will see however, the object never changes forms, remaining solely as a *telephone* object:

```
void main(void)
 {
    touch_tone office("363-1111", 5);
    rotary home("555-1234", 2);

    telephone cellular("555-5555", 3);
```

```
    home.dial("222-3333");
    office.dial("333-4444");

    cellular = home;
    cellular.dial("555-1234");

    cellular = office;
    cellular.dial("555-5678");
}
```

When you compile and execute this program, your screen will display the following output:

```
C:\> NOPOLY  <ENTER>
Click click click with rotary: 222-3333 Volume: 2
Beep beep beep with touch tone: 333-4444 Volume: 5
Use a rotary or touch-tone phone to call: 555-1234 Volume: 2
Use a rotary or touch-tone phone to call: 555-5678 Volume: 5
```

As you can see, when the program assigns the *rotary* and *touch_tone* objects to *cellular*, the actual form of the *cellular* object does not change. In other words, the *cellular* object continues to use the standard *telephone dial* function.

Note: To save book pages, this program code does not contain the class definitions and member functions. However, the source file NOPOLY.CPP on this book's companion disk contains the complete program code.

UNDERSTANDING POLYMORPHISM

Polymorphism is a difficult way to say multiple forms. A polymorphic object is an object capable of changing from one form to another throughout the its lifetime. Polymorphism is a powerful programming tool because it lets you write code for that behaves correctly for many different object types. In most cases, the actual object type is not known, even at run time. As you will learn in Chapter 13, polymorphism can occur due to behind the scenes operations performed by the compiler. For now, however, simply understand that C++ virtual functions let you write code that supports polymorphism, code where an object can change from one type to another as the program executes.

WHAT POLYMORPHISM IS NOT

Do not confuse polymorphism with function overloading. For example, the following program, OVERONLY.CPP, overloads the *dial* function within the *rotary* and *touch_tone* classes. Because the base class definition does not use the *virtual* keyword, the member declarations within the derived classes simply overload the function declaration. The functions are not virtual:

```
#include <iostream.h>
#include <string.h>

class telephone {
  public:
    telephone(char *number, int volume);
    int dial(char *outgoing_number);      Function is not virtual
  protected:
    char phone_number[32];
    int volume;
};

telephone::telephone(char *number, int volume)
 {
   strcpy(telephone::phone_number, number);
   telephone::volume = volume;
 }

int telephone::dial(char *outgoing_number)
 {
   cout << "Use a rotary or touch-tone phone to call: " <<
     outgoing_number;

   cout << " Volume: " << volume << endl;
   return(1);
 }

class touch_tone: public telephone {
  public:
    touch_tone(char *number, int volume) : telephone(number,
      volume) { };
    int dial(char *outgoing_number);
};

int touch_tone::dial(char *outgoing_number)
 {
   cout << "Beep beep beep with touch tone: " << outgoing_number;
   cout << " Volume: " << volume << endl;

   return(1);
 }

class rotary: public telephone {
  public:
    rotary(char *number, int volume) : telephone(number,
      volume) { };
```

```
    int dial(char *outgoing_number);
};

int rotary::dial(char *outgoing_number)
 {
   cout << "Click click click with rotary: " << outgoing_number;
   cout << " Volume: " << volume << endl;

   return(1);
 }

void main(void)
 {
    touch_tone office("363-1111", 5);
    rotary home("555-1234", 2);

    telephone *cellular = new telephone("111-2222", 3);

    home.dial("222-3333");
    office.dial("333-4444");

    cellular->dial("123-4567");

    cellular = &office;

    cellular->dial("890-1234");
 }
```

As you can see, the program assigns a pointer to an office object to the *cellular* pointer. When you compile and execute this program, your screen will display the following output:

```
C:\> OVERONLY  <ENTER>
Click click click with rotary: 222-3333 Volume: 2
Beep beep beep with touch tone: 333-4444 Volume: 5
Use a rotary or touch-tone phone to call: 123-4567 Volume: 3
Use a rotary or touch-tone phone to call: 890-1234 Volume: 5
```

As you can see, the *cellular* object's *dial* member function does not change following the pointer assignment. In other words, the object is not polymorphic.

USING THE BASE CLASS MEMBER FUNCTION

In the previous examples, each derived class (*rotary* and *touch_tone*) both provided *dial* functions that replaced the virtual base class member function.

In some cases, a derived class will not replace the virtual function, but will use the base class function instead. Assume, for example, that you are writing a simulator program for Rolls Royce, which creates car, truck, and even jet engines. Your program might use the *engine* class, shown here:

```
class engine {
  public:
    engine(char *name, int fuel_type);
    virtual void get_fuel(int gallons);
  private:
    char name[64];
    int fuel_type;
};
```

As you can see, the class defines the *get_fuel* member function as a virtual function (they each use different fuel). By default, the *engine* function displays a message instructing the user to add regular or unleaded fuel, as shown here:

```
void engine::get_fuel(int gallons)
 {
   cout << "Please add " << gallons << " of regular or unleaded" <<
           endl;
 }
```

For a jet engine, however, the program would prompt the user for JP4 or some other type of jet fuel. Likewise, for a truck, the program asks the user to use diesel fuel. Finally, for a motorcycle engine, the program simply uses the default or base class function. The following program, ENGINE.CPP, implements the virtual *engine* class:

```
#include <iostream.h>
#include <string.h>

class engine {
  public:
    engine(char *name, int fuel_type);
    virtual void get_fuel(int gallons);
  private:
    char name[64];
    int fuel_type;
};

engine::engine(char *name, int fuel_type)
 {
   strcpy(engine::name, name);
   engine::fuel_type = fuel_type;
 }
```

```
void engine::get_fuel(int gallons)
 {
   cout << "Please add " << gallons << " of regular or unleaded" <<
           endl;
 }

class jet_engine : public engine {
  public:
    jet_engine(char *name, int fuel_type) : engine(name,
      fuel_type) {};
    void get_fuel(int gallons)
      {
         cout << "Please add " << gallons << " of JP4 jet fuel" <<
                 endl;
      };
};

class truck_engine : public engine {
  public:
    truck_engine(char *name, int fuel_type) : engine(name,
      fuel_type) {};
    void get_fuel(int gallons)
      {
         cout << "Please add " << gallons << " of diesel fuel" <<
                 endl;
      };
};


void main(void)
 {
   engine rolls("Rolls Royce", 1);
   jet_engine F100("Jet aircraft", 2);
   truck_engine truck("Delivery truck", 3);
   engine harley("Harley Davidson", 1);

   rolls.get_fuel(20);
   F100.get_fuel(1000);
   truck.get_fuel(40);
   harley.get_fuel(5);
 }
```

As you can see, the *rolls* and *harley* objects use the base class *engine* member function. When you compile and execute this program, your screen will display the following output:

```
C:\> ENGINE  <ENTER>
Please add 20 of regular or unleaded
Please add 1000 of JP4 jet fuel
```

```
Please add 40 of diesel fuel
Please add 5 of regular or unleaded
```

As you may have noticed, this program does not illustrate polymorphism—no object takes on more than one form.

The following program, however, USER_ENG.CPP, uses the object pointer *user_engine* to display the engine prompt for the user-selected engine. The program begins by prompting the user to select an engine. Based on the user's selection, the *user_engine* pointer takes on the form of a specific engine object:

```
#include <ctype.h>

void main(void)
 {
   engine rolls("Rolls Royce", 1);
   jet_engine F100("Jet aircraft", 2);
   truck_engine truck("Delivery truck", 3);
   engine harley("Harley Davidson", 1);

   engine *user_engine;

   int not_done = 1;

   while (not_done)
    {
      char user_choice;

      cout << "Select an engine type" << endl;
      cout << "S Standard\t Jet engine\tD Diesel\tQ Quit: " << endl;

      cin >> user_choice;

      user_choice = toupper(user_choice);

      switch (user_choice) {
        case 'S': user_engine = &rolls;
                break;
        case 'J': user_engine = &F100;
                break;
        case 'D': user_engine = &truck;
                break;
        case 'Q': not_done = 0;
                user_engine = (engine *) 0;
                break;
        default: user_engine = (engine *) 0;
                break;
      };
```

```
        if (user_engine)
         {
           user_engine->get_fuel(5);
           cout << endl << endl << endl;
         }
     }
 }
```

Note: To save book pages, this program code does not contain the class definitions and member functions. However, the source file USER_ENG.CPP on this book's companion disk contains the complete program code.

As you can see, the program assigns a different engine type to the pointer associated with *user_engine*, based on the user's input. Because the object can point to one of several different object types, the *user_engine* pointer is polymorphic. The compiler can in no way determine which object the pointer will point to at any given time. As such, polymorphism occurs during run time, using behind the scenes compiler support that we will discuss in Chapter 13.

RULES FOR POLYMORPHIC FUNCTIONS

If you do not precede a base-class member function with the *virtual* keyword, polymorphism will not occur. In addition, if the return type or the parameter types of a derived class function (whose name matches that of a virtual function) are not the same, polymorphism does not occur. For example, the following program, MISMATCH.CPP, changes the type of the gallons parameter from *int* to *long*. As a result, polymorphism does not occur with the *engine* pointer:

```
#include <iostream.h>
#include <string.h>

class engine {
  public:
    engine(char *name, int fuel_type);
    virtual void get_fuel(int gallons);
  private:
    char name[64];
    int fuel_type;
};

engine::engine(char *name, int fuel_type)
 {
   strcpy(engine::name, name);
   engine::fuel_type = fuel_type;
 }
```

***int** definition of **gallons** parameter*

```
void engine::get_fuel(int gallons)
 {
   cout << "Please add " << gallons << " of regular or unleaded" <<
           endl;
 }

class jet_engine : public engine {
  public:
    jet_engine(char *name, int fuel_type) : engine(name,
      fuel_type) {};
    void get_fuel(long gallons)
      {                                  long definition of gallons parameter
         cout << "Please add " << gallons << " of JP4 jet fuel" <<
                 endl;
      };
};

void main(void)
 {
   engine rolls("Rolls Royce", 1);
   jet_engine F100("Jet aircraft", 2);

   engine *engine_ptr;

   engine_ptr = &rolls;
   engine_ptr->get_fuel(20);

   engine_ptr = &F100;
   engine_ptr->get_fuel(1000);
 }
```

Because the parameter types of the *get_fuel* member functions do not match, polymorphism does not occur. Thus, when you compile and execute this program, your screen will display the following output:

```
C:\> MISMATCH  <ENTER>
Please add 20 of regular or unleaded
Please add 1000 of regular or unleaded
```

Experiment with this program, changing the type *long* back to *int*. As you will find, polymorphism will occur, and the program will display the following output:

```
C:\> MISMATCH  <ENTER>
Please add 20 of regular or unleaded
Please add 1000 of JP4 jet fuel
```

VIRTUAL FUNCTIONS AND MULTILEVEL INHERITANCE

In Chapter 2 you examined inheritance in detail. Depending on your class structures, there may be times when you use multiple levels of inheritance. For example, assume that you create a *pay_phone* class that is based on the *rotary* class presented earlier in this chapter:

```
class pay_phone: public rotary {
  public:
    pay_phone(char *number, int volume, int cost): rotary(number,
      volume) {
      pay_phone::cost = cost;
    }
    int dial(char *outgoing_number);
  private:
    int cost;
};
```

Next, assume that the pay phone requires its own *dial* function, which first prompts the user to insert 25 cents. You can declare the *dial* member function as virtual within the *rotary* within the *rotary* class like this:

```
class rotary: public telephone {
  public:
    rotary(char *number, int volume) : telephone(number,
      volume) { };
    virtual int dial(char *outgoing_number);
};
```

By defining the function as *virtual*, your program can create objects with their own *dial* member functions, as well as objects that use the default or *rotary dial*. The following program, PAYPHONE.CPP, for example, creates a polymorphic object that can be either a rotary phone or a pay phone:

```
#include <iostream.h>
#include <string.h>

class telephone {
  public:
    telephone(char *number, int volume);
    virtual int dial(char *outgoing_number);
  protected:
    char phone_number[32];
    int volume;
};

telephone::telephone(char *number, int volume)
 {
```

```
   strcpy(telephone::phone_number, number);
   telephone::volume = volume;
 }

int telephone::dial(char *outgoing_number)
 {
   cout << "Use a rotary or touch-tone phone to call: " <<
           outgoing_number;

   cout << " Volume: " << volume << endl;
   return(1);
 }

class rotary: public telephone {
  public:
    rotary(char *number, int volume) : telephone(number,
      volume) { };
    virtual int dial(char *outgoing_number);
};

int rotary::dial(char *outgoing_number)
 {
   cout << "Click click click with rotary: " << outgoing_number;
   cout << " Volume: " << volume << endl;

   return(1);
 }

class pay_phone: public rotary {
  public:
    pay_phone(char *number, int volume, int cost): rotary(number,
      volume) {
      pay_phone::cost = cost;
    }
    int dial(char *outgoing_number);
  private:
    int cost;
};

int pay_phone::dial(char *outgoing_number)
 {
   cout << "Please deposit " << cost << " cents" << endl;

   return(rotary::dial(outgoing_number));
 }

void main(void)
 {
    pay_phone street("363-1111", 5, 25);
    rotary home("555-1234", 2);
```

```
    telephone *phone;

    phone = &home;
    phone->dial("222-3333");

    phone = &street;
    phone->dial("333-4444");
}
```

As you can see, the phone pointer is assigned to point at the two different object types. When you compile and execute this program, your screen will display the following output:

```
C:\> PAYPHONE  <ENTER>
Click click click with rotary: 222-3333 Volume: 2
Please deposit 25 cents
Click click click with rotary: 333-4444 Volume: 5
```

As you can see, the *pay_phone* class replaces the *dial* member function. Take time to examine how the *pay_phone* class defines the *dial* function:

```
int pay_phone::dial(char *outgoing_number)
{
    cout << "Please deposit " << cost << " cents" << endl;

    return(rotary::dial(outgoing_number));
}
```

As you can see, the function first displays the message to the user to deposit the correct amount. Next, the function uses the global resolution operator (::) to invoke the *dial* function defined by the *rotary* class, returning the value returned by *rotary::dial*. As before, take time to experiment with this program. Remove the *virtual* keyword from the front of the function declaration in *rotary::dial*. When you compile and execute the program you will find that polymorphism does not occur.

Understanding Pure Virtual Functions

Abstraction is the process of temporarily ignoring underlying details so you can focus on the larger problem at hand. When programmers create their first prototypes of large programs, they often insert simple function definitions for complex functions they will later define. For example, programmers in Washington D.C., might create a function similar to the following:

```
void health_care_program(void)
  {
     cout << "Health care program function-to be completed later" <<
             endl;
  }
```

By placing simple functions such as this within your program, you can get parts of the program up and running. In some cases, you can even demonstrate such prototypes to the end users.

When you create classes, there may be times when you create base classes from which the classes your program will later use are defined. An *abstract class* is a class definition whose purpose is to lay the foundation from which other classes can be derived. Your programs will normally not instantiate objects of an abstract class. Instead, your classes will inherit abstract class characteristics.

When you use abstract classes, there will be many times when the abstract classes use virtual functions that can be used or replaced by a derived class. Depending on your class definition, there may be times when you will define a virtual function whose meaning the derived class must define. Such functions, which must be defined by the derived class, are called *pure virtual functions.* To create a pure virtual function, the abstract class initializes the function to zero. For example, the following *abstract_telephone* class defines the *dial* member as a pure virtual function:

```
class abstract_telephone {
  public:
    abstract_telephone(char *number, int volume);
    virtual int dial(char *outgoing_number) = 0;
  protected:
    char phone_number[32];
    int volume;
};
```

Pure virtual function

Within a derived class, you must specify a function for each pure virtual function. The following program, VIRTDIAL.CPP, uses a pure virtual function for *dial*:

```
#include <iostream.h>
#include <string.h>

class abstract_telephone {
  public:
    abstract_telephone(char *number, int volume);
    virtual int dial(char *outgoing_number) = 0;
  protected:
    char phone_number[32];
    int volume;
};
```

```
abstract_telephone::abstract_telephone(char *number, int volume)
 {
   strcpy(abstract_telephone::phone_number, number);
   abstract_telephone::volume = volume;
 }

class touch_tone: public abstract_telephone {
  public:
    touch_tone(char *number, int volume) :
      abstract_telephone(number, volume) { };
    int dial(char *outgoing_number);
};

int touch_tone::dial(char *outgoing_number)
 {
   cout << "Beep beep beep with touch tone: " << outgoing_number;
   cout << " Volume: " << volume << endl;

   return(1);
 }

void main(void)
 {
    touch_tone office("363-1111", 5);
    office.dial("333-4444");
 }
```

When you compile and execute this program, your screen will display the following output:

```
C:\> VIRTDIAL  <ENTER>
Beep beep beep with touch tone: 333-4444 Volume: 5
```

As before, take time to experiment with this program. If you remove the function *touch_tone::dial*, the program will compile, but your linker will display error messages stating the function is not found. As you have read, your derived classes must specify definitions for pure virtual functions.

UNDERSTANDING PURE VIRTUAL FUNCTIONS

As you examine C++ class definitions, you may encounter virtual member functions that are initialized to zero. Such functions, called pure virtual functions, are used within abstract classes to specify a function that classes derived from the abstract class must later specify. If the derived class does not later specify a definition for the pure virtual function, the linker will display error messages and will not build an executable program.

Putting It All Together

This chapter examined polymorphism and virtual functions in detail. Before you continue with Chapter 9, make sure that you have learned the following

- ✓ Polymorphism is the ability of an object to take on two or more different forms during a program's execution. C++ supports polymorphism through the use of virtual functions.
- ✓ A virtual function is like a variable function, an operable class member function that is designed to be replaced later by an as yet unknown derived member function. You precede the function by the *virtual* keyword.
- ✓ When your programs derive a class from a base that uses a virtual function, the derived class can replace the virtual function with a function of its own or it can use the function defined by the base class.
- ✓ When a derived class defines a member function whose name matches that of a base-class function, the return type and parameter types must exactly match those of the base class function, or polymorphism will not occur.
- ✓ A pure virtual function is a virtual function the base class initializes to 0. The derived class must provide a definition for a pure virtual function.

Chapter 9
Getting Up to Speed with Rules of Scope

Within your programs, names identify variables, functions, classes, types, and so on. A name's *scope* defines the locations throughout your program at which a name has meaning. For example, variables with *local scope* have meaning throughout the function within which they are defined. Likewise, variables with *global scope* have meaning throughout your program, following the variable's declaration. As you will learn in this chapter, the proper use of scope often requires more than local and global variables. By the time you finish this chapter, you will understand the different aspects of scoping within C++. Take time to examine each program closely. Many of the subtle concepts the programs illustrate can only be appreciated through careful examination. When you finish this chapter, you will have learned

- What the scope of a name (identifier) is
- What local and global scope are
- How to indicate the scope of an identifier
- What the four types of scope are
- What function scope is
- What file scope is
- What class scope is
- Where C++ lets your programs declare variables
- What happens when a local variable name conflicts with a global variable or a class member variable
- What a variable's lifetime is
- What internal and external linkage are

DECLARATIONS VERSUS DEFINITIONS

When you read books and magazines articles about C and C++, the discussion often uses the terms *definition* and *declaration* interchangeably. As you will learn here, however, the meanings of these two terms are quite different. A declaration specifies the properties of a variable—it specifies a type (such as *int*, *float*, or *char*) and a name. For example, the following statements are valid declarations in C or C++:

```
int age, count;
float salary;
long int miles_to_the_moon;

struct date {
  int day;
  int month;
  int year } birthday;

enum suite { clubs, diamonds, hearts, spades };
```

In general, when a declaration also results in memory being allocated to store the object, the declaration is also a *definition*. Each of the previous declarations allocated storage for an entity, and as such, each declaration is also a definition.

The following declarations, however, do not allocate storage, and as such, are not definitions:

```
extern int error_flag;
extern istream_withassign _Cdecl cin;
extern ostream_withassign _Cdecl cout;

int some_function(int, float, char);    // Function prototype
```

In this case, the declarations specify each variable's type and name. However, the *extern* keyword informs the compiler that the variables are *defined* elsewhere. As a result, the compiler will not allocate memory to store the variable. As the previous function prototype shows, declarations are not restricted to variables. Function prototypes are declarations, in that they introduce the function name to the program. The function statements, on the other hand, define the function.

In the simplest sense, a declaration introduces a name. To the C++ compiler, each name within your program has a type, which determines the set of values the corresponding entity can store and the set of operations that can be performed on the entity. The name's scope specifies the locations throughout your program where the name has meaning. Because of scope, the same name can be used throughout different parts of your program, in different ways.

Basics of Scope

Every entity (variable, function, class, and so on) within your program has a name. The scope of the entity's name defines the locations within your program where the name has meaning. C++ defines four types of scope: local, function, file, and class.

Understanding Declarations and Definitions

Within your program, variables, classes, functions, and all other entities have names. Before the program can reference (use) the entity, the corresponding name must have first been declared. A declaration specifies a name and a type, similar to those shown here:

```
int i, j, k;
float salary;
char string[256];
extern istream_withassign _Cdecl cin;
```

In the simplest sense, if a declaration also allocates storage memory for the corresponding entity, the declaration is also a definition. In the case of the declarations just shown, only the last statement, which uses the *extern* keyword does not allocate storage. As such, the statement is not a definition. More formally, however, a declaration is a definition unless the declaration falls into one of the following categories:

- Declares a function prototype
- Contains the *extern* keyword and no initializer or function body
- Declares a class name
- Declares static class member
- Declares a new type using *typedef*

Understanding Local Scope

Local scope corresponds to items defined within a block of program code (within opening and closing braces) or as formal parameters within a function definition. Variables with local scope are known only within the block within which they are declared, following the actual declaration. For example, the following program, LOCAL.CPP, creates three local variables named *chapter*, *title*, and *book*:

```
#include <iostream.h>

void main(void)
 {
   int chapter = 9;
   char *title = "Getting Up to Speed with Rules of Scope";
   char *book = "Success with C++";
```

Local variable declarations

```
    cout << "Chapter " << chapter << " " << title << endl;
    cout << book << endl;
 }
```

In C, local variables can be defined at the start of any of any block of code. In C++, however, variables can be defined at any location, even intermixed within the program statements. As such, the following program, MIXLOCAL.CPP, is identical in function to the program just shown:

```
#include <iostream.h>

void main(void)
 {
    int chapter = 9;
    char *title = "Getting Up to Speed with Rules of Scope";

    cout << "Chapter " << chapter << " " << title << endl;

    char *book = "Success with C++";
    cout << book << endl;
 }
```

By declaring variables close to the variable's use, you can improve the readability of large programs. A common reason for declaring variables within program statements is to declare the control variables within a *for* loop, as shown here:

Local variable declaration

```
for (int i = 0; i < 50; i++)
    some_array[i] = 0;
```

As you see, the *for* loop declares the variable *i* within the loop's initialization. After the loop ends, the local variable *i* remains defined. The following program, SHOW_I.CPP, defines a variable named *i* within a *for* loop in this way. After the loop ends, the program displays the variable's value:

```
#include <iostream.h>

void main(void)
 {
    for (int i = 0; i < 25; i++)
      cout << i;

    cout << endl << "Value of i is " << i << endl;
 }
```

Declaring Variables Within Your Program Statements

C++ lets your programs declare variables within your program statements, and not just at the start of a statement block. In many cases, you can improve your program readability by declaring variables closer to the variable's use. For example, the following statements declare the *age* and *name* within the program statements:

```
cout << "Type in the employee name and age: ";

int age;
char name[64];

cin >> name >> age;
```

In a similar way, the following statement declares the variable *i* within a *for* statement:

```
for (int i = 0; i < 10; i++)
   cout << i << endl;
```

As is the case with many aspects of software engineering, there will be debate over the proper way to declare variables within your programs for years to come. As a rule, if declaring a variable within your program statements improves your program's readability, do so.

As you have read, local variable names only have meaning within the block within which they are defined. If your program tries to use a variable within a block prior to the local variable's declaration or within a different outside or unrelated block, the variable's name is unknown, and a syntax error will result. The following program, TWOBOOKS.CPP, for example, creates a local variable named *book* and assigns a character string to the variable. Within an *if* statement, the program creates a second local variable named *book*, to which the program assigns a different values. Because each variable has different scope, both variables are distinct, even though the variables share the same name:

```
#include <iostream.h>

void main(void)
 {
   char *book = "Success with C++";
```

*First declaration of the variable **book***

```
    if (book)
     {
       char *book = "Rescued by C++";

       cout << "Start with the book " << book << endl;
     }

    cout << "Then read the book " << book << endl;
  }
```

Second declaration of the variable **book**

Note: This program is presented to illustrate the local scope, ***not*** *good programming practice. As a rule, your functions should not use two (or more) variables with the same name. Use of the same name for different variables normally makes a program difficult to understand.*

Several definitions presented throughout this chapter use wording such as "the entities can be used anywhere within the block within which the entity was declared, following the declaration." What the wording means, is that if you declare a variable within the middle of a block of code, you cannot refer to the variable prior to the declaration. The variable is only known (within that block) following the declaration. The following statements, therefore will generate a syntax error:

```
cout << "This is chapter " << chapter;
int chapter = 9;
```

As you can see, the program tries to use the variable *chapter* before it has been declared.

Understanding Local Scope

Variables with local scope are known only within the block of code within which the variables are declared, following the variable's declaration. C++ lets your programs declare local variables throughout the program, even interspersed within program statements. By declaring variables close to their use, you can improve your program's readability. C++ considers formal function parameters as local variables, which exist only within the function code.

Understanding Function Scope

A *label* defines a location within a function's statements. Using the *goto* statement, your programs can branch to the statement the follows the label. The following program, GOTOLOOP.CPP, uses the *goto* statement and the label *loop* to display the numbers 1 through 50 on your screen display:

```
#include <iostream.h>

void main(void)
 {
   int i = 1;

   loop:
     cout << i++ << endl;

     if (i <= 50)
       goto loop;
 }
```

When your programs use the *goto* statement to branch to a label, the label must reside within the same function as the *goto* statement. In other words, labels have *function scope*. Label names are the only entity that have function scope.

UNDERSTANDING FUNCTION SCOPE

Function scope restricts an identifier's meaning to the function within which the identifier is declared. Label names are the only C++ entity that has function scope. As a result, your programs cannot use the *goto* statement to branch from one function to a label defined in another.

UNDERSTANDING FILE SCOPE

Variables declared within a source file and outside of all program blocks have *file scope*. In the simplest sense, variables with file scope are global variables. Global variables are known throughout the program within all program blocks that follow the declaration. The following program, GLOBAL.CPP, declares the variables *book* and *chapter* as global variables. The program then displays each variable's value within two different functions:

```
#include <iostream.h>

char *book = "Success with C++";
char *chapter = "Getting Up to Speed with Scope";

void show_globals(int count)
 {
   for (int i = 0; i < count; i++)
     cout << book << " " << chapter << endl;
 }
```

```
void main(void)
 {
   cout << "This book: " << book << endl;
   cout << "Chapter 13: " << chapter << endl;

   show_globals(1);
 }
```

Once again, your programs cannot reference a global variable prior to the variable's declaration. The following statements, for example, try to reference the global variable *error_number* within the function *show_error*, before the variable has been declared. If you try to compile similar statements, a syntax error will occur:

```
void show_error(void)
 {
    cerr << "Error in processing # " << error_number << endl;
 }

 int error_number;  // Global variable
```

Understanding File Scope

File scope specifies that variables declared outside of all program blocks will have meanings throughout all the blocks that follow the variable's declaration. Variables with file scope are global. Because global variables are easily accessible throughout your programs, the variables are very susceptible to errors or misuse that leads to errors. As a rule, your programs should greatly restrict the use of global variables.

Understanding Class Scope

Classes exist to support information hiding and encapsulation. Within a class, members are local and can be used only by class member functions (or functions within classes derived from this class), with the dot (.) or indirection operator (–>) , after the scope resolution operator (::), or by classes declared as a *friend*. This section examines several different operations on class members, who have *class scope*.

Understanding Private and Public Class Members

As you read in Chapter 2, class members can be private or public, depending on how you want the program to access the variables. Private members can only be accessed by class member functions (or derived class functions or friends). Public members, on the other hand, can be accessed by throughout your program using the dot or indirection operator. For example, the following program, PUBPRIV.CPP, creates a class named *Book*, which contains the member variables *title*, *author*, and *pages*. The class also supports the *Book* constructor function and the *show_book* member functions:

```
class Book {
 public:
   Book(char *book_title, char *book_author, int book_pages)
     {
       strcpy(title, book_title);
       strcpy(author, book_author);
       pages = book_pages;
     };

   void show_book(void)
     {
       cout << "Book: " << title << endl;
       cout << "Author: " << author << endl;
       cout << "Pages: " << pages << endl;
     }
 private:
   char title[64];
   char author[64];
   int pages;
};
```

As you can see, the class implements its member functions using inline statements. By defining the member variables as *private*, the program restricts member variable access to class member functions. The following statements implement the PUBPRIV.CPP program:

```
#include <iostream.h>
#include <string.h>

class Book {
 public:
   Book(char *book_title, char *book_author, int book_pages)
     {
       strcpy(title, book_title);
       strcpy(author, book_author);
       pages = book_pages;
     };

   void show_book(void)
     {
       cout << "Book: " << title << endl;
       cout << "Author: " << author << endl;
       cout << "Pages: " << pages << endl;
     }
```

```
  private:
    char title[64];
    char author[64];
    int pages;
};

void main(void)
 {
   Book cpp_book("Success with C++", "Jamsa", 528);

   cpp_book.show_book();
 }
```

As you can see, the *Book* class hides all of its member variables from program access by making the variables private. The only way to access the member variables is through the public class member functions, such as the constructor function or the function *show_book*.

Use Private and Public Members

When you create your own classes, the *private* and *public* labels give your programs the ability to control member access, much like variable scope. As a rule, you should declare member variables as private as often as possible, allowing (controlled) variable access only through member functions. Likewise, only those functions your program really must directly access should be public. In other words, use the "need to know" theory to determine which members you declare as private and which you declare as public.

Understanding Controlled Access

When you read about the advantages of making class variables private, you will normally encounter discussion that includes the terms *controlled access.* When class member variables are public, the program can change the variables at any time and in any way. Assume, however, that you have created a nuclear reactor class. One of the member fields is named *melt_down_protection.* When the variable contains the value 1, the nuclear reactor is protected against meltdown. When the variable contains the value 0, however, the reactor is assumed to be turned off, and protection can be shut down. If the member variable is public, a programmer can intentionally change the variable's value using a statement such as:

```
nuke.melt_down_protection = 0;
```

Likewise, the programmer could accidentally change the variable's value through a programming error. For example, the following *if* statement is supposed to test if the variable's value is 0. Unfortunately, because the programmer used the assignment operator (=) instead of a test for equality (==), the member variable is assigned the value 0:

```
if (nuke.melt_down_protection = 0)
```

To avoid such errors, your program should only access the variable using member functions such as *set_melt_down*, which may prompt the user for a password, or *get_melt_down*, which returns the current variable setting. Controlled access therefore, is just that. When you write a program, you know how each member variable is intended to be used. By making those variables private, you can ensure (control) that variables are only accessed as you intended.

With class scope, class member variables can be directly accessed by member functions. For example, consider either the *Book* constructor or the *show_book* member functions previously shown:

```
Book(char *book_title, char *book_author, int book_pages)
  {
    strcpy(title, book_title);
    strcpy(author, book_author);
    pages = book_pages;
  };

void show_book(void)
  {
    cout << "Book: " << title << endl;
    cout << "Author: " << author << endl;
    cout << "Pages: " << pages << endl;
  }
```

As you can see, both functions refer directly to the member variables by name. In the case of the *Book* constructor function, the function assigns parameter values to the member functions. When member functions receive parameters, there may be times when the name of a parameter matches that of a member variable. For example, assume the *Book* constructor function used the parameter names *title*, *author*, and *price*, as shown here:

```
Book(char *title, char *author, int pages)
```

When local variable names (remember formal parameters are local variables) are the same as a class member, the class member becomes *hidden*. Operations within the function that reference the variable name will correspond to the local variable, not to the member variable. In such cases, the function can refer directly to the member functions by using the global resolution operator (::), as shown here:

```
    Book(char *title, char *author, int pages)
      {
        strcpy(Book::title, title);
        strcpy(Book::author, author);
        Book::pages = pages;
      };
```

The following program, UNHIDE.CPP, uses the global resolution operator to unhide member variables that have been hidden by local variables:

```
#include <iostream.h>
#include <string.h>

class Book {
 public:
    Book(char *title, char *author, int pages)
      {
        strcpy(Book::title, title);
        strcpy(Book::author, author);
        Book::pages = pages;
      };

    void show_book(void)
      {
        cout << "Book: " << title << endl;
        cout << "Author: " << author << endl;
        cout << "Pages: " << pages << endl;
      }
 private:
    char title[64];
    char author[64];
    int pages;
};

void main(void)
 {
    Book cpp_book("Success with C++", "Jamsa", 528);

    cpp_book.show_book();
 }
```

In the case of the previous program, the *Book* class used inline functions. As you read in Chapter 2, when a class uses inline functions, each object is assigned its own copy of the function code. In other words, the program gains no benefits from shared program instructions. The following program, NOINLINE.CPP, moves the class functions out of the class definition:

```
#include <iostream.h>
#include <string.h>

class Book {
 public:
   Book(char *title, char *author, int pages);
   void show_book(void);
 private:
   char title[64];
   char author[64];
   int pages;
};

Book::Book(char *title, char *author, int pages)
 {
   strcpy(Book::title, title);
   strcpy(Book::author, author);
   Book::pages = pages;
 };

void Book::show_book(void)
 {
   cout << "Book: " << title << endl;
   cout << "Author: " << author << endl;
   cout << "Pages: " << pages << endl;
 }

void main(void)
 {
   Book cpp_book("Success with C++", "Jamsa", 528);

   cpp_book.show_book();
 }
```

Constructor function for the **Book** class

Member function for the **Book** class

As you can see, the program uses the global resolution operator with the *Book* class name to resolve class member functions. As your programs and object use become more complex, there may be times when the member functions used for one class have the same name as a function name used by another class. By specifying the class name using the global resolution operator, your programs resolve the name conflicts.

Be Aware of Hidden Members

When you pass parameters to class member functions, there may be times when a parameter (or local variable) name conflicts with the name of a class member. When such conflicts occur, C++ essentially hides the class member, associating all references of the conflicting name to the local variable. To unhide a class member in such cases, you must use the global resolution operator (::). For example, the following function *set_salary*, assigns the value specified in the *salary* parameter to the *employee* class *salary* member:

```
void employee::set_salary(float salary)
 {
   employee::salary = salary;
 }
```

As you can see, the function uses the global resolution operator with the class name to unhide the member variable.

Understanding Class Friends

As you have learned, *private* class members let you restrict how a class can be used. As you build programs with related objects, there may be times when you can improve your program's readability or when you can improve information hiding by granting a specific class, called a *friend*, with access to one or more class private members. For example, assume, that your program uses a class named *employee*, which contains private and public members, as shown here:

```
class employee {
  public:
    employee(char *name, float salary, char *ssan);
    void show_employee(void);
    void change_employee(void);
  private:
    char name[256];
    float salary;
    char ssan[256];
};
```

Next, assume that your program has a *manager* class that needs to access directly the private members of a specific worker objects. One solution would be make all of the *employee* member fields as public, which would make the members accessible to the functions within the *manager* class. Unfortunately, by making the members public, the fields would become accessible to the entire program. A better solution would be make the members only accessible to the *manager* class by specifying the *manager* as a friend of the class, like this:

```
class employee {
  public:
    employee(char *name, float salary, char *ssan);
    void show_employee(void);
    void change_employee(void);
    friend manager;
  private:
    char name[256];
    float salary;
    char ssan[256];
};
```

Specifying **manager** class objects as a friend

The following program, MGR_UPD.CPP, creates *employee* and *manager* objects. The program then passes to the *employee* object to the *manager* member function *update_employee*, which updates the object. To enable the function to change the *employee* object, the program passes the object to the function by address:

```
#include <iostream.h>
#include <string.h>

class manager;

class employee {
  public:
    employee(char *name, float salary, char *ssan);
    void show_employee(void);
    void change_employee(char *name, float salary, char *ssan);
    friend manager;
  private:
    char name[256];
    float salary;
    char ssan[256];
};

employee::employee(char *name, float salary, char *ssan)
 {
   strcpy(employee::name, name);
   strcpy(employee::ssan, ssan);
   employee::salary = salary;
 }

void employee::show_employee(void)
 {
   cout << "Name: " << name << endl;
   cout << "Salary: " << salary << endl;
   cout << "SSAN: " << ssan << endl;
 }
```

```
void employee::change_employee(char *name, float salary, char *ssan)
 {
   strcpy(employee::name, name);
   strcpy(employee::ssan, ssan);
   employee::salary = salary;
 }

class manager {
  public:
    void update_employee(employee *emp, char *name, float salary,
      char *ssan);
    // Other members
};

void manager::update_employee(employee *emp, char *name,
  float salary, char *ssan)
 {
   emp->change_employee(name, salary, ssan);
 }

void main(void)
 {
   employee worker("Jamsa", 25000.0, "538-66-5444");

   manager the_boss;

   worker.show_employee();

   the_boss.update_employee(&worker, "Jones", 33456.0,
     "111-22-3333");

   worker.show_employee();
 }
```

Note the declaration of the *manager* class at the start of the program:

```
class manager;
```

The program uses this declaration to allow the *employee* object to reference the class as a friend. As you can see, the program passes the *employee* object to the function *update_employee* by address, which lets the program change the object's member variables. Experiment with this program and remove the *friend* statement from within *employee* class declaration. When you remove the statement, you also remove the *manager* object's access to the *change_employee* function, which results in a syntax error.

By specifying the *manager* class as a friend, the previous program provided *manager* objects with full access to *employee* object member fields. Unfortunately, by declaring the *manager* class as a friend, *manager* objects can fully access *employee* object members in any way they want. In many cases, you might want to restrict the friend's access to specific functions. For example, the following *employee* class declaration restricts the access of manager friend objects to the function *update_employee*:

```
class employee {
  public:
    employee(char *name, float salary, char *ssan);
    void show_employee(void);
    void change_employee(char *name, float salary, char *ssan);
    friend void manager::update_employee(employee *emp, char *name,
      float salary, char *ssan);
  private:
    char name[256];
    float salary;
    char ssan[256];
};
```

By restricting a friend's access in this way, you better control how your program can access an object, which in turn makes your program easier to understand and reduces the chance of errors.

Allowing Special Object Access to Friends

As the number of objects you use within your programs increases, there may be times when you can improve your program's performance or improve your program's readability by providing a class of objects with special access to an object's members. By declaring another class as an object's friend, within a class declaration, you provide the friend with access to the object's private members. The following *comedian* object class, for example, declares *agent* class objects as a *friend*. In this way, *agent* objects have access to the *comedian*'s private members:

```
class agent;
class comedian {
    public:
          comedian(char *name, char *joke);
          void show_comedian(void);
          friend agent;
   private:
          char *name[64];
          char *best_joke[256];
};
```

Note the simple declaration of the *agent* class that precedes the *comedian* class declaration. By declaring the *agent* in this way, the *comedian* class can reference the *agent* class before it is formally declared. In some cases, you might want to restrict a friend's access to a specific function. To do so, specify the function within the class declaration, as shown here:

```
class comedian {
    public:
          comedian(char *name, char *joke);
          void show_comedian(void);
          friend void agent::pay_comic(void);
   private:
          char *name[64];
          char *best_joke[256];
};
```

In this case, only the *agent* member function *pay_comic* would have access to the *comedian's* private member variables.

Understanding Protected Members

Chapter 4 discusses inheritance in detail. As you learned, when you derive one class from another (the base class), the derived class has access to the base class public members but not the private members. To provide derived class objects with a middle level of access, C++ supports *protected members.* Protected members can be accessed by derived classes, but not by the rest of the program. The following program, PROTECT.CPP, derives the *document* class using the *file* base class:

```
#include <iostream.h>
#include <string.h>

class file {
  public:
    file(char *name, int type);
  protected:
    void show_file_info(void);
    int attributes;
  private:
    char name[64];
    int type;
};

file::file(char *name, int type)
 {
   strcpy(file::name, name);
   file::type = type;
 }
```

```
void file::show_file_info(void)
 {
   cout << "Filename: " << name << endl;
   cout << "Type: " << type << endl;
 }

class document : public file {
  public:
    document(char *name, int type, int attributes);
    void show_document(void);
    void print_document(void) { /* statements */ };
    void save_document(void) { /* statements */ };
  private:
    int error_status;
};

document::document(char *name, int type, int attributes) :
   file(name, type)
 {
   document::attributes = attributes;
 }

void document::show_document(void)
 {
   show_file_info();
   cout << "Attributes: " << attributes << endl;
 }

void main(void)
 {
   document spreadsheet("WORKSHEET.DAT", 1, 255);

   spreadsheet.show_document();
 }
```

As you see, the file class declares the *attributes* and *show_file_info* members as *protected*. Experiment with this program, trying to access these two members directly from within *main*. You will find, the only way to access the protected members is within *file* or *document* class member functions.

Using Protected Members

When your programs use C++ inheritance to derive a class from a base class, you may have base class members that you want derived objects to access, but that you don't want accessible to the rest of your program. In such cases, you can use protected members. Protected class members are accessible within the base or derived class member functions, but not outside of such functions.

How Various Qualifiers Affect Scope

As you know, when you declare variables, C++ lets you add qualifiers to type declarations, such as *long*, *short*, and so on. In addition, you can precede your variable declarations with *storage class specifiers*, such as *static*, *auto*, *extern*, and *register*. This section examines the *extern* and *static* specifiers and their impact on variable, function, and class member scope. You will find that, by using these qualifiers, you can control access to various identifiers.

Using the extern Qualifier

As you have learned, declarations and definitions are often distinguished by the allocation of storage space. When you precede a declaration with the *extern* keyword, you tell the C++ compiler that you will be using an identifier that has been defined at some other location (either in the program source file, a header file, or within a library file). The following program, EXTERN.CPP, uses the variable *title*, which is defined outside of the program:

```
#include <iostream.h>

void show_title(void);

void main(void)
 {
   extern char *title;

   cout << "The title is " << title << endl;

   show_title();
 }
```

As you can see, the program declares the variable *title* as *extern*. In this way, the C++ compiler does not allocate space for the variable. In this case, the variable title is actually defined within the source file, SHOWTITL.CPP, which also defines the function *show_title*:

```
#include <iostream.h>

char *title = "Success with C++";

void show_title(void)
 {
   cout << "The title of this book is " << title << endl;
 }
```

Assuming you are using the Borland C++ compiler, you can compile the program as follows:

```
C:\> BCC  EXTERN.CPP  SHOWTITL.CPP  <ENTER>
```

When you execute the program, your screen will display the following:

```
C:\> EXTERN  <ENTER>
The title is Success with C++
The title of this book is Success with C++
```

Take time to experiment with this program, possibly removing the *extern* from in front of the declaration within the file EXTERN.CPP or by moving the declaration into of title into the function *show_title*. In each case, your changes will very likely result in syntax errors. External variables amplify the problems introduced by global variables, in that they can be changed in many ways, some of which might not be obvious to a programmer who is examining the program code. Worse yet, because the changes can be made from within multiple source files, the changes can be very difficult to track or detect.

To reduce a global variable's vulnerability, you might want your program to restrict access to the variable to the source file within which the variable is defined. In such cases, your programs can precede the declaration with the *static* specifier. For example, the following statement restricts the scope of the variable *title* to the file SHOWTITL.CPP:

```
static char *title = "Success with C++";
```

If you make add the *static* specifier to the variable declaration within the file and then recompile the two programs, the linker will display an error message about the unresolved *title* identifier.

Initializing an External Variable

When you precede a variable declaration with the *extern* keyword, your declaration is normally not a definition, because the compiler does not allocate storage for the variable. That is, unless, you initialize the variable. For example, the following program, NOEXTERN.CPP, uses initializes the external variable *title* with the string "Rescued by C++". Because of the initialization, the compiler will allocate storage for the variable:

If you compile and link this program with SHOWTITL.CPP, your program will display the following output:

```
C:\> NOEXTERN  <ENTER>
The title is Rescued by C++
The title of this book is Success with C++
```

As you can see, the program uses two different *title* variables. Depending on your linker, the linker might detect the duplicate identifiers.

UNDERSTANDING STATIC CLASS MEMBERS

You have learned that, when you declare class objects, each object gets its own member variables. For example, if your program uses two or more *date* objects, each object can have its own *month*, *day*, and *year* variables. Depending on your object's purpose, there may be times when you will want two or more objects to share the same member variable. For example, assume that you have objects of type *Nuke*, each of which tests for a different situation within a nuclear reactor. Next, assume that when an error condition occurs, the object sets the member variable *melt_down* to 1. By sharing the *melt_down* variable among *Nuke* objects, all program objects can instantly be aware of a meltdown situation. To share an object member variable with other objects, you simply precede the variable declaration with the *static* keyword:

```
class Nuke {
 public:
   Nuke(char *name, int limit);
   void show_status(void);
   void set_melt_down(void);
 private:
   static int melt_down;
   char name[64];
   int limit;
};
```

Based on this declaration, objects of type *Nuke* will share the *melt_down* member variable but will have individual copies of the member variables *name* and *limit*. In this case, the member variable is declared as *private*. However, C++ fully supports private and public shared member variables. Next, following the class declaration, you must declare a variable outside of the class that will hold the variable's value:

```
int Nuke::melt_down = 0;
```

In this case, the declaration also assigns an initial value to the variable, but such an initialization is not required. The following program, MELTDOWN.CPP, illustrates the use of the shared member variable:

```
#include <iostream.h>
#include <string.h>

class Nuke {
 public:
   Nuke(char *name, int limit);
   void show_status(void);
   void set_melt_down(void);
```

```
 private:
   static int melt_down;
   char name[64];
   int limit;
};

int Nuke::melt_down = 0;

Nuke::Nuke(char *name, int limit)
 {
   strcpy(Nuke::name, name);

   Nuke::limit = limit;
 }

void Nuke::show_status(void)
 {
   cout << "Name: " << name;
   cout << " limit: " << limit;
   cout << " meltdown: " << melt_down << endl;
 }

void Nuke::set_melt_down(void)
 {
    melt_down = 1;
 }

void main(void)
 {
   Nuke rods("Check Rods", 1001);
   Nuke fission("Check Fission", 2002);

   rods.show_status();
   fission.show_status();

   rods.set_melt_down();

   rods.show_status();
   fission.show_status();
 }
```

When you compile and execute this program, your screen will display the following output:

```
C:\> MELTDOWN  <ENTER>
Name: Check Rods limit: 1001 meltdown: 0
Name: Check Fission limit: 2002 meltdown: 0
Name: Check Rods limit: 1001 meltdown: 1
Name: Check Fission limit: 2002 meltdown: 1
```

As you can see, when the *rods* object sets the value of the shared *melt_down* value to 1, the *fission* object immediately sees the change.

Sharing an Object Member Variable

Depending on your object's use, there may be times when two or more objects need to share the same member variable. In such cases, your programs can create a shared member variable by preceding the variable's declaration within the object with the *static* keyword. For example, in the following *Employee* class, objects share the variables *company_name* and *health_plan*:

```
class Employee {
    public:
        Employee(char *name, long identifier, int job);
        void show_employee(void);
    private:
        char name[64];
        long identifier;
        int job;
        static char company_name[64];
        static char health_plan[25];
};
```

Next, outside of the class declaration, you must specify declarations for the shared variables, as shown here:

```
char Employee::company_name[64];
char Employee::health_plan[25];
```

Each object your program later creates of type *Employee* will share these two variables.

Inline versus Out-of-Line Member Functions

When you declare a class, you have the choice of declaring member functions as *inline functions*, whose statements appear within the class declaration itself, or outside of the class. For example, the previous MELTDOWN.CPP program, used *out-of-line functions* such as the *Nuke* constructor shown here:

```
Nuke::Nuke(char *name, int limit)
 {
   strcpy(Nuke::name, name);
   Nuke::limit = limit;
 }
```

The program could have just as easily declared the function as inline, as shown here:

```
class Nuke {
 public:
   Nuke(char *name, int limit) {
      strcpy(Nuke::name, name);
      Nuke::limit = limit;
    }
  void show_status(void);
   void set_melt_down(void);
 private:
   static int melt_down;
   char name[64];
   int limit;
};
```

When you declare a function as inline, each object you create gets its own unique copy of the function code. When you use out-of-line functions, on the other hand, each function shares one copy of the function. In most cases, you will want to take advantage of such code sharing to reduce your program's memory overhead.

SHARING MEMBER FUNCTION CODE

When you declare class member functions, you have two choices. You can declare the function statements as inline statements, or you can declare the statements out of line (outside of the class declaration itself). The advantage of using out-of-line function declarations is that each object you create shares a copy of the program code. As such, if you create 100 objects, only one function is created, which objects share. In this way, your program's memory requirements is reduced.

REVISITING THE GLOBAL RESOLUTION OPERATOR

When your programs use global variables, there may be times when a local variable name conflicts with that of a global variable. In such cases, C++ associates all references to the name with the local variable. For example, the following program, USELOCAL.CPP, defines the global variable *number*, assigning the variable the value 1001. Within *main*, the program uses the local variable number within a *for* loop, causing a name conflict. When the program displays *number's* value, the program displays the value of the local variable, in essence, hiding the global variable:

```
#include <iostream.h>

int number = 1001;   // Declare global variable

void main(void)
 {
   for (int number = 1; number < 5; number++)
     cout << number << endl;

   cout << "Value of number is " << number << endl;
 }
```

When you compile and execute this program, your screen will display the following output:

```
C:\> USELOCAL  <ENTER>
1
2
3
4
Value of number is 5
```

As you can see, the program used the local variable *number*, disregarding the global variable. In cases when you want to force the program to use the global variable, you can precede the variable name with the global resolution operator (::). The following program, USEGLOB.CPP, for example, uses the global resolution operator to display the value of the global variable *number* following the *for* loop:

```
#include <iostream.h>

int number = 1001;   // Declare global variable

void main(void)
 {
   for (int number = 1; number < 5; number++)
     cout << number << endl;

   cout << "Value of number is " << ::number << endl;
 }
```

When you compile and execute this program, your screen will display the following output:

```
C:\> USEGLOB  <ENTER>
1
2
```

```
3
4
Value of number is 1001
```

As you can see, the program displays the value of the global variable *number* as desired. When your programs use the global resolution operator (::) to resolve a global variable in this way, C++ will always reference the global variable. Consider, for example, the following program, WHICHNUM.CPP, which uses three different variables named *number*:

```
#include <iostream.h>

int number = 1001;   // Global variable

void main(void)
 {
   for (int number = 1; number < 5; number++)
    {
      int number = 1;

      cout << "local number " << number << " ::number is " <<
              ::number << endl;
    }
 }
```

As you can see, within the innermost block of code, the program uses the global resolution operator. Using the global resolution operator, the program refers to the global variable, not the variable *number* defined in the next outer loop. If you compile and execute this program, your screen will display the following output:

```
C:\> WHICHNUM  <ENTER>
local number 1 ::number is 1001
local number 1 ::number is 1001
local number 1 ::number is 1001
local number 1 ::number is 1001
```

As you might have noticed, using variables with the same name for different purposes can lead to programs that are very difficult to understand. To avoid such confusion, make sure that you use meaningful names for each of your variables. In most cases (with the exception of counter and index variables), simply using meaningful names will eliminate many naming conflicts. Second, avoid the use of global variables whenever possible. Finally, if such conflicts occur, make sure that you fully understand C++ rules of scope, as well as variable lifetimes, discussed next.

Understanding an Identifier's Lifetime

A variable's *lifetime* defines when the variable is in scope. Normally, a variable's life begins when the variable is defined. Likewise, the variable's life ends when the variable goes out of scope. For example, when your program declares local variables within a function, the variables come to life when the function is invoked and the variable's lifetime normally ends when the function ends. In a similar way, if a program defines a global variable, the variable's lifetime begins at the definition and continues until the program ends.

After the discussion presented in this chapter, you might be thinking that a variable's lifetime is pretty simple. Unfortunately, the use of qualifiers, such as *static*, can add complexity to the concept of a variable's lifetime. For example, the following function *use_count* uses the *static* variable *counter* to track the number of times the function is invoked:

```
long use_count(void)
 {
   static long counter = 0;

   // Statements

   return(counter);
 }
```

In this case, *counter's* lifetime begins the first time the function is invoked, which in turn initializes the variable. Unlike other local variables declared within the function, whose lifetimes end with the function's return, *counter's* lifetime will then continue until the program ends.

As you have learned, C++ lets you declare variables at any location throughout your program. The following *if* statement, for example, declares a similar *static* counter variable:

```
if (some_condition)
 {
   static int if_counter = 0;

   // Statements

   if_counter++;
  }
```

To determine ways to improve your program's performance, your program might use a similar variable to determine how many times a particular code fragment is executed. In this case, the variable's lifetime begins the first time the *if* statement is executed and ends when the program ends.

A common practice within C++ programs is to declare a variable within a *for* loop, as shown here:

```
for (int i = 0; i < 10; i++)
    some_operation();
```

When you declare a variable in this way, the variable's lifetime begins when the loop is executed for the first time and ends when the block containing the for loop completes. Next, the following statement that defines the variables *i* and *j* within two nested *for* loops:

```
for (int i = 0; i < 3; i++)
  for (int j = 0; j < 3; j++)
    cout << i << ' ' << j << endl;
```

When this code fragment executes, your screen will display the following values:

```
01
02
03
10
11
12
20
21
22
```

As you can see, the code treats the variable's *i* and *j* correctly. At first glance, you might state that the code also creates the variables *i* and *j*, which continue to live throughout the current block of code. As it turns out, the variable *i* lives throughout the remainder of the current block. When the outer *for* loop ends, so too ends the lifetime of the variable *j*. The following program, SYNTAX.CPP, tries to display both variable's values after the loops end. If you try to compile this program, your compiler will generate a syntax error stating that the variable *j* is unknown:

```
#include <iostream.h>

void main(void)
 {
   for (int i = 0; i < 3; i++)
     for (int j = 0; j < 3; j++)
       cout << i << ' ' << j << endl;

   cout << "Ending values i: " << i << " j: " << j << endl;
 }
```

Unknown identifier ***j***

When you work with different variables, take time to determine each variable's lifetime. By better understanding a variable's scope and lifetime, you will better understand operations the compiler performs behind the scenes, which may in turn, lead to you writing more efficient code.

Understanding Linkage

When your programs are short, such as the programs presented in this book, you will normally include all of your program code in one source file. As your programs become longer, you might find that your code is easier to understand if you logically divide the code into multiple files. In addition, you can often reduce your program development time by separately compiling different parts of your program. In this way, should you make changes to part of your program, you only need to recompile one source file. Next, you can use the linker to *link* the previously compiled object files. In Chapter 17 you will learn how to build a class library. For now, however, you will simply compile and then link two related source files. To being, create the file STR_LEN.CPP, which contains the following function:

```
int str_len(char *string)
 {
   int length = 0;

   while (*string++)
     length++;

   return(length);
 }
```

Compile the program file to create the object code file STR_LEN.OBJ. If you are using Borland C++, you would use the following command:

```
C:\> BCC -c STR_LEN.CPP  <ENTER>
```

Note: The command-line option "–c" tells the compiler to only compile the file and not to link it. Without the "–c" option on the command line the compiler will attempt to create STR_LEN.EXE. (The "–c" is case sensitive; it must be lowercase.)

Next, create the program HOWLONG.CPP, which uses the function, as shown here:

```
#include <iostream.h>

int str_len(char *);
```

```
void main(void)
 {
   char *string = "Success with C++";

   cout << "The string " << string << " contains " <<
           str_len(string) << " characters" << endl;
 }
```

As before, compile the program to produce an object file:

```
C:\> BCC -c HOWLONG.CPP  <ENTER>
```

Using your linker, combine the object files to create an executable program named HOWLONG.EXE. If you are using Borland C++, you can use the following BCC command to link the files:

```
C:\> BCC  HOWLONG.OBJ  STR_LEN.OBJ  <ENTER>
```

***Note:** Many compilers, such as Borland C++ will let you specify the names of C++ and object files you want to compile and then link. Thus, if you are using Borland C++, you can compile the program HOWLONG.CPP and link the file STR_LEN.OBJ using the following command:*

```
C:\> BCC HOWLONG.CPP STR_LEN.OBJ  <ENTER>
```

If you examine the program HOWLONG.CPP, you will find that the program includes a function prototype for the *str_len* function. Even though the *str_len* function resides in a different file, you must declare the function before its first use.

When your programs use multiple source or object files, you need to understand *linkages*, which are used by the compiler and linker to resolve variable references. C++ defines two types of linkages, internal and external. When an identifier name is local to a source file, the identifier has *internal linkage*. When an identifier's scope exceeds the file, the identifier has *external linkage*. Assume, for example, that a source file defines the global variable *error_number*, as shown here:

```
int error_number;  // Global

void main(void)
 {
   // Statements
 }
```

In this case, the global variable's scope exceeds the source file, and as such, the variable has external linkage. For example, create (or use from the companion disk to this book) the following program ERRORNUM.CPP:

```
void show_error_number(void);

int error_number = 1001;

void main(void)
 {
   show_error_number();
 }
```

As you can see, the program assigns a value to the global variable and then invokes the function *show_error_number* to display the variable's value. As before, the program includes a prototype for the function, even though the function is declared in a different file.

Next, create (or use from the companion disk) the file SHOWERR.CPP, which defines the function *show_error_number*:

```
#include <iostream.h>

extern int error_number;

void show_error_number(void)
 {
   cout << "Error number: " << error_number << endl;
 }
```

In this case, the file uses the *extern* statement to tell the compiler that the variable *error_number* is defined in another file. After compilation, the linker must resolve the variable reference.

When you create multifile programs that rely on external links such as this, you need to ensure that you correctly specify the external variable type. In most cases, the compiler cannot detect a mistyped external variable, which can result in an error that is very difficult to detect. For example, the following file, WRONGERR.CPP, incorrectly declares the external *error_number* variable as type *float*:

```
#include <iostream.h>
                                        Incorrect type specified
extern float error_number;

void show_error_number(void)
 {
   cout << "Error number: " << error_number << endl;
 }
```

Next, the following file, BAD_INIT.CPP, assigns an initial value to the external *error_number* variable. Unfortunately, when the compiler performs the initialization, the declaration becomes a definition, hiding the previous external global variable:

```
#include <iostream.h>

extern int error_number = 2002;

void show_error_number(void)
 {
   cout << "Error number: " << error_number << endl;
 }
```

If you compile and link BAD_INIT.CPP to the ERRORNUM program, the program will display the following (incorrect) output:

```
C:\> ERRORNUM  <ENTER>
Error number: 2002
```

Depending on your linker, the duplicate identifier name may be detected. If not, you might have difficulty trying to debug the cause of the error. To understand better the processing performed, you might want to change the ERRORNUM.CPP program to display *error_number's* value, as shown here:

```
#include <iostream.h>

void show_error_number(void);

int error_number = 1001;

void main(void)
 {
   show_error_number();
   cout << "In main: " << error_number << endl;
 }
```

In this case, the program's output becomes the following:

```
C:\> ERRORNUM  <ENTER>
Error number: 2002
In main 1001
```

Finally, just as you use private class members to prevent object members from being accessed from outside of the object, there may be times when you want to restrict a variable's or function's scope to the current source file. When you precede a global variable name with the *static* keyword, the identifier's linkage becomes *internal* to that source file. In other words, the identifier cannot be referenced from outside the current source file. The following program, INTERNAL.CPP, defines two functions named *internal* and *external.* Because the *internal function* is preceded with the *static* keyword, the function's scope is local to the source file. Because the *external function* is not preceded by the *static* keyword, the function has external linkage:

```
#include <iostream.h>

static void internal(char *message)
 {
   cout << message << endl;
 }

void external(char *message)
 {
   cout << message << endl;
 }

void some_function(void);

void main(void)
 {
   internal("Using the internal function");
   external("Using the external function");

   some_function();
 }
```

Note that the function also uses the function *some_function*, which is declared outside of the source file. The following file, SOMEFUNC.CPP, defines *some_function*:

```
void external(char *);

void some_function(void)
 {
   external("Using external from outside the source file");
 }
```

As you can see, the function uses the *external* function to display a message. When you compile and link these two files and run the INTERNAL program, your screen will display the following output:

```
C:\> INTERNAL  <ENTER>
Using the internal function
Using the external function
Using external from outside the source file
```

If you change the SOMEFUNC.CPP file to use the *internal* function, the program will not link, and the linker will display a message stating that it could not resolve the reference to *internal*. Because the *internal* function has internal linkage, the function cannot be used outside of its source file.

As you begin to work with multifile programs and libraries, you need to keep linkage in mind. As you can see, errors in linkage can be as difficult to detect as errors in scope.

Putting It All Together

This chapter has examined the C++ rules of scope in detail. If you have not already done so, take time to experiment with the programs presented in this chapter and note the impact of your changes. In Chapter 10 you will examine C++ references, which provide an alias or second name for a variable. Before you continue with Chapter 10, make sure that you have learned the following:

- ✓ An identifier's scope defines the location within your program where the identifier has meaning.
- ✓ Before a program can use an identifier, the identifier must be declared. In general, a declaration specifies a type and a name. If the declaration also allocates storage, the declaration is normally also considered to be a definition.
- ✓ C++ supports four types of scope: local, function, file, and class.
- ✓ Local scope corresponds to items defined within a block of code (opening and closing braces).
- ✓ Function scope only corresponds to labels. A *goto* statement cannot branch to a label outside of the current function (a nonlocal *goto*).
- ✓ File scope corresponds to global variables and function identifiers that are known throughout the source file (or multiple files).
- ✓ Class scope corresponds to member variables and member functions that are only accessible to class objects.
- ✓ C++ lets your programs declare variables throughout your code, not just at the beginning of a program block. In many cases, declaring a variable closer to its use improves your program's readability.
- ✓ If a local variable name conflicts with a global variable or a class member variable, the compiler will associate references to the name with the local variable. To access the global or class variable, you must use the global resolution operator (::).
- ✓ A variable's lifetime defines when the variable is in scope. Normally, a variable's life begins when the variable is defined.
- ✓ C++ supports internal and external linkage. Identifiers with internal linkage are known only within the source file within which they are defined. Identifiers with external linkage can be accessed from within multiple source files.

Chapter 10
Getting Up to Speed with References

If you are an experienced C programmer, you are now probably comfortable (or beginning to feel comfortable) with most pointer operations. As such, you should now be ready to master C++ *references*—which are kind of like an address and kind of a like a value. This chapter examines C++ references in detail. However, as you will learn, in most cases, you will continue to use standard pointer operations, just as you have in the past.

Programmers understand (for the most part) pointer operations. However, there are times when you work with complex variables, such as structures or objects, when using references is very efficient. In addition, in Chapter 11 you will learn how to create your own I/O stream manipulators such as *hex* or *endl*. As you will find, the manipulators work with references to specific I/O streams.

When you finish this chapter, you will have learned

- What a reference is
- The pitfalls of aliases
- What you must do to create a reference
- The operations your programs can perform on a reference
- How the C++ compiler views a reference
- Uses for references
- What hidden objects are

By understanding functions that receive or return references, the I/O stream manipulators will be very straightforward.

A Reference Is Simply an Alias

As you know, a variable name corresponds to a storage location in memory, which is accessible using a specific address. A C++ *reference* is simply a second name (or *alias*) for the memory location. Before you can use a reference, you must declare the reference within your program. Like all declarations, a reference has a name and a type. When you declare a reference, you must assign to the reference the variable for which the reference is to serve as an alias. Reference declarations place the ampersand (&) character immediately after the variable type, such as *int&* . The following statements, for example, declare *alias* as a reference to the variable *count*:

```
int count;

int&  alias = count;     // Create the reference
```

Variable the reference is to alias
Reference name (alias)
Reference of type **int**

The following program, FIRSTREF.CPP, creates a reference named *alias* for the variable *count*. The program displays the *count's* value using the variable and the reference. The program then increments *count's* value by incrementing *alias*:

```
#include <iostream.h>

void main(void)
 {
   int count = 1000;

   int& alias = count;  // Create the reference

   cout << "count's value is " << count << " and " << alias << endl;

   alias++;             // Increment count's value

   cout << "count's value is " << count << " and " << alias << endl;
 }
```

A reference is nothing more than an alias (or second name) for a variable. After your program creates a reference, your program can use either the reference or the variable to refer to the same memory location. In this case, the program not only displays *count's* value using the reference, the program also uses the reference to increment *count's* value.

When you compile and execute this program, your screen will display the following:

```
C:\> FIRSTREF  <ENTER>
count's value is 1000 and 1000
count's value is 1001 and 1001
```

You can create references for variables of any type (*float*, *long*, and even *struct*). The following program, REFTYPES.CPP, for example, creates references for several different data types, using the references to manipulate each variable's value:

```
#include <iostream.h>

void main(void)
 {
   float pi = 22.0 / 7.0;

   float& pi_alias = pi;

   struct Date { int month; int day; int year; }
                today = { 9, 30, 94 };

   Date& birthday = today;

   cout << "Pi is " << pi << " or " << pi_alias << endl;

   cout << "My birthday is " << birthday.month << '/' <<
          birthday.day << '/' << birthday.year << endl;
 }
```

As you can see, the program creates two references, one of type *float* and one based on the structure type *Date*. When you compile and execute this program, your screen will display the following:

```
C:\> REFTYPES  <ENTER>
Pi is 3.142857 or 3.142857
My birthday is 9/30/94
```

The purpose of these first two programs is to illustrate that a reference is simply an alias or a second name for a variable. Normally, you would not use references in the manner shown here. By referring to the same memory location using two or more names, your programs can quickly become difficult to understand. As you will learn, however, references are most convenient for passing and returning values to and from functions, particularly complex values such as structures or objects.

Creating a Reference

A reference is a second name or alias for a variable. References have a name and a type (such as *int*, *float*, or even a class or structure). To create a reference, you must declare the reference, much like you would declare a variable. For example, the following statements create a reference named *hillary* for a variable of type *president* named *bill*:

```
struct president { char name[64]; int age; short qualifications;
                 } bill;

president& hillary = bill;
```

Unlike a variable, however, the value your program assigns to a reference cannot be changed. Once you assign a value to a reference, that value remains in affect for the duration of the program block's execution.

A Reference Is Not a Variable

Although a reference appears very much like a variable, in that you must specify a name, type, and assign a value, a reference is not a variable. Once you assign a value to a reference, you cannot change the alias. In other words, once you alias one variable, you cannot use the same reference to alias a different variable.

The following program, REF_FUNC.CPP, uses a reference variable within a function. When you use a local reference in this way, the reference value remains in effect for the duration of the function. Each time you invoke the function, the reference corresponds to the new parameter to which it is assigned. The function cannot, however, change the reference's value:

```
#include <iostream.h>

void use_reference(int value)
 {
   int& alias = value;

   cout << "The parameter value using alias is " << alias << endl;
 }

void main(void)
 {

   for (int i = 0; i < 5; i++)
     use_reference(i);
 }
```

When you compile and execute this program, your screen will display the following output:

```
C:\> REF_FUNC  <ENTER>
The parameter value using alias is 0
The parameter value using alias is 1
The parameter value using alias is 2
The parameter value using alias is 3
The parameter value using alias is 4
```

As you can see, the reference is assigned to the new parameter with each function invocation.

Reference Syntax You Might Encounter

All of the references presented in programs throughout this book consistently place the ampersand (&) immediately after the type name, as shown here:

```
int value;

int& alias = value;
```

C++, however, lets you place the ampersand between the type and reference name, or even next to the reference name. The following declarations, therefore, are identical:

```
int& alias = value;      int & alias = value;      int &alias = value;
```

Although you may encounter all three formats when you examine other programs, you should choose one format and stick to its use. In so doing, your programs become more consistent and, normally, easier to understand.

Rules for Working with References

As you have learned, a reference creates a second name or alias for a variable. Using the alias, you can perform many of the same operations you can perform on the variable itself. For example, you can perform arithmetic operations and value assignments, you can display the value, and you can even test the value within conditional operators. However, unlike variables, there are many operations you cannot perform on the reference itself.

You cannot

- Get the address of a reference using the C++ address (&) operator
- Assign a pointer to a reference
- Compare two reference values
- Create offsets from a reference value
- Change a reference's value

Do not misunderstand the rule about using a reference within a conditional operation. For example, the following program, TESTREF.CPP, uses the reference *alias* within an *if* statement to test whether the value contained in memory referenced by *alias* is 1001:

```
#include <iostream.h>

void main(void)
 {
   int value = 1001;

   int& alias = value;

   if (alias == 1001)
     cout << "alias contains the value 1001" << endl;
   else
     cout << "alias does not the value 1001" << endl;
 }
```

As you can see, the program uses the reference within a conditional test. You cannot, however, use a conditional test to determine whether two references are aliases for the same memory location. Instead, you can simply compare the values within each reference's corresponding memory address. For example, the following program TEST2REF.CPP, uses an *if* statement to compare the values referenced by *alias_one* and *alias_two*:

```
#include <iostream.h>

void main(void)
 {
   int one = 1;
   int& alias_one = one;

   int uno = 1;
   int& alias_two = uno;

   if (alias_one == alias_one)
     cout << "The references contain the same value " <<
             alias_one << endl;
   else
     cout << "The alias values differ " << alias_one << " and " <<
             alias_two << endl;
 }
```

As you can see, the *if* statement compares the values of each reference. If you compile and execute this program, your screen will display the following output:

```
C:\> TEST2REF  <ENTER>
The references contain the same value 1
```

As you can see, the *if* examines the values contained in the memory locations aliased by each reference, as opposed to the memory addresses corresponding to each reference. In this case, the two references are unrelated. It just so happens that the memory locations that correspond to the each reference contains the value 1.

Is the Reference a Value or an Address?

When programmers first learn about references, many try to equate references to an address. The best way to visualize a reference is a *resolved address.* To the C++ compiler, a reference is an address. When the compiler creates your program's object code, the compiler treats references as addresses. Within your program, however, the reference corresponds to the value at a specific address. In other words, a reference lets your program manipulate a value contained in a specific memory location without requiring your program to work with pointers. Any operation your programs can perform with a reference can also be performed using pointers.

References are easy to use within your programs because the compiler is doing all the "dirty work" of resolving addresses and values behind the scenes. Because a reference is not really a variable and not really a pointer, there are certain operations your programs simply can't perform on a reference.

One of the best ways to "get a glimpse" at what the compiler is doing behind the scenes with references is to produce an assembly language listing of your program. If you are using Borland's C++ compiler for example, you can produce an assembly language listing using the –S switch, as shown here:

```
C:\> BCC  -S  FILENAME.CPP  <ENTER>
```

The syntax for Microsoft Visual C++ is as follows:

```
C:\> CL  /Fa /Fs  FILENAME.CPP  <ENTER>
```

Note: With both compilers, the command-line switches are case sensitive.

After you create the assembly language listing, edit the file's contents and note the instructions the compiler uses to resolve addresses.

Using References as Parameters

References let your programs achieve the benefits of pointers without the syntactical overhead (in other words, you don't have worry about passing parameters by address and using pointers to access the parameter's value). The following program, REFPARAM.CPP, for example, passes a reference to the function *change_value.* Within the function, the statements use a reference to change the value of the variable aliased by the reference:

```
#include <iostream.h>

void change_value(int& value)
 {                                     Reference-based parameter
   value = 1001;
 }

void main(void)
 {
   int count = 1;

   int& alias = count;

   cout << "count's value is " << count << " or " << alias << endl;

   change_value(alias);
                                       Passing the reference as a parameter
   cout << "count's value is " << count << " or " << alias << endl;
 }
```

As you can see, the program passes the reference *alias* to the function *change_values.* Within the function, a second reference, named *value* is used. When you compile and execute this program, your screen will display the following output:

```
C:\> REFPARAM  <ENTER>
count's value is 1 or 1
count's value is 1001 or 1001
```

Admittedly, the program eliminates the need to work with pointers and addresses. However, the program introduces one more names (in this case *alias*) that programmers who are reading your program must remember. As a rule, the fewer variable names and references a programmer must recall to understand your program, the easier your program will be to read and modify.

Using pointers, you can achieve the exact result, as shown by the following program, PTRPARAM.CPP:

```
#include <iostream.h>

void change_value(int *value)
 {                                     Pointer-based argument
   *value = 1001;
 }
```

```
void main(void)
 {
   int count = 1;

   cout << "count's value is " << count << endl;

   change_value(&count);
                                    Passing an argument by address
   cout << "count's value is " << count <<  endl;
 }
```

In a similar way, the following program, REF_EXCH.CPP, passes two references to the function *exchange_values*, which in turn, exchanges the values:

```
#include <iostream.h>

void exchange_values(int &a, int& b)
 {                                  Two reference-based parameters
   int temp;     // Not a reference

   temp = a;
   a = b;
   b = temp;
 }

void main(void)
 {
   int one = 1;
   int two = 2;

   int& one_alias = one;
   int& two_alias = two;

   cout << "Before exchange: one is " << one << " and two is " <<
          two << endl;

   exchange_values(one_alias, two_alias);
                                    Passing references as parameters
   cout << "After exchange: one is " << one << " and two is " <<
          two << endl;
 }
```

As before, the program eliminates the need to work with pointers and addresses, but adds the overhead of two references (*one_alias* and *two_alias*). As the number of variables and references used within your program increases, so, too, does your program's difficulty to understand. Note that, within the function *exchange_values*, the function declares the variable *temp* as an *int* and not a reference to an *int*. Keep in mind that the statement following the declaration assigns the value contained in the memory location aliased by the variable *a* to the variable *temp*, which in this case, is the value 1. If the function had instead declared *temp* as a reference, as follows, *temp* would have become an alias for the variable *a*:

```
int &temp = a;      // Create an alias
```

You might want to experiment with this program to ensure that you understand why *temp* should not be a reference. The following program, PTR_EXCH.CPP, performs a similar exchange using pointers. As you will see, the *temp* variable is not a pointer to an *int*, but rather, a variable of type *int*, for a similar reason:

```
#include <iostream.h>

void exchange_values(int *a, int *b)
 {
   int temp;     // Not a pointer

   temp = *a;
   *a = *b;
   *b = temp;
 }

void main(void)
 {
   int one = 1;
   int two = 2;

   cout << "Before exchange: one is " << one << " and two is " <<
           two << endl;

   exchange_values(&one, &two);

   cout << "After exchange: one is " << one << " and two is " <<
           two << endl;
 }
```

Using References with Structure Parameters and Objects

A common use for references is to pass structure parameters to functions or to return such complex variables. For example, the following program, SHOWDATE.CPP, uses the function's *get_date* and *show_date* to prompt the user for and then to display the current date. The program stores the date in a structure of type *Date*, as shown here:

```
struct Date {
  int month;
  int day;
  int year;
};
```

As you will see, the program passes a reference to a variable of type *Date* to the function *get_date* and the structure variable itself to *show_date*:

```
#include <iostream.h>

struct Date {
 int month;
 int day;
 int year;
};

void get_date(Date& date)
 {
   cout << "Type in today's month: ";
   cin >> date.month;

   cout << "Type in today's day: ";
   cin >> date.day;

   cout << "Type in today's year: ";
   cin >> date.year;
 }

void show_date(Date date)
 {
   cout << "Today's date is: " << date.month << '/' << date.day <<
          '/' << date.year << endl;
 }

void main(void)
 {
   Date today;

   Date& todays_date = today;

   get_date(todays_date);

   show_date(today);
 }
```

As you can see, the program passes a reference to the *get_date* function but passes the structure itself to the *show_date* function. Because the *get_date* function changes structure members, the function must work with either pointers or a reference to the structure.

Using a reference, the function eliminates the need for pointer operations such as those shown here:

```
void get_date(Date *date)
 {
   cout << "Type in today's month: ";
   cin >> date->month;

   cout << "Type in today's day: ";
   cin >> date->day;

   cout << "Type in today's year: ";
   cin >> date->year;
 }
```

Comment Your Reference Operations

Most C and C++ programmers are familiar with pointer operations. If you choose to use references, make sure you comment your operations in detail. Otherwise, programmers who read your program code might find themselves constantly asking the difference between similar variable names (the variable and its reference). In the case of the previous SHOWDATE.CPP, program, you might comment *main* as follows:

```
void main(void)
 {
   Date today;

   Date& todays_date = today;   // Create an alias for today that
                                // eliminates pointer operations
                                // Within functions that change
                                // structure members

   get_date(todays_date);       // Todays_date is a reference that
                                // aliases the today structure

   show_date(today);            // Pass the actual date structure--
                                // not the reference
 }
```

When a function returns a structure, there is considerable overhead that occurs, due to the fact that function members must be copied from the stack into the new structure to which they are being assigned. Assume, for example, that the function *get_date* returned a structure of *Date*, as shown in the following program, RET_STRU.CPP:

```
#include <iostream.h>

struct Date {
 int month;
 int day;
 int year;
};

Date get_date(void)
 {
   Date date;

   cout << "Type in today's month: ";
   cin >> date.month;

   cout << "Type in today's day: ";
   cin >> date.day;

   cout << "Type in today's year: ";
   cin >> date.year;

   return(date);
 }

void show_date(Date date)
 {
   cout << "Today's date is: " << date.month << '/' << date.day <<
          '/' << date.year << endl;
 }

void main(void)
 {
   Date today;

   today = get_date();

   show_date(today);
 }
```

Function returns a structure of type **Date**

Assigning the return value

You might find it interesting to generate an assembly language for the previous program in order to determine how the compiler actually manipulates the stack to pass and return the structure.

To eliminate the stack manipulation overhead, you can use a reference to the structure, as shown in the following program, RET_REF.CPP:

```
#include <iostream.h>

struct Date {
 int month;
 int day;
 int year;
};

Date& get_date(Date &date)
 {
   cout << "Type in today's month: ";
   cin >> date.month;

   cout << "Type in today's day: ";
   cin >> date.day;

   cout << "Type in today's year: ";
   cin >> date.year;

   return(date);
 }

void show_date(Date& date)
 {
   cout << "Today's date is: " << date.month << '/' << date.day <<
           '/' << date.year << endl;
 }

void main(void)
 {
   Date today;

   Date& todays_date = today;  // Alias for today

   todays_date = get_date(todays_date);

   show_date(todays_date);
 }
```

As you can see, both functions, *get_date* and *show_date* work with structure references. As a result, the program becomes more consistent. In addition, you can modify *main*, making the program more compact by combining statements, as shown here:

```
todays_date = get_date(todays_date);
show_date(todays_date);
```

```
show_date(get_date(todays_date));
```

The previous *get_date* function received a reference as a parameter and later returned the same reference. As you will learn, many I/O stream manipulators are written to behave in the same way. The manipulators will receive a reference to a stream parameter, perform an operation, and later return the reference.

USING REFERENCES WITH OBJECTS

As you examine functions in other C++ programs, you might encounter functions that use references for objects or that return references to objects. For example, in Chapter 11 you will learn to create your own I/O stream manipulators, such as *hex*, *dec*, or *oct*. At that time, you will define manipulator functions that work with an I/O stream similar to that shown here in the program DECOCTHE.CPP:

```
#include <iostream.h>
#include <iomanip.h>

ios& dec(ios& stream)          // Returns a reference
 {                             // Reference-based parameter
   stream.setf(ios::dec);
   return(stream);
 }

ios& oct(ios& stream)
 {
   stream.setf(ios::oct);
   return(stream);
 }

ios& hex(ios& stream)
 {
   stream.setf(ios::hex);
   return(stream);
 }

void main(void)
 {
   cout << oct << "Value 10 in octal is " << 10 << endl;
   cout << dec << "Value 10 in decimal is " << 10 << endl;
   cout << hex << "Value 10 in hexadecimal is " << 10 << endl;
 }
```

When C++ encounters the manipulator in an output operation, C++ invokes the corresponding manipulator function. As you can see, the functions receive a reference to an I/O stream as a parameter and then return a reference to the same stream:

```
ios& dec(ios& stream)        // Returns a reference to an I/O stream
 {                           // Receives a reference to an I/O stream
   stream.setf(ios::dec);
   return(stream);
 }
```

The following *tab* function, for example, inserts a tab character within an output stream:

```
ostream& tab(ostream& stream)
 {
   stream << '\t';
   return(stream);
 }
```

As you can see, the manipulator simply inserts the tab character into the specified output stream. When the operation is complete, the function returns the reference to the stream. To use the manipulator, your program simply includes the manipulator within the output stream, as shown here:

```
cout << tab << "Indenting the program output" << endl;
```

Be Aware of Hidden Objects

When your program uses references, you need to ensure that the reference type corresponds to that of the variable the reference is to alias. For example, if you are creating an alias to a variable of type *int*, you should declare the reference as type *int*:

```
int value;

int& alias = value;
```

If the reference type does not match that of the variable type, the compiler will create a *hidden object*, which is assigned the value of variable. For example, the following program, WRONGREF.CPP, creates a reference named *wrong_type* of type *long* to which it assigns an alias to a variable of type *int*:

```
#include <iostream.h>

void main(void)
 {
   int value = 1;                 // Variable of type int

   long& wrong_type = value;      // Reference of type long
```

```
   cout << "Starting values: " << value << " and " << wrong_type <<
           endl;

   value++;

   cout << "Ending values: " << value << " and " << wrong_type <<
           endl;
}
```

When you compile and execute this program, your screen will display the following output:

```
C:\> WRONGREF  <ENTER>
Starting values: 1 and 1
Ending values: 2 and 1
```

As you can see, the variable and its alias contain different values! When the C++ compiler encountered the reference to the type *long*, the compiler created storage for a second object, to which it associated to the reference *wrong_type*. After the compiler allocated the storage, it assigned to the storage location the value of the variable to which the alias was to be created (which in this case is the value 1). Experiment with the previous program, performing operations on the variable *value*, as well as the reference *wrong_type*. As you will find, the variable and alias are unrelated.

Most programs will never have a use for such hidden objects. Unfortunately, hidden objects such as this can result in errors that are very difficult to debug. As such, you need to be aware of this compiler idiosyncrasy.

Putting It All Together

As you examine C++ programs you might encounter functions that make extensive use of references. In the simplest sense, a reference is an alias or second name that your programs can use to refer to a variable. In Chapter 11, for example, you will create manipulator functions that receive a reference to an I/O stream as a parameter and later return a reference to the stream. Before you continue with Chapter 11, make sure you have learned the following:

- ✓ A reference is an alias or second name your programs can use to refer to a variable.
- ✓ Using one or more aliases can make your programs more difficult to understand by increasing the number of identifiers (names) a programmer who is reading your program must understand.

- ✓ To create a reference, you must specify a name and type, placing the ampersand (&) immediately after the type name. In addition, you must assign an initial value to the reference.
- ✓ A reference is not a variable. As such, C++ restricts the different operations your programs can perform on a reference.
- ✓ To the C++ compiler, a reference is an address. To your program, a reference is best viewed as the value contained at the resolved address.
- ✓ Using references, your programs can eliminate many pointer operations within functions. As such, many C++ programs use references to pass or return structures and objects to or from a function.
- ✓ Any operation your program performs with a reference can be performed using pointer operations.
- ✓ If the reference type does not match the variable type for which the reference is to serve as an alias, the C++ compiler will create a hidden object. Such objects can be very difficult to detect.

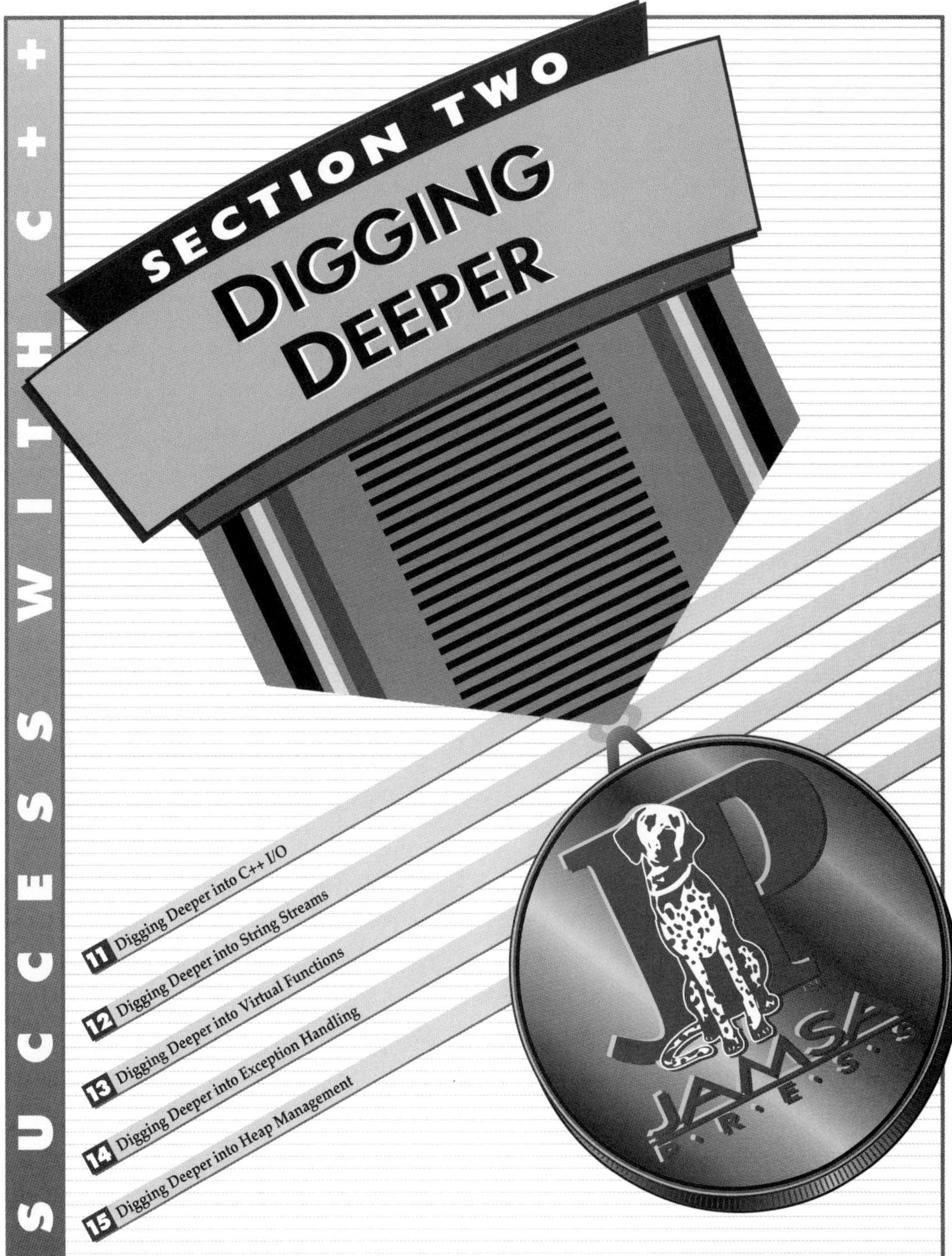
SUCCESS WITH C++
SECTION TWO
DIGGING DEEPER
11 Digging Deeper into C++ I/O
12 Digging Deeper into String Streams
13 Digging Deeper into Virtual Functions
14 Digging Deeper into Exception Handling
15 Digging Deeper into Heap Management
JAMSA PRESS

Chapter 11
Digging Deeper into C++ I/O

In Chapter 1 you examined C++ I/O streams and their use within your programs. At that time, you learned how to use the various manipulators and member functions. This chapter takes a closer look at the classes that make up the C++ I/O streams. You will examine the base and derived classes in detail. By the time you finish this chapter, you will be able to examine and understand fully header files such as IOSTREAM.H and IOMANIP.H. In addition, you will learn how to create your own I/O manipulators. Finally, this chapter examines the behind-the-scenes flow of data that occurs when your program performs an I/O operation.

When you finish reading this chapter, you will have learned

- How your programs can create manipulators that use parameters
- How you can simplify a manipulator's use in other programs.
- The effect of tying one stream to another and how to do it
- Where the C++ file streams are defined
- How your programs perform formatted I/O operations
- How to perform unformatted I/O operations

Note: Your compiler may use additional header files for many of the stream definitions described in this chapter. For example, Borland C++ version 4.0 uses IOSTREAM.H for practically all stream-related definitions. In addition to IOSTREAM.H, Microsoft Visual C++ version 1.0 uses IOS.H, ISTREAM.H, and OSTREAM.H. This chapter uses Borland C++ as a point of reference; you will need to refer to the specific header files used by your compiler.

Understanding the I/O Stream Relationship

As you have learned, the header file IOSTREAM.H defines the I/O stream classes. If you have not already done so, print a copy of the file at this time. As you examine the file's contents, you will find classes defined in terms of the classes *ios*, *istream*, and *ostream*. As Figure 11.1 shows, the *ios* class is the base class, from which the *istream* and *ostream* classes are derived. The *istream* and *ostream* classes add to the *ios* base class the extraction (>>) and insertion (<<) operators.

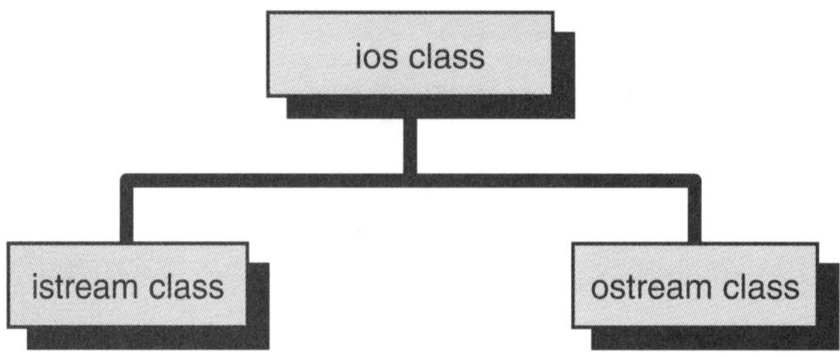

Figure 11.1 The classes ***istream*** *and* ***ostream*** *are derived from the* ***ios*** *base class.*

The *istream* and *ostream* classes implement the extraction and insertion operators. If you examine the header file IOSTREAM.H, you will find prototypes for the insertion and extraction operators, as shown here:

```
istream _FAR & _Cdecl operator>> (istream _FAR & (_Cdecl *_f)(istream _FAR &));
istream _FAR & _Cdecl operator>> (ios _FAR & (_Cdecl *_f)(ios _FAR &) );
istream _FAR & _Cdecl operator>> (  signed char _FAR *);
:  :  :  :  :  :
istream _FAR & _Cdecl operator>> (unsigned char _FAR *);

ostream _FAR & _Cdecl operator<< (short);
ostream _FAR & _Cdecl operator<< (unsigned short);
ostream _FAR & _Cdecl operator<< (int);
:  :  :  :  :  :
ostream _FAR & _Cdecl operator<< (unsigned int);
```

As you can see, the file provides operators for the common data types, such as *short*, *unsigned short*, and *int*. In Chapter 1, your programs made extensive of the *cin* and *cout* I/O streams to perform keyboard and screen I/O. In addition, Chapter 1 briefly discussed the *cerr* and *clog* streams, which let your programs display messages to the standard error device. If you examine the header file IOSTREAM.H, you will find declarations similar to the following that define these streams:

```
extern istream_withassign _Cdecl cin;
extern ostream_withassign _Cdecl cout;
extern ostream_withassign _Cdecl cerr;
extern ostream_withassign _Cdecl clog;
```

As you can see, the *cin* input stream is defined in terms of the *istream_withassign* class. Likewise, *cout*, *cerr*, and *clog* are defined in terms of the output stream class *ostream_withassign*. As Figure 11.2 shows, these two class types are actually derived from the *ostream* and *istream* classes.

In general, objects of the *_withassign* class support an assignment (=) operator member function, which can be used to assign the stream to a different source or target. For example, *cin* and *cout* are normally associated with the keyboard and screen display. If you redirect the program's input or output, however, the stream connection will change.

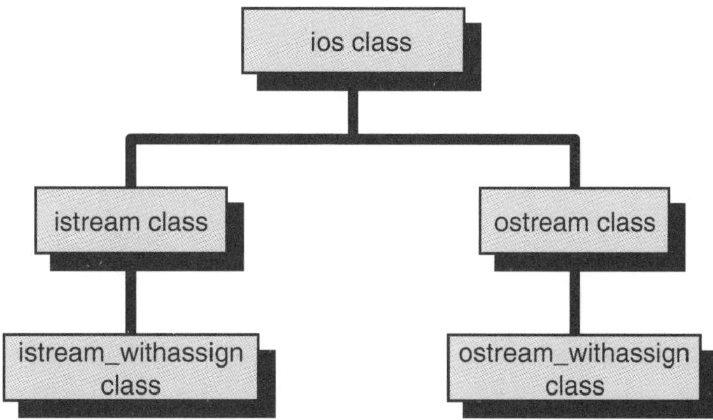

Figure 11.2 The class types ***ostream_withassign*** *and* ***istream_withassign*** *are derived from* ***ostream*** *and* ***istream****.*

The following program, CHSTREAM.CPP, uses the assignment operator with the *cout* stream to write *cout's* output to the file COUT.DAT, which is currently connected to a file stream:

```
#include <fstream.h>

void main(void)
 {
   ofstream output("COUT.DAT");

   cout << "About to assign cout to the file" << endl;

   cout = output;

   cout << "This is not written to the screen, but rather, the file!"
        << endl;
 }
```

When you compile and execute this program, your screen will display the first message. The second message, however, will not appear on the screen, but rather, will be written to the file COUT.DAT.

In a similar way, the following COUT_PRN.CPP, assigns the *cout* stream to a file that corresponds to the printer device. When you compile and execute this program, the program will write its output to the printer device:

```
#include <fstream.h>

void main(void)
 {
   ofstream cprn("PRN");

   cout << "About to assign cout to the printer" << endl;

   cout = cprn;

   cout << "This is not written to the screen, but rather, the printer!"
        << endl;
 }
```

Understanding I/O Streams

A *stream* is best defined as a series of bytes moving from one source to another. The header file IOSTREAM.H defines the C++ I/O stream classes. The classes are based on the *ios* class with provides the variables and member functions required for most input and output operations. The header file then derives the *istream* and *ostream* classes which in turn implement the extraction (>>) and insertion (<<) operators that your programs use for input and output operations. Most C++ programs make extensive use of the *cin*, *cout*, *cerr*, and *clog* I/O streams. These streams are normally defined as *istream_withassign* or *ostream_withassign*, which means the objects support an assignment (=) operator member function that lets a new stream to be connected:

```
extern istream_withassign _Cdecl cin;

extern ostream_withassign _Cdecl cout;
```

Creating Your Own I/O Manipulators

As you have learned, a manipulator is a function that you can place within an insertion or extraction operation. In Chapter 1 you used the manipulators defined within the header file IOMANIP.H. As it turns out, you can create your own manipulators for use with input or output streams. For example, the following statement uses a manipulator named *beep* that sounds the computer's built-in speaker:

```
cout << beep << "Important message" << endl;
```

The following statements create the *beep* manipulator:

```
ostream& beep(ostream& stream)
 {
   stream << '\007';
   return(stream);
 }
```

As you can see, the function returns an object of type *ostream*—actually, the same output stream the function receives as the parameter stream. Within the function statements, the function inserts the ASCII bell character (ASCII value 7) into the stream. The function then returns a reference to the updated stream. When the program encounters a manipulator within an extraction or insertion operation, the program invokes the function that corresponds to the manipulator. In the following statement, for example, the program invokes the *beep* function twice:

```
cout << beep << "Important message" << beep << endl;
```

The following program, BEEPMAN.CPP, uses the manipulator to sound the computer's built-in speaker before displaying a message:

```
#include <iostream.h>

ostream& beep(ostream& stream)
 {
   stream << '\007';
   return(stream);
 }

void main(void)
 {
   cout << beep << "This is an important message" << endl;
 }
```

Creating Your Own Manipulator

Throughout this book, you have used the I/O manipulators presented in the header file IOMANIP.H. In addition to using these manipulators, your programs can create their own. To create a manipulator, you declare the manipulator as function that returns a reference to an object of type *istream* or *ostream.* As you can see here, the function's first parameter corresponds to the stream:

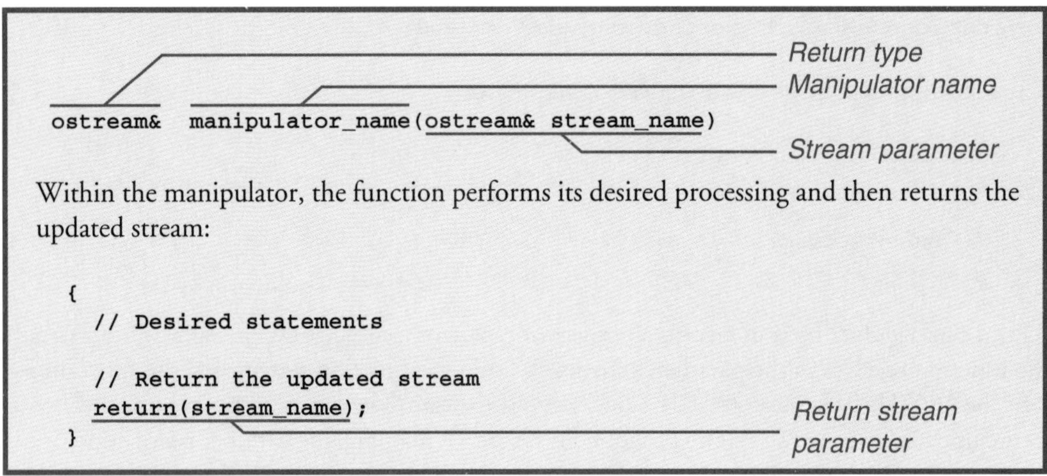

The following program, TAB_MAN.CPP, for example, uses a manipulator named *tab*, which inserts a tab character into the output stream:

```
#include <iostream.h>

ostream& tab(ostream& stream)
 {
   stream << '\t';
   return(stream);
 }

void main(void)
 {
   cout << "Hello" << tab << "world!" << endl;
 }
```

In Chapter 1 you learned to use the *ios::scientific* and *ios::fixed* flags to select fixed or scientific output format for the display of a floating-point value. For example, the following program, FIXEDSCI.CPP, uses these flags to display the value 123.456:

```
#include <iostream.h>
#include <iomanip.h>

void main(void)
 {
   float value = 123.456;

   cout << setiosflags(ios::fixed) << value << endl;
   cout << setiosflags(ios::scientific) << value << endl;
 }
```

When you compile and execute this program, your screen will display the following output:

```
C:\> FIXEDSCI  <ENTER>
123.456001
1.234560e+02
```

If you use these flags on a regular basis, you should consider creating the *fixed* and *scientific* manipulators, shown here:

```
ostream& fixed(ostream& stream)
 {
   stream << setiosflags(ios::fixed);
   return(stream);
 }

ostream& scientific(ostream& stream)
 {
   stream << setiosflags(ios::scientific);
   return(stream);
 }
```

The following program, FIXSCI_2.CPP, uses the *fixed* and *scientific* manipulators to display the value 123.456:

```
#include <iostream.h>
#include <iomanip.h>

ostream& fixed(ostream& stream)
 {
   stream << setiosflags(ios::fixed);
   return(stream);
 }

ostream& scientific(ostream& stream)
 {
   stream << setiosflags(ios::scientific);
   return(stream);
 }

void main(void)
 {
   float value = 123.456;

   cout << fixed << value << endl;
   cout << scientific << value << endl;
 }
```

The following program, DECOCTHE.CPP, creates and uses the familiar *dec*, *oct*, and *hex* manipulators:

```
#include <iostream.h>
#include <iomanip.h>

ios& dec(ios& stream)
 {
   stream.setf(ios::dec);
   return(stream);
 }

ios& oct(ios& stream)
 {
   stream.setf(ios::oct);
   return(stream);
 }

ios& hex(ios& stream)
 {
   stream.setf(ios::hex);
   return(stream);
 }

void main(void)
 {
   cout << oct << "Value 10 in octal is " << 10 << endl;
   cout << hex << "Value 10 in decimal is " << 10 << endl;
   cout << dec << "Value 10 in hexadecimal is " << 10 << endl;
 }
```

The following program, SHOWBASE.CPP, creates the *showbase* manipulator, which directs the stream to precede hexadecimal values with 0x and octal values with 0:

```
#include <iostream.h>
#include <iomanip.h>

ios& showbase(ios& stream)
 {
   stream.setf(ios::showbase);
   return(stream);
 }

void main(void)
 {
   cout << showbase;
   cout << oct << "Value 10 in octal is " << 10 << endl;
   cout << hex << "Value 10 in decimal is " << 10 << endl;
   cout << dec << "Value 10 in hexadecimal is " << 10 << endl;
 }
```

When you compile and execute this program, your screen will display the following output:

```
C:\> SHOWBASE  <ENTER>
Value 10 in octal is 012
Value 10 in decimal is 0xa
Value 10 in hexadecimal is 10
```

Finally, the following program, SHOW_PO.CPP, creates the *showpoint* and *showpos* manipulators, which direct the stream to display the decimal point for floating-point numbers and to precede positive numbers with a plus sign:

```
#include <iostream.h>
#include <iomanip.h>

ios& showpoint(ios& stream)
 {
   stream.setf(ios::showpoint | ios::fixed);
   return(stream);
 }


ios& showpos(ios& stream)
 {
   stream.setf(ios::showpos);
   return(stream);
 }


void main(void)
 {
   cout << 10.0 / 2 << endl;
   cout << showpoint;
   cout << 10.0 / 2 << endl;

   cout << 1 << ' ' << 2 << ' ' << endl;
   cout << showpos;
   cout << 1 << ' ' << 2 << ' ' << endl;
 }
```

When you compile and execute this program, your screen will display the following output:

```
C:\> SHOW_PO  <ENTER>
5
5.000000
1 2
+1 +2
```

MANIPULATORS THAT SUPPORT MULTIPLE PARAMETERS

Each of the previous manipulators have been fairly simple, in that they do not support parameters. The following *spaces* manipulator lets you insert a specific number of spaces (blank characters) into an output stream:

```
cout << spaces(5) << "Just skipped 5 spaces" << endl;
```

To create a manipulator that supports parameters, you essentially create two functions. The first function is very similar to those you have created to this point:

```
ostream& spaces(ostream& stream, int space_count)
 {
   for (int i = 0; i < space_count; i++)
     stream << ' ';

   return(stream);
 }
```

As you can see, the function returns a reference to an output stream and receives a reference as the parameter value. In addition, the function receives a second parameter named *space_count* of type *int.* The second function uses the OMANIP macro that is defined in the header file IOMANIP.H, as shown here:

```
OMANIP(int) spaces(int space_count)
 {
   OMANIP(int) type(spaces, space_count);
   return(type);
 }
```

During compilation, the preprocessor expands the macro to create the function that your program actually calls when it manipulator is encountered. As you can see, this function invokes the first function, specifying the required two parameter values.

The following program, SPACEMAN.CPP, uses the *spaces* manipulator to insert a different number of spaces into an output stream:

```
#include <iostream.h>
#include <iomanip.h>

ostream& spaces(ostream& stream, int space_count)
 {
   for (int i = 0; i < space_count; i++)
     stream << ' ';
```

```
    return(stream);
  }

OMANIP(int) spaces(int space_count)
  {
    OMANIP(int) type(spaces, space_count);
    return(type);
  }

void main(void)
  {
    for (int i = 1; i <= 5; i++)
      cout << "Skipping " << i << spaces(i) << "spaces" << endl;
  }
```

Note: Some compilers may not fully support the OMANIP macro. If you experience syntax errors when you compile the program, refer to your compiler documentation.

When you compile and execute this program, your screen will display the following output:

```
C:\> SPACEMAN  <ENTER>
Skipping 1 spaces
Skipping 2  spaces
Skipping 3   spaces
Skipping 4    spaces
Skipping 5     spaces
```

In a similar way, the following program, NEWLINES.CPP, creates a manipulator named *newlines*, which directs the stream to print the number of blank lines specified:

```
#include <iostream.h>
#include <iomanip.h>

ostream& newlines(ostream& stream, int count)
  {
    for (int i = 0; i < count; i++)
      stream << endl;

    return(stream);
  }

OMANIP(int) newlines(int count)
  {
    OMANIP(int) type(newlines, count);
    return(type);
  }
```

```
void main(void)
 {
   for (int i = 1; i <= 5; i++)
     cout << "Skipping " << i << newlines(i) << "lines" << endl;
 }
```

Note: Some compilers may not fully support the OMANIP macro. If you experience syntax errors when you compile the program, refer to your compiler documentation.

MANIPULATORS THAT USE PARAMETERS

When you create your own manipulators, there will be many times when your program needs to pass a value to the manipulator. To create a manipulator that supports a parameter, you actually create two functions. The first function specifies the manipulator name, parameters, and statements. For example, the following *beeps* manipulator lets your program specify the number of times you want the manipulator to sound the computer's bell:

```
ostream& bells(ostream& stream, int bell_count)
 {
   for (int i = 0; i < bell_count; i++)
     stream << '\a';

   return(stream);
 }
```

The second function declaration uses the *OMANIP* macro defined in the header file IOMANIP.H:

```
OMANIP(int) bells(int bell_count)
 {
   OMANIP(int) type(bells, bell_count);
   return(type);
 }
```

To sound the computer's speaker three times, use the *bells* manipulator, as shown here:

```
cout << bells(3);
```

Finally, the following program, SETFILL.CPP, creates a *setfill* manipulator, similar to that discussed in Chapter 1:

```
#include <iostream.h>
#include <iomanip.h>

ostream& filler(ostream& stream, int fillchar)
 {
   stream.fill((char)fillchar);
   return(stream);
 }

OMANIP(int) filler(char fillchar)
 {
   OMANIP(int) type(filler, fillchar);
   return(type);
 }

void main(void)
 {
   cout << "Hello" << filler('.') << setw(15) << "world!" << endl;
 }
```

Note: Some compilers may not fully support the OMANIP macro. If you experience syntax errors when you compile the program, refer to your compiler documentation.

When you compile and execute this program, your screen will display the following output:

```
C:\> SETFILL  <ENTER>
Hello.........world!
```

Using this same technique, you can create a wide variety of manipulators. Take time now, for example, to create manipulators that right- and left-justify program output.

Building Your Own Manipulator File

As you have learned, the header file IOMANIP.H contains the function prototypes for several common manipulators. Depending on the number and the complexity of the manipulators you create, you might simply want to place the manipulators (with complete function definitions) into a header file, such as MY_MANIP.H. If you don't want other users to access the manipulator code, simply place the manipulator function prototypes within the file and place the actual manipulator code in an object library. Chapter 17 talks about the steps you should follow to create a class library. As it turns out, you can follow similar steps to create a library for your manipulator functions.

UNDERSTANDING A TIED I/O STREAM

In Chapter 1 you learned that the *cout* and *clog* I/O streams perform buffered output. As such, output written to these streams will not appear on the screen until the buffer is full, the program ends, the program flushes the buffer, or in the case of *cout*, the program performs an input operation from *cin*. In this case, *cin* is *tied* to the *cout* output stream. If you examine the header file IOSTREAM.H, you will find that the *ios* class supports a member function named *tie*. If your program invokes *tie* with no parameters, *tie* will return a pointer to the output stream to which the input stream is tied. The following program, SHOWTIE.CPP, uses the *tie* function to verify that *cin* is tied to the *cout* output stream:

```
#include <iostream.h>

void main(void)
 {
   if (*(cin.tie()) == cout)
     cout << "cin is tied to cout" << endl;
   else
     cout << "cin not tied to cout" << endl;
 }
```

The *tie* member function also lets your programs tie an input stream to an output stream. The following program, TIE_CON.CPP, for example, opens a file that corresponds to the console device. Next, the program ties *cin* to the file stream. The program then writes a message to the stream and waits three seconds. When the program performs an input operation to *cin*, the message is flushed:

```
#include <fstream.h>
#include <time.h>

void main(void)
 {
   time_t start_time, current_time;

   ofstream screen("CON");

   cin.tie(&screen);

   screen << "Hello C++ world!--Press Enter to continue";
   time(&start_time);

   do {
     time(&current_time);
   } while ((current_time - start_time) < 3);
```

```
    cin.get();
    screen.close();
  }
```

Your programs can also tie one output stream to another. In this way, when the tied output buffer is flushed, so too is the output buffer to which the stream is tied. By default, C++ ties *cerr* to *cout* and *clog* to *cout*. In this way, if *cerr* is flushed, so too is *cout*. Likewise, if *clog* is flushed, so too is *cout*. The following program, SHOWTIES.CPP, shows how C++ ties streams by default:

```
#include <iostream.h>

void main(void)
 {
   if (*(cin.tie()) == cout)
     cout << "cin is tied to cout" << endl;

   if (*(cerr.tie()) == cout)
     cout << "cerr is tied to cout" << endl;

   if (*(clog.tie()) == cout)
     cout << "clog is tied to cout" << endl;

   if (*(cout.tie()) == NULL)
     cout << "cout is not tied" << endl;
 }
```

When you compile and execute this program, your screen will display the following:

```
C:\> SHOWTIES  <ENTER>
cin is tied to cout
cerr is tied to cout
clog is tied to cout
cout is not tied
```

Adding More Pieces to the Picture

In Chapter 3 you examined C++ file streams. As you learned, the header file FSTREAM.H defines the file stream classes *ifstream*, *ofstream*, and *fstream*. When your program needs to perform file input operations, your program creates objects of type *ifstream*. Likewise, for file output operations, your programs use objects of type *ofstream*. Finally, if your program needs to read and write to the same file, your programs use objects of type *fstream*. If you examine the declarations of these classes within FSTREAM.H, you will find that these classes are actually based on classes *istream*, *ostream*, and *iostream* as Figure 11.3 shows.

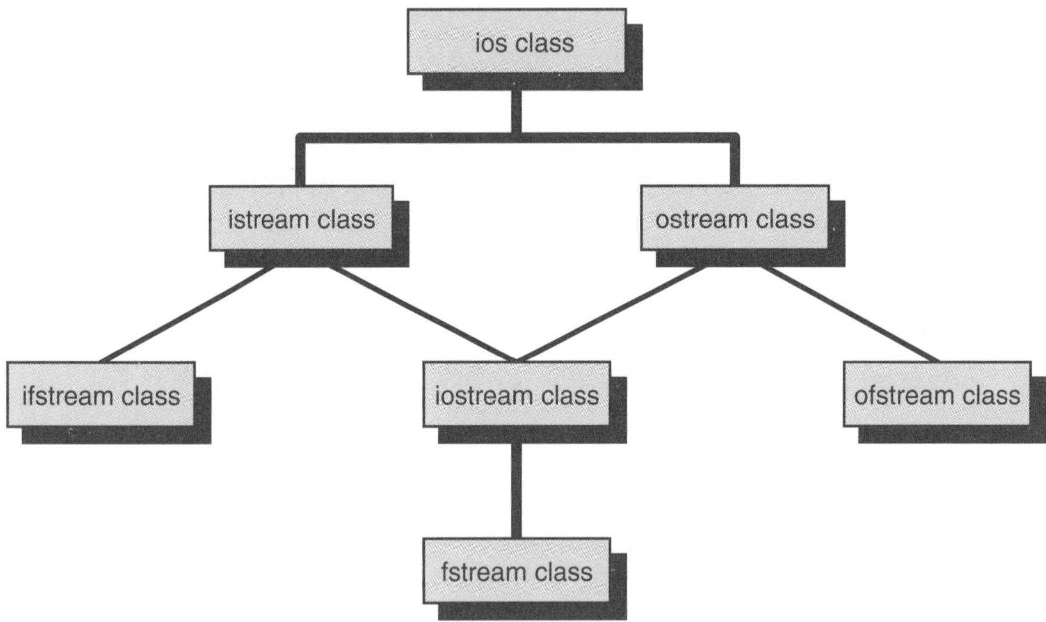

Figure 11.3 *The* ***ifstream, ofstream,*** *and* ***fstream*** *classes are derived from the* ***istream, ostream,*** *and* ***iostream*** *classes.*

The *ifstream* and *ofstream* classes add the *open* and *close* member functions to their base classes. The *iostream* class adds a read and write capability to those it has inherited from the *istream* and *ostream* classes. The *fstream* class, in turn, adds *open* and *close* functions to those provided by the *iostream* class.

UNDERSTANDING FORMATTED AND UNFORMATTED OUTPUT

When you perform I/O operations, you can use formatted or unformatted I/O classes. All of the classes discussed in this chapter have performed formatted I/O. Table 11.1 lists the C++ formatted I/O classes.

Class Name	Description
ios	The base class for input and output streams
istream	Derived from *ios*, adds the extraction operator
ostream	Derived from *ios*, adds the insertion operator

Table 11.1 *C++ formatted I/O classes.* *(continued on next page)*

Class Name	Description
iostream	Derived from *istream* and *ostream*, adds read and write operations
istream_withassign	Derived from *istream*, adds an assignment operator
ostream_withassign	Derived from *ostream*, adds an assignment operator
ifstream	Derived from *istream*, adds open and close methods
ofstream	Derived from *ostream*, adds open and close methods
fstream	Derived from *iostream*, adds open and close methods
stdiostream	Derived from *ios*, adds a connection to a file from *stdio*

***Table 11.1** C++ formatted I/O classes. (continued from previous page)*

When your programs perform formatted I/O, the I/O classes convert integer and floating-point values to their ASCII counterparts. For example, the following statement outputs the values 22, 33, and 44:

```
cout << 22 << " " << 33 << " " << 44 << endl;
```

To display the value 22, for example, the program outputs the ASCII values 50 (the ASCII value for the character '2') two times. Likewise, to output the value 33, the program outputs the ASCII character 51 two times.

When your programs perform *unformatted* output, on the other hand, the program outputs each value's actual binary representation, with no translations. Table 11.2 lists the C++ unformatted I/O classes.

Class Name	Description
streambuf	The base class for buffered I/O that implements read and write pointers and simple I/O operations
filebuf	Derived from *streambuf*, adds open and close methods
stdiobuf	Derived from *streambuf*, adds a connection a file from *stdio*

***Table 11.2** C++ unformatted I/O classes.*

To help you better understand the unformatted classes, consider the hierarchy diagram shown in Figure 11.4.

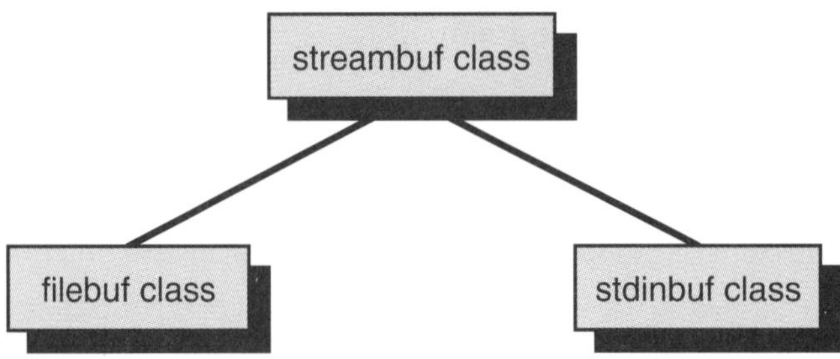

Figure 11.4 The C++ unformatted I/O classes.

The header file IOSTREAM.H defines the unformatted I/O classes. When your programs perform unformatted I/O, your programs essentially work with buffered data, as discussed next.

Understanding Buffered I/O

The *streambuf* class provides the base for buffered I/O operations in C++. When you perform buffered I/O, your programs will normally read or write information to a specific buffer (storage location) that resides in memory, as shown in Figure 11.5.

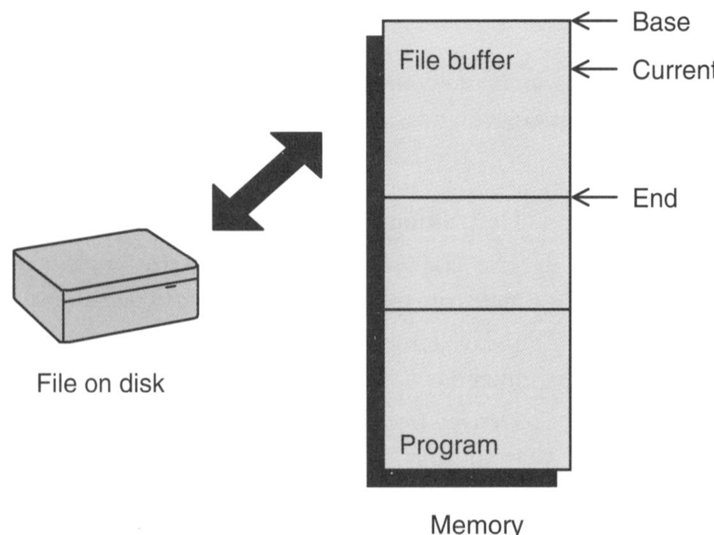

Figure 11.5 Buffered I/O places data into a storage location in memory.

As you can see, several pointers are used to control the buffer. If you examine the header file IOSTREAM.H, you will find that the file defines many different member functions for the class. Many of these functions manipulate the buffer pointers or the characters to which the pointers point. Your programs should not create objects of type *streambuf*. Instead, your programs can open files using the *filebuf* class. In most cases, however, your programs won't actually perform buffered I/O using objects of type *filebuf*. Instead, your programs will use *ifstream* and *ofstream* objects, as discussed in Chapter 3. As it turns out, the *ios* class uses a pointer to an object of type *streambuf* to gain support for buffered I/O. It is important to note that the *ios* class is not derived from the *streambuf* class, but instead, use a pointer to an object of type *streambuf*.

To manipulate objects of the *filebuf* class, you need to understand the purpose of the *streambuf* member functions. If you examine the file IOSTREAM.H, you will find member function prototypes similar to the following:

```
int  _Cdecl sgetc();                          // Peek at next character in
                                              // the buffer
int  _Cdecl snextc();                         // Advance to and return next
                                              // character in the buffer
int  _Cdecl sbumpc();                         // Return the current
                                              // character in the buffer
                                              // and advance the pointer
void _Cdecl stossc();                         // Advance to the next
                                              // character in the buffer
int  _Cdecl sgetn(char _FAR *, int);          // Get next n characters in
                                              // the buffer
int  _Cdecl sputbackc(char);                  // Return a character to the
                                              // buffer
int  _Cdecl in_avail();                       // Number of available
                                              // characters in the buffer
int  _Cdecl sputc(int);                       // Put one character into the
                                              // buffer
int  _Cdecl sputn(const char _FAR *, int); // Put n characters into
                                              // the buffer
int  _Cdecl out_waiting();                    // Number of unflushed
                                              // characters in output
                                              // buffer
```

In addition to the member functions listed here, the *streambuf* class defines functions that let your programs seek or move from one location in the buffer to another and functions that synchronize the buffer for input and output operations. When your programs perform buffered file operations using *filebuf* objects, you will use one or more of these functions. To help you understand these functions better, Table 11.2 lists each function's purpose and return value.

Function Name	Purpose
sgetc	Peeks at the next character in the buffer. If no character is available, EOF is returned. The *get* pointer is not moved.
snextc	Moves the *get* pointer forward one character and returns the next character.
sbumpc	Returns the current character and then advances the *get* pointer. If no character is available, EOF is returned.
stossc	Moves the *get* pointer forward one character.
sgetn	Returns the next *n* characters from the buffer. The function returns the number of characters returned. If no characters are available, EOF is returned..
sputbackc	Places the last character taken from the buffer back into the buffer.
in_avail	Returns the number of available characters.
sputc	Places the specified character into the buffer and advances the *put* pointer.
sputn	Places *n* characters from a string into the buffer, advancing the *put* pointer.
out_waiting	Returns the number of characters in the output buffer

***Table** 11.2 The purpose of **filebuf** member functions*

Opening a File for Buffered I/O Operations

In most cases, your programs will use the *ifstream* and *ofstream* classes for file input and output operations. However, by examining file operations that use the *filebuf* class, you will understand buffered file I/O better. Opening a file for buffered I/O operations using *filebuf* is very similar to opening a file stream for input or output operations. To begin, you declare an object of type *filebuf*, as shown here:

```
filebuf  buffer_file;
```

Next, open the file using the *open* member function, as shown here:

```
buffer_file.open("FILENAME.EXT", ios::in);
```

The following program, OPENBUF.CPP, opens the file specified in the command line for buffered input. If the file is successfully opened, the program displays a message and then closes the file. If the file is not opened, the program displays an error message so stating:

```
#include <fstream.h>

void main(int argc, char **argv)
 {
   filebuf buffered_file;

   buffered_file.open(argv[1], ios::in);

   if (buffered_file.is_open())
    {
      cout << "File successfully opened" << endl;
      buffered_file.close();
    }
   else
     cerr << "Error opening the file: " << argv[1] << endl;
 }
```

As you can see, the program uses the *close* method to close the file when it is no longer needed. The following program, SHOWBUF.CPP, opens a file for buffered input. The program then displays the file's contents a character at a time.

```
#include <fstream.h>

void main(int argc, char **argv)
 {
   filebuf buffered_file;

   int letter;

   buffered_file.open(argv[1], ios::in);

   if (buffered_file.is_open())
    {
      while ((letter = buffered_file.sgetc()) != EOF)
        {
          cout.put((char)letter);
          buffered_file.snextc();
        }

      buffered_file.close();
    }
   else
     cerr << "Error opening the file: " << argv[1] << endl;
 }
```

The program uses the *sgetc* member function to peek at the next character in the buffer. If the end of file has not been encountered, the program displays the character and then advances the pointer to the next character using the *snextc* function.

In a similar way, the following program, EASYSHOW.CPP, opens a buffered file. The program then displays the file's contents using the insertion operator to display the file's buffer. If you examine the header file IOSTREAM.H, you will find that the insertion operator is overloaded for operations that use an address to a *streambuf*. The function that corresponds to this overload extracts the characters from the buffer, placing them into the output stream:

```
#include <fstream.h>

void main(int argc, char **argv)
 {
   filebuf buffered_file;
   buffered_file.open(argv[1], ios::in);
   if (buffered_file.is_open())
    {
      cout << &buffered_file;
      buffered_file.close();
    }
   else
     cerr << "Error opening the file: " << argv[1] << endl;
 }
```

Connecting All the Pieces

To understand fully how the various I/O classes work together, you need to keep in mind that I/O classes have public functions your programs can invoke and private members that work behind the scenes to control I/O operations. When your program opens a file for input, for example, an object of type *ifstream* is created. As you have read, *ifstream* (which adds open and close members) is based on the *istream*. The *istream* class, in turn, is based on the *ios* base class—adding the extraction operator to the base class. When your program performs an input operation using the stream, the data must be placed somewhere. As it turns out, the data is placed into a buffer in memory that corresponds to a *streambuf* object. The *streambuf* object contains pointers and functions that control access to the data. Keep in mind, however, that the *ios* class is not derived from the *streambuf* class, but rather, uses a pointer to a *streambuf* object.

Putting It All Together

Almost every C++ program you create will make extensive use of I/O and file streams. This chapter has taken a close look at I/O streams—not just their use, but also the interrelationships between the different class types. Before you continue with Chapter 12, make sure that you have learned the following:

- ✓ The header file IOSTREAM.H defines the stream I/O classes. Within the file, you find a series of related class definitions.
- ✓ The *ios* class defines the base class for I/O operations. The classes *istream* and *ostream* in turn, add the extraction and insertion operators to the *ios* class. Within the IOSTREAM.H file, you will find member functions that define these operations.
- ✓ The *cin* stream is defined as *istream_withassign*. Likewise, the *cout*, *cerr*, and *clog* streams are defined as *ostream_withassign*. Classes defined as *_withassign* contain an assignment operator (=), which your programs can use to assign a different stream to a class object.
- ✓ C++ programs implement manipulators much as programs overload operators—using functions. To create a manipulator for an I/O stream, your program creates a function that receives a reference to a stream as a parameter and then manipulates the stream in some way. The function then returns the stream reference.
- ✓ Your programs can create manipulators that use parameters. The easiest way to create such a manipulator is to use the *OMANIP* macro defined in the header file IOMANIP.H.
- ✓ If you create a series of manipulators, you should store the manipulators in a header file, simplifying the manipulator's use in other programs.
- ✓ To help your programs control I/O buffers, your programs can *tie* one stream to another. For example, the *cin* stream is tied to *cout*. If the *cout* stream contains buffered output that has not yet been displayed, the output will immediately appear when your program performs input from *cin*.
- ✓ The header file FSTREAM.H defines the C++ file streams. Within that file, you will find class definitions for *ifstream*, *ofstream*, and *fstream*. These classes add the open and close capabilities to those they inherit from the *istream*, *ostream*, and *iostream* classes.
- ✓ When your programs perform formatted I/O operations, information output is first converted to its ASCII format. Likewise, information input is converted from ASCII to the desired format. Unformatted I/O operations, on the other hand, do not convert values.
- ✓ To perform unformatted I/O operations, your programs can use *Filebuf* objects.

Chapter 12
Digging Deeper into String Streams

Throughout this book, your programs have made extensive use of I/O streams to perform keyboard, screen, and file I/O operations. C++ also provides a set of *string streams* that your programs can use to buffer characters for formatted output or for performing numeric conversions. For example, if a string contains the ASCII representation of a number such as 1001, you can use a stream to convert the characters to a value of type *int*. This chapter examines string streams in detail. As you will learn, using these streams is very similar to many of the operations you have performed with I/O streams. When you finish this chapter you will have learned

- What a string stream is and what it does
- Where the class definitions for the string streams are
- What the three primary string stream classes your programs use are
- What input string streams are
- What output string streams are
- How streams support member functions
- What a dynamic buffer is

Looking at the File STRSTREA.H

C++ defines the string stream classes within the header file STRSTREA.H. Take time now to print a copy of the file's contents. You can use the file's contents as a reference throughout this chapter's discussion.

To use a string stream, you must include the header file at the start of your programs, as shown here:

```
#include <strstrea.h>
```

If you examine the file's contents, you will find that the header file defines several classes. The three most commonly used string stream classes are briefly described in Table 12.1. The sections that follow describe these classes in detail.

Stream	Purpose
istrstream	Supports input string formatting operations for member-based strings
ostrstream	Supports output string formatting operations for memory-based strings
strstream	Supports input and output formatting operations for memory-based strings

Table 12.1 String stream classes defined in header file STRSTREA.H.

Putting Input String Streams to Use

The best way to understand string streams and their use is to examine a few simple programs that use them. String streams can support input or output operations. In general, an input string stream supports the extraction operator (>>), letting your programs input variables from the stream's buffer. An output string stream, on the other hand, supports the insertion operator (<<). Using the insertion operator, your programs can write characters, strings, numbers, and even special characters to the stream. Input string streams are often used to convert an ASCII representation of a number to an integer or floating-point representation. For example, assume that the character string *number* contains the value 1.2345, as shown in Figure 12.1.

1	.	2	3	4	5

Figure 12.1 An ASCII representation of a floating-point value.

Before your program can work (perform mathematical operations) with the value, it must first convert the value from ASCII to floating-point. In C, your program might use the *atof* run-time library function, as shown in the following program, ATOF.C:

```
#include <stdlib.h>
#include <stdio.h>

void main(void)
 {
   char *number = "1.2345";
   float value;

   value = atof(number);

   printf("The value is %f\n", value);
   printf("The value squared is %f\n", value * value);
 }
```

When you compile and execute this program, your screen will display the following output:

```
C:\> ATOF  <ENTER>
The value is 1.234500
The value squared is 1.523990
```

Within your C++ programs you can still use functions such as *atof* to perform such conversions.

The down side of using these functions is that you must remember the function names (such as *atoi*, *atof*, *atol*, and so on). Therefore, some C programmers use the *sscanf* function to read values from a character string, eliminating the need to remember the different function names. The following program, SSCANF.C, reads the floating-point value from the ASCII string, performing the desired conversion:

```
#include <stdio.h>

void main(void)
 {
   char *number = "1.2345";
   float value;

   sscanf(number, "%f", &value);

   printf("The value is %f\n", value);
   printf("The value squared is %f\n", value * value);
 }
```

Converting values using *sscanf* is very similar to reading values from an input string stream. The difference, however, is that with string streams, you don't need to consider the formatting characters, such as %f. Instead, you simply use the extraction operator (>>). The following program, INPUTSTR.CPP, illustrates how your programs can use a string stream to convert the floating-point value:

```
#include <strstrea.h>
#include <iostream.h>

void main(void)
 {
   char *number = "1.2345";
   float value;

   istrstream buffer(number);

   buffer >> value;

   cout << "The value is " << value << endl;
   cout << "The value squared is " << value * value << endl;
 }
```

The program creates an input string stream named *buffer* using the following statement:

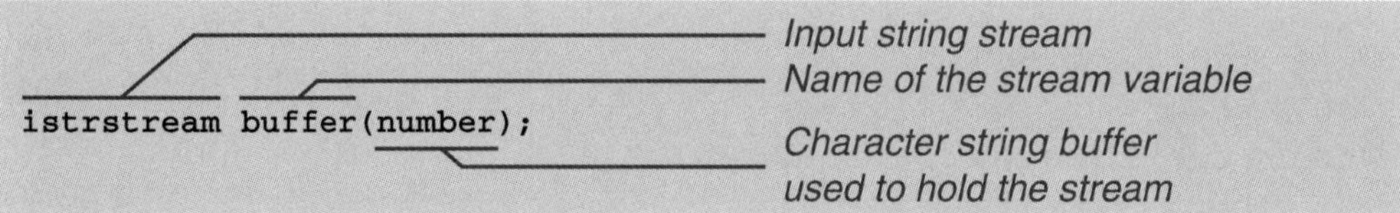

When you pass only a character string buffer to the *istrstream* constructor, the function uses the specified buffer. The buffer length will correspond to the string's NULL termination character. The following statements, on the other hand, create a 256-byte buffer:

```
char string[256];

istrstream buffer(string, sizeof(string));
```

When you specify a buffer size during the object's creation, the stream will support the number of characters specified.

Understanding Input String Streams

A string stream is a buffer (in memory) that contains characters. Input string streams are so named because your programs can use the extraction operator (>>) to read values from the stream into variables. To create an input stream, your programs must declare an object of type *istrstream*, as shown here:

```
char string[256];
char *book = "Success with C++";

istrstream buffer(string, sizeof(string));
istrstream  text(book);
```

The first stream declaration (*buffer*) specifies the stream's buffer size. In the case of the second declaration (*text*), the buffer size corresponds to the NULL terminator at the end of the string "Success with C++". Using the extraction operator, your programs can read data from the stream into a variable, as shown here:

```
buffer >> value;
text >> word;
```

Input string streams are often used to convert an ASCII representation of a number to the corresponding integer or floating-point value.

Reading Multiple Values from an Input String Stream

When your programs read data from an input stream, such as *cin* or a file stream, your programs can read multiple values at one time using the extraction operator:

```
cout << "Type your first and last name: ";

cin >> first >> last;
```

When you work with input string streams, there may also be times when the string's buffer contains multiple values. For example, assume that the string buffer contains the values 1, 100, and 1001, as shown in Figure 12.2.

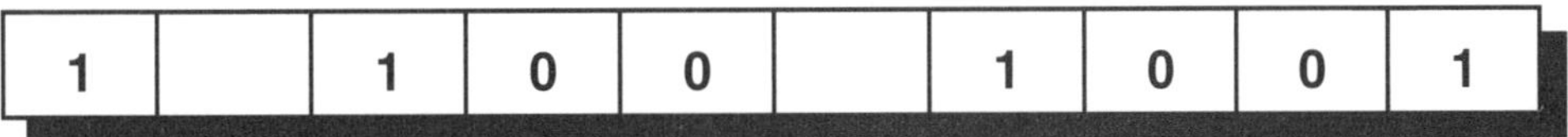

***Figure 12.2** Multiple integer values in a string buffer.*

Using the extraction operator, your program can read all three values, as shown here:

```
int a, b, c;

buffer >> a >> b >> c;
```

The following program, THREEVAL.CPP, uses the extraction operator to read three values from a string buffer:

```
#include <iostream.h>
#include <strstrea.h>

void main(void)
 {
   char *string = "1 100 1001";

   istrstream buffer(string);

   int a, b, c;

   buffer >> a >> b >> c;

   cout << "The values are " << a << ' ' << b << ' ' << c << endl;
 }
```

When you compile and execute this program, your screen will display the following output:

```
C:\> THREEVAL  <ENTER>
The values are 1 100 1001
```

In this case, the program read all three variables using one statement. The program could also have read the variables using the following statements:

```
buffer >> a;
buffer >> b;
buffer >> c;
```

In some cases, your program will not know the number of values the buffer contains. If your program tries to read an empty buffer, the stream will set the *fail* flag. The following program, STR_FAIL.CPP, reads integer values from an input string stream until the stream is empty:

```
#include <iostream.h>
#include <strstrea.h>

void main(void)
 {
   char *string = "1 2 3 4 5 6 7 8 9";

   int value;

   istrstream buffer(string);

   while (! buffer.fail())
     {
       buffer >> value;
       if (! buffer.fail())
         cout << value << endl;
     }
 }
```

As you can see, the program loops until the stream's *fail* flag becomes set. Within the loop, note that the program tests the state of the flag immediately after each input operation. If the input is successful, the program outputs the value read. When you compile and execute this program, your screen will display the following output:

```
C:\> STR_FAIL  <ENTER>
1
2
3
4
```

```
5
6
7
8
9
```

In the previous program, the buffer contained multiple values of type *int*. In some cases, however, buffer may contain values of different types. For example, the following program, DIFFTYPE.CPP, reads values of type *int*, *float*, and *long* from the input string stream:

```
#include <iostream.h>
#include <strstrea.h>

void main(void)
 {
   char *numbers = "1001 1.2345 123456789L";

   int count;
   float rate;
   long distance;

   istrstream buffer(numbers);

   buffer >> count;
   buffer >> rate;
   buffer >> distance;

   cout << "The int count is " << count << endl;
   cout << "The float rate is " << rate << endl;
   cout << "The long distance is " << distance << endl;
 }
```

When you compile and execute this program, your screen will display the following output:

```
C:\> DIFFTYPE  <ENTER>
The int count is 1001
The float rate is 1.2345
The long distance is 123456789
```

When your program uses the extraction operator to read data from an input string stream, the compiler determines the type of value to extract, based on your variable type. For example, in the previous program, the compiler knew to extract first a value of type *int*, followed by a *float* and a *long*. To perform these operations, the compiler calls a function that reads and converts a value of the correct data type. In some cases, however, the values the buffer contains might not correspond to those your program expects. For example, assume that rather than containing the following numbers:

"1001 1.2345 123456789L"

the buffer begins with a character string:

"ABC 1001 1.2345 123456789L"

When function called to convert a value of a specific type encounters an invalid character, the function immediately ends the conversion, returning the value it has created to the point of the error. The function will not advance the pointer passed the point of the error. If the first character in the stream is invalid, the function sets the stream's fail flag. The following program, BAD_DATA.CPP, illustrates how your programs can use the *fail* function to determine whether or not an I/O operation was successful:

```
#include <iostream.h>
#include <strstrea.h>

void main(void)
 {
   char *numbers = "ABC 1001 1.2345 123456789L";

   int count;
   float rate;
   long distance;

   istrstream buffer(numbers);

   buffer >> count;

   if (buffer.fail())
    {
     cerr << "Error reading the int value for count" << endl;
     buffer.clear();
    }

   buffer >> rate;

   if (buffer.fail())
    {
     cerr << "Error reading the float value for rate" << endl;
     buffer.clear();
    }

   buffer >> distance;

   if (buffer.fail())
    {
```

```
      cerr << "Error reading the long value for distance" << endl;
      buffer.clear();
     }
    cout << "The int count is " << count << endl;
    cout << "The float rate is " << rate << endl;
    cout << "The long distance is " << distance << endl;
  }
```

As you can see, the program uses the *fail* member function to test the success of each I/O operation. If an error has occurred, the program displays an error message and then clears the flag. If a conversion function encounters an invalid character, the function stops the conversion without advancing the stream pointer. Thus, all three input operations in this case fail when they encounter the first letter A. If you compile and execute this program, your screen will display the following:

```
C:\> BAD_DATA  <ENTER>
Error reading the int value for count
Error reading the float value for rate
Error reading the long value for distance
The int count is 0
The float rate is 1.3705e-034
The long distance is 0
```

As you can see, the program displays an error message for each I/O operation, and the values assigned to the variables are not correct.

Reading Multiple Values from an Input String Stream

An input string stream is simply a buffer of characters from which your programs can input values using the extraction operator. Depending on the stream's contents, there may be times when your program reads multiple values from the stream in one statement:

```
buffer >> day >> month >> year;
```

When the C++ compiler encounters a stream I/O operation, the compiler invokes a function to extract a value of the specified type. If the function is successful, it converts the value's ASCII representation to the a value of the correct type. If an error occurs during the conversion, the function sets the stream's *fail* flag and immediately ends the conversion, returning the value it has created to that point. The function will not advance the stream pointer past the invalid character.

Using Input String Stream Member Functions

The previous programs have used the extraction operator to read values from an input string stream. The most common use of an input stream is to convert a value from its ASCII representation. However, depending on your program's needs and the stream's contents, there may be times when you will want to read the stream's contents a character at a time, or even the entire buffer in one operation. The following program, IN_GET.CPP, reads a stream's contents one character at a time using the *get* member function:

```
#include <iostream.h>
#include <strstrea.h>

void main(void)
 {
   char *string = "Success with C++";

   istrstream buffer(string);

   for (char letter = buffer.get(); ! buffer.eof();
        letter = buffer.get())
     cout.put(letter);
 }
```

As you can see, the program uses the *get* member function to read a character from the stream and the *eof* function to determine when the stream is empty.

Depending on the information the stream's buffer contains, there may be times when you will want to read past a series of characters before you begin an extraction operation. Using the *get* member function in this way, you can read the stream's contents a character at a time. In a similar way, the following program, READALL.CPP, reads the entire stream buffer using the *getline* member function:

```
#include <iostream.h>
#include <strstrea.h>

void main(void)
 {
   char *string = "Success with C++";

   istrstream buffer(string);

   char book[256];

   buffer.getline(book, sizeof(book));

   cout << book << endl;
 }
```

Putting Output String Streams to Use

Just as there are times when your programs need to convert ASCII representations of values using input string streams, there will also be times when your programs want to format values within a string. In C, programmers use functions such as *itoa* (*int* to ASCII) to convert a numeric value to ASCII. The following program, ITOA.C, for example, illustrates such a conversion:

```
#include <stdio.h>
#include <stdlib.h>

void main(void)
 {
   char buffer[256];

   int value = 1001;

   itoa(value, buffer, 10);

   printf("Value in ASCII is %s\n", buffer);
 }
```

Likewise, some C programs use the *sprintf* function to create an ASCII representation of a value. The following program, SPRINTF.C, for example, uses the *sprintf* function to create an ASCII representation of the value 1.2345:

```
#include <stdio.h>

void main(void)
 {
   char buffer[256];

   float value = 1.2345;

   sprintf(buffer, "%f", value);

   printf("The value in ASCII is %s\n", buffer);
 }
```

Using C++, your programs can convert a value to ASCII using an output string stream. Creating an output string stream is very similar to using an input string, in that you declare an object of type *ostrstream* to which you associate a buffer, as shown here:

```
char string[256];

ostrstream buffer(string, sizeof(string));
```

Output string streams are so named, because your programs can use the insertion operator to place ASCII characters into the stream. The following program, OUT_STR.CPP, illustrates how your programs might use an output string stream:

```
#include <strstrea.h>
#include <iostream.h>
#include <iomanip.h>

void main(void)
 {
   char string[256];
   ostrstream buffer(string, sizeof(string));

   float price = 29.95;
   int programs = 300;

   buffer << "Success with C++ $";
   buffer << setprecision(2) << price << " with over ";
   buffer << programs << " programs" << ends;

   cout << string << endl;
 }
```

In this case, the program uses three statements to write characters to the output string stream. As you can see, the output statements use the *setprecision* and *ends* manipulators. As you have learned, the *setprecision* manipulator controls the number of digits displayed to right of the decimal point. The *ends* manipulator inserts a NULL character within the stream's buffer that marks the end of the string. The output stream in the previous program used a 256-byte buffer that corresponds the array *string*.

When your programs output data to a string stream, they cannot place more data into the stream's buffer than the buffer can hold. If a program tries to overwrite a buffer, the streams *fail* flag is set and the characters are ignored. The following program, OUT_FAIL.CPP, for example, tries to write the letters A through Z to a stream whose buffer size is ten bytes. Using the stream's *fail* member, the program detects the error and displays an error message:

```
#include <iostream.h>
#include <strstrea.h>
#include <stdlib.h>

void main(void)
 {
   char string[10];
```

```
   ostrstream buffer(string, sizeof(string));

   for (char letter = 'A'; letter <= 'Z'; letter++)
    {
      buffer << letter;

      if (buffer.fail())
        {
          cerr << endl << "Error writing the character " <<
                  letter << endl;
          exit(1);
        }
      else
        cout << letter;
    }
 }
```

When you compile and execute this program, your screen will display the following output:

```
C:\> OUT_FAIL  <ENTER>
ABCDEFGHIJ
Error writing the letter K
```

Using a Dynamic Buffer

The previous programs used a fixed-size buffer that corresponded to the array *string*. If your programs do not specify a buffer and buffer size when you create an output string stream, the *ostrstream* constructor function will allocate a buffer dynamically, using the *new* operator. The following statement, for example, creates an output string stream named *buffer* that uses a dynamic array:

```
ostrstream buffer;
```

The following program, DYNAMIC.CPP, for example, creates an output string stream whose size is dynamic. The program then writes the letters of the alphabet to the buffer 100 times (2600 bytes). Using the *ends* manipulator, the program terminates the stream and then displays the letters by sending the characters to *cout*:

```
#include <iostream.h>
#include <strstrea.h>

void main(void)
 {
```

```
    ostrstream buffer;

    for (int count = 0; count < 100; count++)
      for (char letter = 'A'; letter <= 'Z'; letter++)
        buffer << letter;

    buffer << ends;

    cout << buffer.rdbuf();
  }
```

As you can see, the program does not specify a character string buffer to be used with the stream. Instead, the *ostrstream* allocates the memory dynamic from the heap using the *new* operator. To display the stream's contents, the program must access the buffer that contains the characters. To do so, the program uses the *rdbuf* member function. The *rdbuf* function returns a pointer to the start of the buffer.

When an output stream uses a dynamic buffer, the buffer's size can grow throughout the program's lifetime, behind the scenes. The stream will allocate as memory as required until the heap runs out of space. The following program, EAT_HEAP.CPP, creates an output string stream that uses a dynamic buffer. The program then fills the buffer with the letters of the alphabet until the heap runs out of space:

```
#include <iostream.h>
#include <strstrea.h>

void main(void)
  {
    ostrstream buffer;

    long count = 0L;

    cout << "Working...";

    while (! buffer.fail())
      for (char letter = 'A'; letter <= 'Z'; letter++, count++)
        buffer << letter;

    cout << "The number of characters buffered was " << count <<
            endl;
  }
```

CREATING A DYNAMIC OUTPUT STRING STREAM

To create an output string stream, your programs declare an object of type *ostrstream.* Normally, your programs will assign a character string buffer to the stream, as shown here:

```
char string[256];

ostrstream buffer(string, sizeof(string));
```

If your program does not specify a buffer, the *ostrstream* constructor function will automatically allocate a stream buffer from the heap. If your program assigns more characters to the dynamic buffer than the buffer can hold, the buffer size is automatically increasing the buffer size, by allocating memory from heap. When your program is ready to use the buffered data, your program can obtain a pointer to the buffer using the *rdbuf* member function, as shown here:

```
cout << buffer.rdbuf();
```

USING OUTPUT STRING STREAM MEMBER FUNCTIONS

Several of the preceding programs have used the *fail* and *rdbuf* functions with output string streams. Depending on your program requirements, there may be times when you want to work with a string buffer's contents one character at a time or the entire buffer at one time. The following program, OUT_CHAR.CPP, uses the *put* member function to place the letters of the alphabet in the buffer one character at a time:

```
#include <iostream.h>
#include <strstrea.h>

void main(void)
 {
   ostrstream buffer;

   for (char letter = 'A'; letter <= 'Z'; letter++)
     buffer.put(letter);

   buffer.put((char)NULL);

   cout << buffer.rdbuf() << endl;
 }
```

The previous programs have placed characters into the string stream without concern for the number of characters the buffer currently contains. If your program needs to know the number of characters a buffer contains, your programs can use the *pcount* member function. The following program, PCOUNT.CPP, for example, uses the pcount function to display the number of characters the buffer contains at various points throughout the program's execution:

```
#include <iostream.h>
#include <strstrea.h>

void main(void)
 {
   ostrstream buffer;

   cout << "The buffer currently contains " << buffer.pcount() <<
           " bytes " << endl;

   buffer << "Success with C++";

   cout << "The buffer currently contains " << buffer.pcount() <<
           " bytes " << endl;

   buffer << " " << 1 << " 2 " << 3 << endl << ends;

   cout << "The buffer currently contains " << buffer.pcount() <<
           " bytes " << endl;

   cout << buffer.rdbuf() << endl;
 }
```

Understanding How str Freezes a Dynamic Buffer

When your programs use a dynamic output string stream, they normally use the *rdbuf* function to get a pointer to the stream's buffer. As it turns out, your programs can also use the *str* member function to obtain a pointer to the buffer. The following program, USE_STR.CPP, uses the *str* member function to display a buffer's contents:

```
#include <iostream.h>
#include <strstrea.h>

void main(void)
 {
   ostrstream buffer;

   buffer << "Success with C++";

   cout << buffer.str() << endl;
 }
```

When your program invokes *str*, your program *freezes* the buffer, and you should not place other characters in the buffer. Here's why: When your program uses a dynamic buffer, the buffer size can increase as your program's needs require. To increase the buffer size, the stream functions might need to move the buffer to different heap locations. The functions can "get away" with moving the buffer because your program itself does not care where the buffer is located. Once your program invokes the *str* function, however, the functions give up ownership to the buffer, giving the buffer to your program. As such, the functions freeze your buffer, preventing the buffer's growth or movement. Once you freeze the buffer, therefore, you should not place additional characters in to the buffer. In addition, when your program no longer needs the buffer, your program should use the *delete* operator to release the buffer. Because of these complexities, most programs will use the *rdbuf* function instead of *str*.

Using an Input/Output String Stream

In Chapter 3 you learned how to open files for read and write operations. In a similar way, there may be times when your programs need to perform input and output operations on a string stream. To create a string stream capable of supporting input (extraction) and output (insertion), your programs must create objects of type *strstream*, as shown here:

```
strstream buffer;
```

The following program, INOUTSTR.CPP, creates a string stream for input and output operations. The program then outputs a floating-point value to the buffer and later inputs the value into a variable of type *float*:

```
#include <iostream.h>
#include <strstrea.h>

void main(void)
 {
   strstream buffer;

   float value;

   buffer << 1.2345;

   buffer >> value;

   cout << "The value is " << value << endl;
 }
```

Depending on your program's requirements, there may be times when your program performs user input, processes the data, and then assigns the data to a variable. For example, the program may first test the data to ensure that it contains numbers or text as required before trying to assign the data to program variables.

When your program uses *strstream* objects, your programs can use dynamic buffers as just shown, or the programs can specify a buffer as follows:

```
char string[64];

strstream buffer(string, sizeof(string));
```

Depending on the processing your program performs, there may be times when you want the program to append data to values to specific characters in the buffer. For example, the buffer might initially contain the characters "Hello". Your program in turn, can append more text to the buffer. To append output text to a buffer's contents, simply include the *ios::ate* or *ios::app* flags, as shown here:

The following program, HELLO.CPP, appends text to a buffer that contains the word "Hello,":

```
#include <iostream.h>
#include <strstrea.h>

void main(int argc, char **argv)
 {
   char string[256] = "Hello, ";

   strstream buffer(string, sizeof(string), ios::app);

   buffer << argv[1] << endl;

   cout << buffer.str();
 }
```

To display a message using HELLO, you would invoke the program with a word as follows:

```
C:\> HELLO world!  <ENTER>
Hello, world!
```

Understanding the Stream Relationships

In Chapter 11 you examined the relationship between several of the I/O streams. As it turns out, the string stream classes defined in the header file STRSTREA.H are also related. Figure 12.3, for example, illustrates how the string streams are related to the I/O classes discussed in Chapter 11.

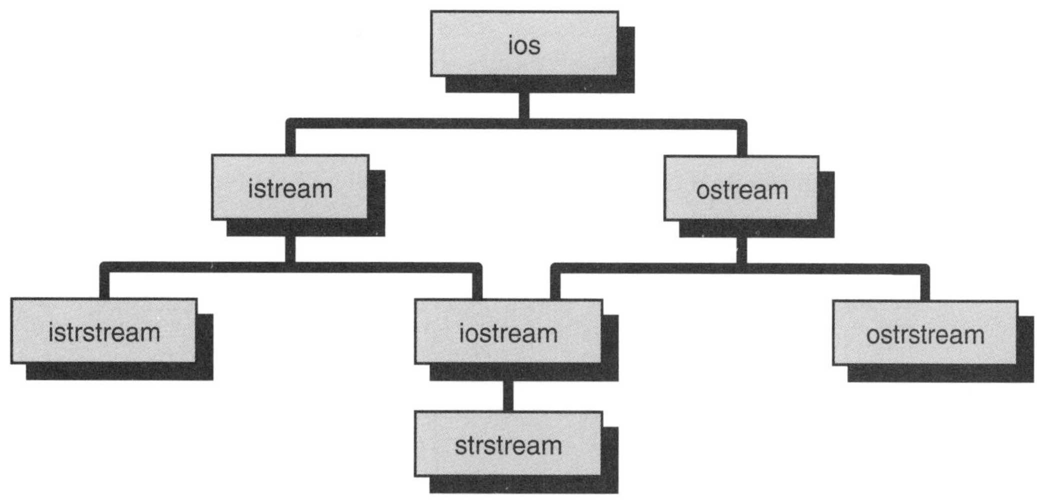

Figure 12.3 The relationship between the I/O and string stream classes.

Putting It All Together

A string stream is a sequence of characters contained in a memory buffer that is typically used for data conversions and formatted I/O. This chapter examined string streams and related operations in detail. Before you continue with Chapter 13, make sure that you have learned the following:

- ✓ A string stream is a character-based buffer that resides in memory. Using stream operators (the insertion and extraction operators), your programs can perform input and output operations to string streams.
- ✓ The header file STRSTREA.H contains the class definitions for the string streams.
- ✓ The three primary string stream classes your programs will use are *istrstream*, *ostrstream*, and *strstream*. The *istrstream* class lets your programs perform input operations from the stream. Likewise, *ostrstream* class supports output operations. Objects of type *strstream* support input and output operations.
- ✓ Input string streams are so named because your programs can use the extraction operator (>>) or stream member functions to input values from the stream, assigning the values to variables.

- ✓ Output string streams are so named because your programs can use the insertion operator (<<) or stream member functions to output values to the stream.
- ✓ Because the string streams are defined by classes, the streams support member functions. If you examine the header file STRSTREA.H, you will find that member functions correspond to the I/O functions discussed in Chapter 1.
- ✓ When you create output string stream objects, your programs can specify a buffer within which the stream will store its data. Likewise, your programs can direct the stream to use a dynamic buffer, which the stream functions allocate from the heap. If your program uses a dynamic buffer, the program may grow the buffer size (behind the scenes) throughout your program's execution.

Chapter 13
Digging Deeper into Virtual Functions

In Chapter 8 you learned how C++ programs use virtual functions to achieve polymorphism. Throughout Chapter 8 you read that virtual functions are possible due to the behind-the-scenes operations the compiler performs. This chapter examines some of those behind-the-scenes operations to help remove some of the mystery that accompanies the virtual functions. By the time you finish this chapter you will understand the following:

- What static linkages and dynamic linkages are
- What a virtual function table is
- The price you pay for the added flexibility of virtual functions

LOOKING AT A SIMPLE EXAMPLE

As you learned in Chapter 8, polymorphism lets an object take on two or more forms. The following program, SHAPES.CPP, uses virtual functions to create a polymorphic *shape* object pointer. To begin, the program creates the following *shape* base class:

```
class shape {
  public:
    shape(char *name, int x, int y);
    virtual void draw(void);
  protected:
    char name[64];
    int x;
    int y;
};
```

As you can see, the program declares the *draw* function as a virtual function. Next, the program derives *circle* and *square* objects, as shown here:

```
class circle : public shape {
  public:
    circle(char *name, int x, int y, int radius);
    void draw(void);
  private:
```

```
    char name[64];
    int radius;
};

class square : public shape {
  public:
    square(char *name, int x, int y, int side);
  private:
    char name[64];
    int side;
};
```

Using virtual functions, the program assigns different shapes to the *graphic* object pointer. The following statements implement the SHAPES.CPP program:

```
#include <iostream.h>
#include <string.h>

class shape {
  public:
    shape(char *name, int x, int y);
    virtual void draw(void);
  protected:
    char name[64];
    int x;
    int y;
};

class circle : public shape {
  public:
    circle(char *name, int x, int y, int radius);
    void draw(void);
  private:
    char name[64];
    int radius;
};

class square : public shape {
  public:
    square(char *name, int x, int y, int side);
  private:
    char name[64];
    int side;
};

shape::shape(char *name, int x, int y)
 {
   strcpy(shape::name, name);
   shape::x = x;
```

```
    shape::y = y;
  }

void shape::draw(void)
  {
    cout << "Drawing the shape: " << name << endl;
  }

circle::circle(char *name, int x, int y, int radius) :
    shape(name, x, y)
  {
    circle::radius = radius;
  }

void circle::draw(void)
  {
    cout << "Circles are being drawn: ";
    cout << "x " << x << " y " << y << " radius " << radius << endl;
  }

square::square(char *name, int x, int y, int side) :
    shape(name, x, y)
  {
     square::side = side;
  }

void main(void)
  {
    circle ball("Circle", 10, 20, 30);

    square box("Square", 40, 50, 40);

    shape *graphic = &ball;

    graphic->draw();

    graphic = &box;

    graphic->draw();
  }
```

As you can see, the *graphic* pointer takes on two forms, the *circle* and the *square*.

When you compile and execute this program, your screen will display the following output:

```
C:\> SHAPES  <ENTER>
Circles are being drawn: x 10 y 20 radius 30
Drawing the shape: Square
```

Polymorphism Is Not Function Overloading

As you learned in Chapter 8, polymorphism is not function overloading. For example, the following program, SUMARRAY.CPP, overloads the *sum_array* function:

```
#include <iostream.h>

float sum_array(float *array, int num_elements)
 {
   float sum = 0.0;

   for (int i = 0; i < num_elements; i++)
     sum += array[i];

   return(sum);
 }

long sum_array(int *array, int num_elements)
 {
   long sum = 0L;

   for (int i = 0; i < num_elements; i++)
     sum += array[i];

   return(sum);
 }

void main(void)
 {
   int int_array[5] = {1, 2, 3, 4, 5};
   float float_array[5] = {1.1, 2.2, 3.3, 4.4, 5.5};

   cout << "Values in int array: " << sum_array(int_array, 5) <<
           endl;
   cout << "Values in float array: " << sum_array(float_array, 5) <<
           endl;
 }
```

When you compile and execute this program, your screen will display the following output:

```
C:\>  SUMARRAY  <ENTER>
Values in int array: 15
Values in float array: 16.5
```

During compilation, the C++ compiler determines which function your program is using, based on the parameters your program passes to the function or the function's return type. The compiler then substitutes the correct function for each invocation. Such compiler-based substitutions are called *static linkages.* They are performed *before* your program runs. When your program performs polymorphism, on the other hand, the substitutions are made *when* your program executes. Such run-time substitutions are called *dynamic linkages.*

Understanding Dynamic Linkage

From the compiler's perspective, function overloading is actually very easy because the compiler knows before your program runs, how each program is used. In the case of the following program, ASKSHAPE.CPP, however, the object that is assigned to the *graphic* object pointer is not known until the program is running. In this case, the program asks the user to select the *circle* or *square* object. Based on the user's selection, the program assigns one of the objects to the pointer:

```
#include <ctype.h>

void main(void)
 {
   circle ball("Circle", 10, 20, 30);

   square box("Square", 40, 50, 40);

   shape *graphic;

   char choice;

   do {
     cout << "Type C for circle S for square: ";
     cin >> choice;
     choice = toupper(choice);

     if (choice == 'S')
       graphic = &box;
     else if (choice == 'C')
       graphic = &ball;
   } while ((choice != 'C') && (choice != 'S'));

   cout << endl << endl;

   graphic->draw();
 }
```

Note: To save book pages, the previous ASKSHAPE.CPP program did not include the class declarations and member functions. However, the source file provided on this book's companion disk provides a complete program.

As you can see, depending on the user's choice, the program assigns a different object pointer to the *graphic* pointer. In other words, during the program's execution (run time), the program must determine the correct object address. To determine such addresses, the program uses a *virtual function table* behind the scenes. This virtual function table is built by the compiler.

UNDERSTANDING VIRTUAL FUNCTION TABLES

A virtual function table is a table C++ uses behind the scenes when your program executes to locate the correct member function when a program uses polymorphism. The table contains entries for objects that use virtual classes. When your program uses such a function, C++ looks up the correct function address within table and then invokes the function.

Each time a class uses one or more virtual functions, the C++ compiler adds a special pointer to the class that points to the virtual table. The following program, TABLEPTR.CPP, uses the *sizeof* operator to display the size of two very similar classes. The only difference between the two classes is that the first uses a virtual class member. As a result, the first class has a special pointer to the virtual table:

```
#include <iostream.h>

class shape1 {
  public:
    shape(char *name, int x, int y);
    virtual void draw(void);
  protected:
    char name[64];
    int x;
    int y;
};

class shape2 {
  public:
    shape(char *name, int x, int y);
    void draw(void);
  protected:
    char name[64];
    int x;
    int y;
};

void main(void)
 {
   cout << "Size of virtual class: " << sizeof(shape2) << endl;
   cout << "Size of nonvirtual class: " << sizeof(shape1) << endl;
 }
```

When you compile and execute this program in Borland C++, your screen will display the following output:

```
C:\> TABLEPTR  <ENTER>
Size of virtual class: 68
Size of nonvirtual class: 70
```

As you can see, the class that uses the virtual function is larger due to the special pointer.

Understanding the Overhead of Virtual Functions

Although virtual class functions add a great deal of flexibility to your programs, the use of virtual functions is not without its cost. Each time your program uses an object that contains one or more virtual functions, a special pointer is used to access a virtual table, which in turn points to the correct function address. Because a virtual function invocation requires additional memory indirection, it is slower than a standard function invocation. The following program, OVERHEAD.CPP, invokes two similar functions five million times each, tracking the amount of time required for each function. The first function is a virtual function, whereas the second function is a standard function call:

```
#include <iostream.h>
#include <string.h>
#include <time.h>

class shape {
  public:
    shape(int x) { shape::x = x; };
    virtual void draw(void);
  protected:
    int x;
};

class circle {
  public:
    circle(int x) { circle::x = x; };
    void draw(void);
  private:
    int x;
};

void shape::draw(void)
 {
   return ;
 }
```

```
void circle::draw(void)
 {
   return ;
 }

void main(void)
 {
   time_t start_time, stop_time;

   circle ball(1);

   shape box(2);

   long int i;

   cout << "Working..." << endl;

   time(&start_time);
   for (i = 0; i < 5000000L; i++)
     box.draw();
   time(&stop_time);

   cout << "Virtual required: " << stop_time - start_time << endl;

   time(&start_time);
   for (i = 0; i < 5000000L; i++)
     ball.draw();
   time(&stop_time);

   cout << "Standard required: " << stop_time - start_time << endl;
 }
```

Depending on your computer type, the amount of time each function requires may differ slightly. However, given the very fast speed of today's processors, the overhead associated with virtual functions is actually very minimal. As a result, for most applications, the overhead of virtual functions can be ignored.

Understanding Virtual Destructors

Chapter 2 introduced you to constructor and destructor functions. Throughout this book, the programs presented have all made use of constructor functions and some have made use of destructors. When you define constructors and destructor functions, keep the following thought in mind: *constructor functions cannot be virtual functions, however destructor functions can.*

As you have learned, a polymorphic object can take on two or more forms. When the corresponding object is destroyed, the program needs to invoke the correct destructor. For example, consider the following program, BADDESTR.CPP, which uses the polymorphic *graphic* object pointer. The program defines a destructor function for each object type that simply displays a message informing you that the destructor function has been invoked:

```
#include <iostream.h>
#include <string.h>

class shape {
  public:
    shape(char *name, int x, int y);
    virtual void draw(void);
    ~shape(void);
  protected:
    char name[64];
    int x;
    int y;
};

class circle : public shape {
  public:
    circle(char *name, int x, int y, int radius);
    void draw(void);
    ~circle(void);
  private:
    char name[64];
    int radius;
};

shape::shape(char *name, int x, int y)
 {
   strcpy(shape::name, name);
   shape::x = x;
   shape::y = y;
 }

void shape::draw(void)
 {
   cout << "Drawing the shape: " << name << endl;
 }

shape::~shape()
 {
   cout << "In shape's destructor" << endl;
 }
```

```
circle::circle(char *name, int x, int y, int radius) :
   shape(name, x, y)
 {
   circle::radius = radius;
 }

void circle::draw(void)
 {
   cout << "Circles are being drawn: ";
   cout << "x " << x << " y " << y << " radius " << radius << endl;
 }

circle::~circle(void)
 {
   cout << "In circle's destructor" << endl;
 }

void main(void)
 {
   shape *graphic = new circle("Circle", 10, 20, 30);

   graphic->draw();
   delete graphic;
 }
```

As you can see, the program creates a *circle* object, assigning a pointer to the object to the polymorphic *graphic* variable. After the program draws the object, the program uses the *delete* operator to destroy the object. Unfortunately, because *graphic* is a pointer to the *shape* class, the program invokes the *shape* destructor, not that of the *circle* class. As a result, when you compile and execute this program, your screen will display the following output:

```
C:\> BADDESTR  <ENTER>
Circles are being drawn: x 10 y 20 radius 30
In shape's destructor
```

Next, assume that the *circle* class has allocated memory that needs to be released by a destructor function. As you just saw, the program does not invoke the *circle* class destructor.

However, if you change the *shape* class destructor function to a virtual function, the program will invoke the *circle* class destructor and the *shape* class destructor, as shown here:

```
C:\> BADDESTR  <ENTER>
Circles are being drawn: x 10 y 20 radius 30
In circle's destructor
In shape's destructor
```

As you can see, the program invokes each of the correct destructor functions. When your program uses polymorphism, and different classes allocate memory, you should use virtual destructor functions to ensure that the memory is released as required.

PUTTING IT ALL TOGETHER

In Chapter 8, you examined polymorphism and virtual functions in detail. In this chapter you examined a few of the behind-the-scenes operations C++ performs to implement virtual functions. Before you continue with Chapter 15, make sure that you have learned the following:

- ✓ Static linkages are the substitutions the C++ compiler makes, before your program runs, when it determines which function your program wants to use, based on the return types.
- ✓ Dynamic linkages are the substitutions made when your program perform polymorphism, while your programs run.
- ✓ A virtual function table contains entries for objects that use virtual classes.
- ✓ Because a virtual function invocation requires additional memory indirection to access the virtual function table, it is slower than a standard function invocation.
- ✓ When your program use polymorphism and different classes allocate memory, you should use virtual destructor functions to ensure that the memory is released as required.

Chapter 14
Digging Deeper into Exception Handling

When you write programs, you should try to determine the possible errors the program might experience and then include code to handle them. For example, when your programs perform file I/O operations, your programs should test the success of file open, read, and write operations and respond appropriately, should an error occur.

As the complexity of your programs increases, so too does the complexity of the code you must include to handle errors. To make it easier for your programs to test for and handle errors, C++ lets your programs handle exceptions (or errors). In the simplest sense, an *exception* is an error or (somewhat) unexpected event. The code that executes when an exception occurs is the *exception handler.*

This chapter examines C++ exception handling in detail. To support and to perform exception handling, your programs use the *try*, *throw*, and *catch* statements. Unfortunately, many older C++ compilers do not yet support exception handling. If your compiler generates errors while compiling the programs presented in this chapter, check with your compiler manufacturer to determine if a newer version of the compiler is available.

When you finish this chapter, you will have learned

- What an exception and an exception handler are
- Which statements support exception handling.
- How your program uses the *try* statement to enable exception handling.
- How to determine whether a specific exception has occurred
- How your programs use the *throw* statement
- How you can use a class to satisfy naming requirements for program-defined exceptions
- How your programs can define their own default handers
- How your programs can use a list of exceptions like function prototypes to specify what the function may throw

Understanding Exceptions

Think of an exception as a program-defined error. If your function works with arrays, for example, an exception might occur if the programs passes to the function an array index that exceeds the array bounds. When the function tests the index value, the function can generate or *throw* an exception. Likewise, if a function adds two integer values, the function might generate an exception if the result overflows an integer's range of values. The only exceptions that occur within a program are those defined by the program, or defined by libraries used by the programs. Hardware events such as page faults, disk read errors, or other interrupts do not generate exceptions.

To perform exception handling, your programs use the *try*, *throw*, and *catch* keywords. Assume, for example, that your program uses the function *fill_array* to read values from a file into a fixed-size array. If the file contains more values than the array can hold, the function should generate an exception.

Before the program invokes the function, the program uses the *try* statement, as shown here to enable exception handling:

```
try {
    fill_array(some_array, 100);
}
```

After the program enables exception handling, it can test for specific exceptions using the *catch* statement, as shown here:

```
try {
    fill_array(some_array, 100);
}

catch (array_overflow) {
     cerr << "Too many values for array to handle" << end;
     exit(1);
}

catch (file_not_found) {
     cerr << "Could not find the data file" << endl;
     exit(1);
}
```

In this case, the program invokes the function *fill_array* within a *try* statement. Next, using two *catch* statements, the program tests for two possible exceptions. If either exception occurs, the program will perform the corresponding statements (the corresponding exception handler). Only one exception can occur at any time. Thus, the previous program cannot experience the *array_overflow* and *file_not_found* exceptions at the same time.

CATCHING EXCEPTIONS WITHIN YOUR PROGRAM

To detect and handle an exception within your program, you use the *try* and *catch* statements. To enable exception handling for a specific operation, your program uses the *try* statement:

```
try {
   some_operation(a, b, c);
}
```

Next, to determine whether an exception occurred, your program uses the *catch* statement:

```
catch (exception_1) {
   // statements
}

catch (exception_2) {
   // statements
}
```

HOW EXCEPTIONS ARE NAMED

Each exception used within your program has a unique name. Your programs name exceptions by creating exception classes. For example, the following statements defines three exception classes:

```
class open_error { };
class read_error { };
class write_error { };
```

In this case, the exception classes do not have members. In later examples, you will find how member variables let your exception classes return more information about the exception. To generate an exception, your program code throws the exception. For example, the following statement throws the *write_error* exception:

```
throw write_error();  // Include parenthesis after the class name
```

In this way, exceptions are thrown and later caught by the exception handler using a *catch* statement. The following program, COPY_EXP.CPP, uses exceptions to determine file open, read, and write errors. If such an error occurs within the function *perform_copy*, the function throws the corresponding exception. Using the *catch* statement, the program catches each exception type:

```
#include <fstream.h>
#include <stdlib.h>

class open_error { };
class read_error { };
class write_error { };

void perform_copy(char *source_file, char *target_file)
 {
   ifstream source(source_file, ios::binary);

   char line[1];

   if (source.fail())
     throw open_error();
   else
    {
      ofstream target(target_file, ios::binary);

      if (target.fail())
        throw open_error();
      else
        {
          while (! source.eof() && ! source.fail())
            {
              source.read(line, sizeof(line));

              if (source.good())
               {
                 target.write(line, sizeof(line));

                 if (target.fail())
                   throw write_error();
               }
              else if (! source.eof())
                 throw read_error();
            }
          source.close();
          target.close();
        }
    }
 }

void main(int argc, char **argv)
 {
   try {
     perform_copy(argv[1], argv[2]);
   }
```

Define the exception classes

Throw an exception

```
  catch (open_error) {          Catch an exception
    cerr << "Error opening file" << endl;
    exit(1);
  }

  catch (read_error) {
    cerr << "Error reading file" << endl;
    exit(1);
  }

  catch (write_error) {
    cerr << "Error writing file" << endl;
    exit(1);
  }
}
```

Naming and Throwing Exceptions

Each exception within your program has a unique name. You can define an exception by creating an exception class similar to the following:

```
class out_of_memory { };
```

To later activate an exception, the program uses the *throw* keyword and the exception name, as shown here:

```
throw out_of_memory();
```

Note the parentheses that follow the exception name within the *throw* statement. In this case, the exception will be handled by code that catches the *out_of_memory* exception:

```
try {
    some_operation()
}
catch (out_of_memory) {
   // Statements
}
```

Looking at Class-Based Exceptions

In the previous example program, the exception classes were global to the entire program. In many cases, however, the exceptions will be local to a class. For example, assume that your program uses an array class to hold integer values:

```
class Array {
  public:
    Array(int size);
    void fill_array(int num_values);
    void show_array(int num_values);

  private:
    int *buffer;
    int size;
};
```

When your program creates an *Array* object, you must specify the buffer size, as shown here:

```
Array vector(100);
```

In this case, the program will allocate a buffer capable of storing 100 integer values. Next, the function *fill_array* lets your program assign consecutive values to elements of the array. For example, the following statement assigns the values 1 through 25 to the array's first 25 entries (the remaining entries are not changed):

```
vector.fill_array(25);
```

In a similar way, the *show_array* function lets your programs display a specific range of values. The following statement, for example, displays the array's first ten values:

```
vector.show_array(10);
```

The following program, ARRAY.CPP, uses the *Array* class to create a vector of integer values:

```
#include <iostream.h>

class Array {
  public:
    Array(int size);
    void fill_array(int num_values);
    void show_array(int num_values);

  private:
    int *buffer;
    int size;
};

Array::Array(int size)
 {
   buffer = new int[size];
   Array::size = size;
 }
```

```
void Array::fill_array(int num_values)
 {
   for (int i = 0; i < num_values; i++)
     buffer[i] = i;
 }

void Array::show_array(int num_values)
 {
   for (int i = 0; i < num_values; i++)
     cout << buffer[i] << endl;
 }

void main(void)
 {
   Array vector(200);

   vector.fill_array(10);

   vector.show_array(10);
 }
```

As you can see, the program uses the array without testing the index values passed to the functions *fill_array* and *show_array*. Assume, for example, that your program invokes the *fill_array* function using the index value 500:

```
vector.file_array(500);
```

In this case, the program will assign the values 1 through 500 to the array, overwriting the array by 300 integer values. A better program would test the index value to ensure that the value is valid before assigning the integers.

The following program, ARRAYEXC.CPP, uses exception handling to signal an operation that would overflow the array bounds. Because the exceptions are specific to the *Array* class, the exception scope is restricted to the class by defining the exceptions as class members:

```
#include <iostream.h>
#include <stdlib.h>

class Array {
  public:
    Array(int size);
    void fill_array(int num_values);
    void show_array(int num_values);
    class range { };
  private:
    int *buffer;
    int size;
};
```

```
Array::Array(int size)
 {
   buffer = new int[size];
   Array::size = size;
 }

void Array::fill_array(int num_values)
 {
   if (num_values > size)
     throw range();

   for (int i = 0; i < num_values; i++)
     buffer[i] = i;
 }

void Array::show_array(int num_values)
 {
   if (num_values > size)
     throw range();

   for (int i = 0; i < num_values; i++)
     cout << buffer[i] << endl;
 }

void main(void)
 {
   Array vector(200);

   try {
     vector.fill_array(10);
   }
   catch (Array::range) {
     cerr << "Invalid array index in fill_array" << endl;
     exit(1);
   }

   try {
     vector.show_array(500);
   }
   catch (Array::range) {
     cerr << "Invalid array index in show_array" << endl;
     exit(1);
   }
 }
```

As you can see, the program invokes the *show_array* function with an invalid index value of 500. When the function examines this value, it throws the exception, which, in turn, is caught by the *catch* statement.

How to Handle Exceptions

When an exception occurs, your programs need to determine how they will handle the event. In the case of the previous programs, the programs simply displayed error messages and then ended. Depending on your program's purpose, you may not be able simply to end. Instead, your program might need to try to resolve the error. Assume, for example, that your program receives an out of memory exception. Rather than simply ending, your program might want to free memory or maybe even traverse and collapse heap entries (collect garbage), as discussed in Chapter 15. In such cases, your exception handler will need access to pointers whose memory it can free, or the function must be sophisticated enough to traverse the heap, releasing nonessential memory. After your program frees the necessary memory, the program can repeat the operation that originally caused the error.

In some cases, you may simply want your program to end. As it turns out, if your program throws an exception and the exception is not caught, your program will run a default handler which automatically ends the program. The following program, BAD_EXC.CPP, throws the *no_such_device* exception. Because no code catches the exception, the program simply ends:

```
#include <iostream.h>

class no_such_device { };     // Exception class
class file_not_found { };

void show_files(char disk_drive)
 {
   if ((disk_drive < 'A') || (disk_drive > 'Z'))
     throw no_such_device();
   else
     cout << "Would display files here" << endl;
 }

void main(void)
 {
   try {
    show_files('a');
   }
   catch (file_not_found) {
     cerr << "Error finding file" << endl;
   }
 }
```

In this case, the program tests for the *file_not_found* exception. It does not, however, test for the *no_such_device* exception. Because the thrown exception is not caught, the program ends.

RETURNING MORE INFORMATION WITH AN EXCEPTION

When your programs throw an exception, there may be times when you want to include additional information about the cause of the error. For example, the program COPY_EXP.CPP, previously shown, throws the *open_error* exception when it cannot open the source or target file. Unfortunately, the program code catching the exception has no way to determine whether the program could not open the source or target file. A better solution would be to return a value the program could test, such as the value 0 for the source file and the value 1 for the target.

An easy way to provide such support is to add a member variable to the exception class to which the value can be assigned. Second, you must provide a member function within the class that can be thrown with the correct value. The following statements illustrate how you might change the *open_file* exception class:

```
class open_error {
 public:
    int value;
    open_error(int value) { open_error::value = value; };
};
```

As you can see, the class provides the member variable named *value* and a constructor function that assigns a specified value to the variable. When your program later throws the exception, your program can specify a value as a parameter, as shown here:

```
throw open_error(1);  // Error opening target file
```

In this case, the *throw* statement causes an exception object to be created. Thus, the object's constructor function is executed, which assigns the specified value to the member variable. When your program catches an exception, your program actually receives the exception object. As a result, your program can examine the member variables, as shown here:

```
catch (open_error exception) {
   if (exception.value)
    cerr << "Error opening target file" << endl;
  else
    cerr << "Error opening source file" << endl;
  exit(1);
}
```

In this case, the program uses a variable named *exception* to refer to the *open_error* object. By testing the value of the *value* member variable, the program can determine if the error was due to the source or target file. The following program, EXPVALUE.CPP, uses a member variable to determine which file is causing the error:

```
#include <fstream.h>
#include <stdlib.h>

class open_error {
  public:
    int value;
    open_error(int value) { open_error::value = value; };
};

class read_error { };
class write_error { };

void perform_copy(char *source_file, char *target_file)
 {
   ifstream source(source_file, ios::binary);

   char line[1];

   if (source.fail())
     throw open_error(0);
   else
    {
      ofstream target(target_file, ios::binary);

      if (target.fail())
        throw open_error(1);
      else
        {
          while (! source.eof() && ! source.fail())
            {
              source.read(line, sizeof(line));

              if (source.good())
               {
                 target.write(line, sizeof(line));

                 if (target.fail())
                   throw write_error();
               }
              else if (! source.eof())
                 throw read_error();
            }
          source.close();
          target.close();
        }
    }
 }
```

```
void main(int argc, char **argv)
 {
   try {
     perform_copy(argv[1], argv[2]);
   }

   catch (open_error exception) {
     if (exception.value)
       cerr << "Error opening target file" << endl;
     else
       cerr << "Error opening source file" << endl;
     exit(1);
   }

   catch (read_error) {
     cerr << "Error reading file" << endl;
     exit(1);
   }

   catch (write_error) {
     cerr << "Error writing file" << endl;
     exit(1);
   }
 }
```

In a similar way, the following program, EXSTRING.CPP, changes the program just shown to include the filename as a character string within the exception class:

```
#include <fstream.h>
#include <stdlib.h>
#include <string.h>

class open_error {
  public:
    int value;
    char filename[64];
    open_error(int value) {
       open_error::value = value;
       filename[0] = NULL;
    };
    open_error(int value, char *filename) {
       open_error::value = value;
       strcpy(open_error::filename, filename);
    };
};

class read_error { };
class write_error { };
```

```
void perform_copy(char *source_file, char *target_file)
 {
   ifstream source(source_file, ios::binary);

   char line[1];

   if (source.fail())
     throw open_error(0, source_file);
   else
    {
      ofstream target(target_file, ios::binary);

      if (target.fail())
        throw open_error(1, target_file);
      else
        {
          while (! source.eof() && ! source.fail())
            {
              source.read(line, sizeof(line));

              if (source.good())
               {
                 target.write(line, sizeof(line));

                 if (target.fail())
                   throw write_error();
               }
              else if (! source.eof())
                 throw read_error();
            }
          source.close();
          target.close();
        }
    }
 }

void main(int argc, char **argv)
 {
   try {
     perform_copy(argv[1], argv[2]);
   }

   catch (open_error exception) {
     if (exception.value)
       {
         if (exception.filename)
           cerr << "Error opening the target file " <<
                   exception.filename << endl;
         else
```

```
            cerr << "Error opening target file" << endl;
        }
      else
        {
          if (exception.filename)
            cerr << "Error opening the source file " <<
                    exception.filename << endl;
          else
            cerr << "Error opening source file" << endl;
        }

      exit(1);
    }

    catch (read_error) {
      cerr << "Error reading file" << endl;
      exit(1);
    }

    catch (write_error) {
      cerr << "Error writing file" << endl;
      exit(1);
    }
}
```

RETURNING VALUES WITH AN EXCEPTION

When your programs throw an exception, there may be times when you want the program to specify additional information about the exception. One way to do so is to add member variables to the exception class, along with constructor functions that later assign parameters to the members. When the program later catches the exception, it can examine the exception's member variables to determine more information about the exception's cause.

CATCHING MULTIPLE EXCEPTIONS IN ONE CATCH STATEMENT

As you have learned, if your program does not catch a specific exception, the default exception handler is invoked, which normally ends the program. As a result, your programs may have a series of *catch* statements. Depending on how your program handles exceptions, you may find that the handlers are very similar as shown here:

```
catch (file_open_error) {
    cerr << "Error opening file" << endl;
    exit(1);
}
catch (source_file_open_error) {
    cerr << "Error opening file" << endl;
    exit(1);
}
catch (target_file_open_error) {
    cerr << "Error opening file" << endl;
    exit(1);
}
catch (temp_open_error) {
    cerr << "Error opening file" << endl;
    exit(1);
}
```

As you can see, the four different exception handlers each perform similar operations. In this cases where your exceptions are somewhat related, you might want to group them as an enumerated type, as shown here:

```
enum FileException { Open, Source, Target, Temp };
```

Next, within your programs, you can throw a specific error, as shown here:

```
throw FileException(Source);
```

When your program catches the exception, your program can then test the corresponding value, possibly using a *switch* statement. The following program, COMBINE.CPP, uses a *switch* statement to determine which exception has been thrown:

```
#include <iostream.h>
#include <stdlib.h>

enum FileException { Open, Source, Target, Temp };

void some_operation(void)
 {
   throw FileException(1);
 }

void main(void)
 {
```

```
   try {
     some_operation();
   }
   catch (FileException value) {
     switch (value) {
       case Open: cerr << "Open file error" << endl;
                  break;
       case Source: cerr << "Source file error" << endl;
                  break;
       case Target: cerr << "Target file error" << endl;
                  break;
       case Temp: cerr << "Temporary file error" << endl;
                  break;
     };
     exit(1);
   }
 }
```

As you can see, the program catches the exception and creates a variable named *value*. Using a *switch* statement, the program can determine which type of exception occurred. Experiment with this program, changing the value thrown, and watch how the program's output changes.

What Happens When an Exception Is Thrown?

When a function throws an exception, the function's execution immediately ends, almost as if the function had executed a *return* statement. Next, the function call chain is unwound until a function is found that handles the specific exception. When a handler is found (a *catch* statement) execution continues within the corresponding function. For example, the following program, EXPCHAIN.CPP, invokes a series of functions before the function *three* generates an exception. The exception is caught within *main*:

```
#include <iostream.h>

class Exception { };

void three(void)
 {
    cout << "In three, about to throw exception" << endl;
    throw Exception();
 }

void two(void)
 {
   cout << "In two, about to call three" << endl;
   three();
```

```
    cout << "Back in two" << endl;
  }

void one(void)
  {
    cout << "In one, about to call two" << endl;
    two();
    cout << "Back in one" << endl;
  }

void main(void)
  {
    try {
      one();
    }
    catch (Exception) {
      cout << "Caught the exception in main" << endl;
    }

    cout << "Hello, world" << endl;
  }
```

When C++ unwinds the call chain in search of a function that handles an exception, statements within functions that are unwound are not executed. For example, if you compile and execute this program, your screen will display the following output:

```
C:\> EXPCHAIN  <ENTER>
In one, about to call two
In two, about to call three
In three, about to throw exception
Caught the exception in main
Hello, world
```

As you can see, several statements within each function do not execute. Take time to experiment with this program. For example, you might want to change the function *two* to include a hander, as shown here:

```
void two(void)
  {
    cout << "In two, about to call three" << endl;
    try {
      three();
    }
    catch (Exception) {
      cout << "Caught the exception in two" << endl;
    }
    cout << "Back in two" << endl;
  }
```

When you compile and execute the program, your screen will display the following output:

```
C:\> EXPCHAIN  <ENTER>
In one, about to call two
In two, about to call three
In three, about to throw exception
Caught the exception in two
Back in two
Back in one
Hello, world
```

As you can see, once the exception is caught within the function *two*, the function's execution continues, returning control to the function *one*, who in turn returns control to *main*. Because the exception has been handled by the function *two*, the exception is no longer active when control returns to *main*, and the *catch* statement executes.

EXCEPTIONS UNWIND THE FUNCTION CALL CHAIN

When a function throws an exception, the function's execution immediately ends, just as if the function had executed a *return* statement. C++ then searches the call chain for a function that handles the exception. If the next function in the call chain does not handle the exception, that function's execution also immediately ends. If a function has created a local object, the object's destructor function is invoked before the function's execution ends.

BE AWARE OF RUN-TIME LIBRARY EXCEPTIONS

As the use of exceptions evolves, you will encounter run-time and class library functions that throw exceptions. As you read documentation about such functions, note possible exceptions the function may throw. If your program does not catch such an exception, the default exception handler will be invoked, which in many cases will end your program's execution.

SPECIFYING AN EXCEPTION INTERFACE

As you know, function prototypes specify a function's return and parameter types. When your functions throw exceptions, you might want to specify the possible exceptions a function can throw using a statement similar to a function prototype. For example, assume that the function *perform_copy* can throw the *open_error, read_error,* and *write_error* exceptions. You might specify the function prototype as follows:

```
void perform_copy(char *source_file, char *target_file)
  throw (open_error, read_error, write_error);
```

When your program specifies a function's exception in this way, the C++ compiler will automatically associate any functions not specified in the list to the *unexpected* function.

Understanding Nested Exceptions

When your programs throw and catch exceptions, there may be times when an exception handler itself performs operations that require exception handling. For example, consider the following code fragment. To begin, the statements enable exception handling using the *try* statement. The statements then invoke the function *some_operation.* If the operation throws the *out_of_memory* exception, the statements catch the exception and start performing exception handling statements. Within those statements, additional exceptions are tested:

```
try {
     some_operation();
}
catch (out_of_memory) {
     // statements

  try {
        some_other_operation();
  }

  catch (cant_write_to_file) {
        // statements
  }
}
```

Depending on your program's complexity, there may be times when your programs have several levels of similar nested exceptions.

Repeating an Operation

For simplicity, most of the preceding programs simply end when an exception is encountered. In many cases, however, you will want your programs to try to resolve the cause of the error so they can repeat the operation. Earlier in this chapter, the program ARRAYEXC.CPP trapped invalid index values to the functions *fill_array* and *show_array.* The following program, TRYAGAIN.CPP, catches such index exceptions and continually decrements the index value until an acceptable index is found:

```
#include <iostream.h>
#include <stdlib.h>

class Array {
  public:
    Array(int size);
    void fill_array(int num_values);
    void show_array(int num_values);
    class range { };
  private:
    int *buffer;
    int size;
};

Array::Array(int size)
 {
   buffer = new int[size];
   Array::size = size;
 }

void Array::fill_array(int num_values)
 {
   if (num_values > size)
     throw range();

   for (int i = 0; i < num_values; i++)
     buffer[i] = i;
 }

void Array::show_array(int num_values)
 {
   if (num_values > size)
     throw range();

   for (int i = 0; i < num_values; i++)
     cout << buffer[i] << endl;
 }

void main(void)
 {
   Array vector(200);
   int index = 500;

   fill:
```

```
   try {
     vector.fill_array(index);
   }
   catch (Array::range) {
     index -= 1;
     goto fill;
   }

   index = 500;

   show:
   try {
     vector.show_array(index);
   }
   catch (Array::range) {
     index -= 1;
     goto show;
   }
 }
```

Each time an exception is caught, the program subtracts one from the invalid index and then uses the *goto* statement to branch to a location which immediately precedes the *try* statement to allow the operation to be repeated. The program must branch prior to the *try* statement in order to enable exception handling for the next function invocation. Experiment with this program and invoke the function from within the handler, as shown here:

```
   try {
     vector.fill_array(index);
   }
   catch (Array::range) {
     index -= 1;
     vector.fill_array(index);
   }
```

Because exception handling has not been restarted for the operation, the program will invoke the default exception handler, immediately ending.

Handling Uncaught Exceptions

As you have learned, when an exception is thrown and not caught, a default exception handler executes, which normally ends your program's execution. As it turns out, the name of that default handler is *terminate.* The following program, USE_TERM.CPP, simply invokes the *terminate* function to verify the function's existence. Note that the program includes the header file EXCEPT.H. Depending on your compiler, the header filename containing the prototype for the *terminate* function may differ:

```
#include <iostream.h>
#include <except.h>

void main(void)
 {
   terminate();
 }
```

By default, the *terminate* function normally displays a message and then immediately ends. Depending on your program's requirements, there may be times when you will want to create your own function. Using the *set_terminate function*, your program can assign a specific function to the *terminate* function. The following program, HASTA.CPP, uses the *set_terminate* function to invoke the function *my_termination* if an exception is thrown and not caught:

```
#include <iostream.h>
#include <except.h>
#include <stdlib.h>

class my_error { };
class your_error { };

void my_termination(void)
 {
   cerr << "Hasta la vista, baby!" << endl;
   exit(1);
 }

void some_operation(void)
 {
   throw your_error();
 }

void main(void)
 {
   set_terminate(my_termination);
   try {
     some_operation();
   }
   catch (my_error) {
     cerr << "Caught my error !" << endl;
   }
 }
```

In this case, when the *your_error* exception is thrown and not caught, the program invokes the *terminate* function, which as been assigned to the program-defined function. The function, in turn, displays a message and then uses the *exit* function to end the program's execution.

As you have learned, if you specify the exceptions a function can throw and the function later throws an unlisted exception, your program will invoke a default handler function named *unexpected*. The following program, UNEXPECT.CPP, invokes the *unexpected* function to verify the function's existence:

```
#include <iostream.h>
#include <except.h>

void main(void)
 {
   unexpected();
 }
```

Depending on your program's purpose, there may be times when you want the program to invoke a specific function instead of the default handler when a function invokes an unlisted exception. Using the *set_unexpected* function, your programs can do just that. The following program, SET_UNEX.CPP, uses the *set_unexpected* function to install a custom handler that executes when a function invokes an unlisted exception:

```
#include <iostream.h>
#include <except.h>
#include <stdlib.h>

class my_error { };
class your_error { };

void my_unexpected_handler(void)
 {
   cerr << "Shame on someone for throwing an unlisted exception!" <<
           endl;
   exit(1);
 }

void some_operation(void) throw (my_error)
 {
   throw your_error();
 }

void main(void)
 {
   set_unexpected(my_unexpected_handler);
   try {
     some_operation();
   }
   catch (my_error) {
     cerr << "Caught my error !" << endl;
   }
 }
```

PUTTING IT ALL TOGETHER

Exception handling lets your programs catch and handle a wide range of program-defined errors. Depending on your C++ compiler, exception handling may not yet be supported. If you experience problems when trying to compile the programs presented in this chapter, contact your compiler manufacturer to determine if a more recent version of the compiler is available. In Chapter 15 you will learn ways to control and manage the heap. Before you continue with Chapter 15, make sure that you have learned the following:

- ✓ In the simplest sense, an exception is a program defined error. An exception handler is code written to respond to such an error.
- ✓ The C++ *try*, *throw*, and *catch* statements support exception handling.
- ✓ When your program wants to test for exceptions, it uses the *try* statement to enable exception handling.
- ✓ To determine whether a specific exception has occurred, your program uses the *catch* statement.
- ✓ To generate an exception, your programs use the *throw* statement. In other words, when the error occurs, your program throws an exception that is later caught by an exception handler.
- ✓ Each program-defined exception has a unique name. In many cases, you will use a class for each exception. By using a class, your programs can assign values to class member variables in order to provide the exception handler with more information about the exception.
- ✓ If an exception is thrown and not caught, a default handler named *terminate* executes. In most cases, the terminate function displays an error message and ends your program's execution. Using the *set_terminate* function, your programs can define their own default hander. Depending on your compiler, the header file EXCEPT.H may contain the *set_terminate* function prototype.
- ✓ Just as your programs can use function prototypes to specify a function's return type and parameters, your programs can specify a list of exceptions the function may throw. Should the function throw a function that is not contained in the list, C++ will invoke a special handler named *unexpected.* Using the *set_unexpected* function, your programs can define their own default handler. Depending on your compiler, the header file EXCEPT.H may contain the *set_unexpected* function prototype.

Chapter 15
Digging Deeper into Heap Management

In Chapter 7 you learned how to allocate and free memory dynamically using the C++ *new* and *delete* operators. You learned that when you perform dynamic memory allocation, the *new* operator gets the memory from an area called the *heap*. The heap, therefore, is actually just a pool of byte storage locations. As the complexity of your programs that perform dynamic memory allocation increases, there may be times when you need to examine different attributes of the heap itself, in order to track down difficult errors in your program. If you are working in the DOS environment, your programs can use the functions presented in this chapter to examine the heap. If you are working in an environment other than DOS, examine closely the concepts this chapter presents. Your operating system may provide a similar set of functions with which you can examine the heap.

When you finish this chapter, you will know:

- What the heap is and its size
- How the heap manages free and allocated memory regions
- How your programs detect a memory allocation error
- How to detect quickly heap corruptions caused by programming errors

Note: Your compiler may use different function names and slightly different structures for heap operations. This chapter uses Borland C++ as a point of reference—you will need to use the functions and structures that your compiler requires.

Examining the Heap

The heap is simply an region in memory from which your programs can dynamically allocate regions of memory, as shown in Figure 15.1.

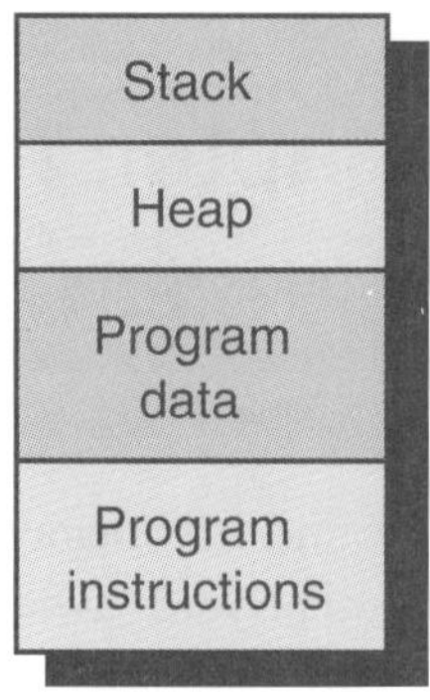

Figure 15.1 The heap is an area in memory from which your programs can allocate memory dynamically.

Assuming that your program allocates three regions in memory whose sizes are 100, 200, and 300 bytes, the heap would appear as shown in Figure 15.2.

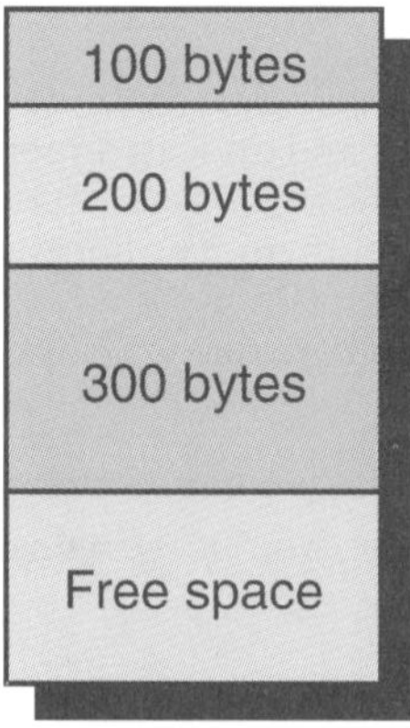

Figure 15.2 Allocating memory from the heap.

Should your program later release the 200 bytes, the heap would appear as shown in Figure 15.3.

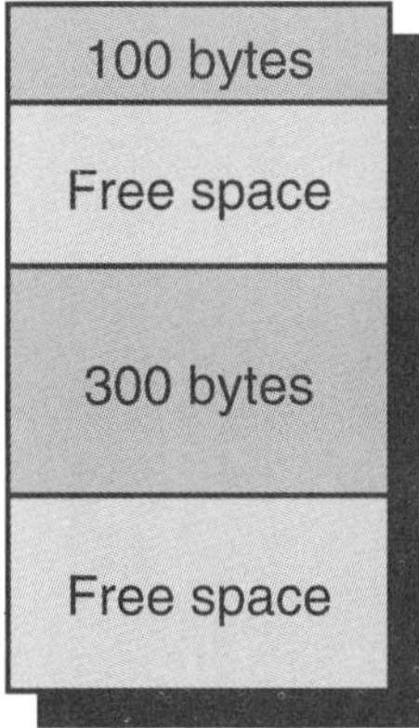

Figure 15.3 Releasing memory from the heap.

To support dynamic memory, the operating system or your programming language provides heap management functions that work behind the scenes. To allocate and release memory from the heap, these functions keep track of each region that has been allocated, as well which regions are available for use. In the case of the DOS-environment, most compilers create a linked list based on *heapinfo* structure, shown here:

```
struct heapinfo {
  void *ptr;
  unsigned int size;
  int in_use;
};
```

The linked list contains a *heapinfo* node for each free memory region, as well as those that are in use. The *ptr* field points to the next node in the linked list. The *size* field specifies the size (in bytes) of the current node's memory region. Finally, the *in_use* field is set to 1 if the memory region is allocated and 0 if the region is available for use. Given the previous allocation of the 100-, 200-, and 300-byte memory regions, the linked would appear as shown in Figure 15.4.

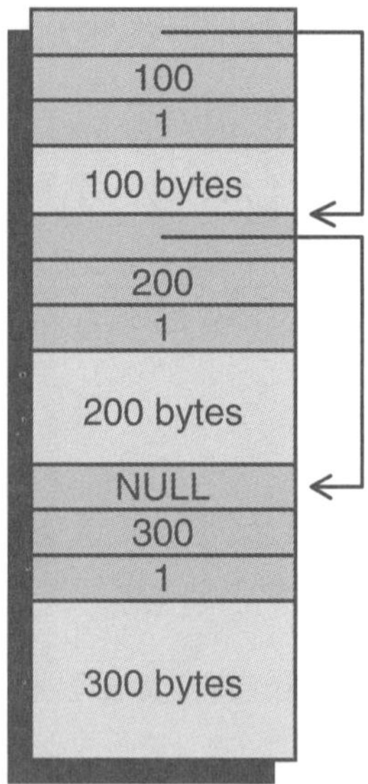

Figure 15.4 The heap space is tracked using a linked list.

If your program were to release the 200-byte region, the value of the second node's *in_use* field would change from 1 (in use) to 0 (available).

To help you better understand the heap's linked list, the following program, HEAPLIST.CPP, allocates memory and then tracks the heap's linked list using the *heapwalk* function. The program then releases to memory regions and displays the new linked list:

```
#include <iostream.h>
#include <alloc.h>

void main(void)
 {
   char *buffer1, *buffer2, *buffer3, *buffer4;

   struct heapinfo node = {NULL, 0, 0};

   buffer1 = new char[1000];
   buffer2 = new char[2000];
   buffer3 = new char[3000];
   buffer4 = new char[4000];

   while (heapwalk(&node) == _HEAPOK)
     {
       cout << "Size " << node.size << " bytes State ";
```

```
        if (node.in_use)
          cout << "In use" << endl;
        else
          cout << "Free" << endl;
      }

    node.ptr = NULL;  // Start at the beginning at the list

    delete buffer2;
    delete buffer4;

    cout << endl << "After memory release" << endl;

    while (heapwalk(&node) == _HEAPOK)
      {
        cout << "Size " << node.size << " bytes State ";

        if (node.in_use)
          cout << "In use" << endl;
        else
          cout << "Free" << endl;
      }
  }
```

When you compile and execute this program, the program's output might confuse you. For example, consider the following output:

```
C:\> HEAPLIST  <ENTER>
Size 516 bytes State In use
Size 40 bytes State In use
Size 520 bytes State In use
Size 40 bytes State In use
Size 520 bytes State In use
Size 40 bytes State In use
Size 520 bytes State In use
Size 14 bytes State In use
Size 16 bytes State In use
Size 8 bytes State In use
Size 1004 bytes State In use
Size 2004 bytes State In use
Size 3004 bytes State In use
Size 4004 bytes State In use

After memory release
Size 516 bytes State In use
Size 40 bytes State In use
Size 520 bytes State In use
```

Memory space allocated for I/O streams

Memory space allocated by the program

```
Size 40 bytes State In use
Size 520 bytes State In use
Size 40 bytes State In use
Size 520 bytes State In use
Size 14 bytes State In use
Size 16 bytes State In use
Size 8 bytes State In use
Size 1004 bytes State In use
Size 2004 bytes State Free
Size 3004 bytes State In use
```

As you can see, the heap contains entries for memory regions other than the buffers allocated by the program. Depending on your compiler, the purpose of these allocated memory regions might differ. For example, these memory regions might correspond to buffers automatically allocated for the I/O streams. Also, note that in this case, the node structure that tracks each region requires four bytes for the *near* memory regions (that use 16-bit pointers) and eight bytes for the *far* memory regions (that use 32-bit pointers). If you are using an operating system other than MS-DOS, the pointer size within the node structure will correspond to the computer's address size, such as four bytes for a 32-bit address. If you are working in the MS-DOS environment, compile this program using the small and large memory models. In the case of the small memory model, the node pointer will use 16-bit pointers. Likewise, in the case of the large memory model, the program will use a 32-bit pointer.

Tracking the Heap's Linked List

The heap is a pool of memory from which your programs can dynamically allocate memory. As your program allocates and releases memory, the heap may contain several different pieces, with some in use and some free. To track regions within the heap, most programming languages use a linked list whose nodes correspond to regions within the list. To help you detect errors within your programs that perform dynamic memory allocations, many run-time libraries provide a set of functions your programs can use to traverse the heap's linked list. By individually examining the heap entries, you can quickly detect many programming errors.

Testing Heap Entry Validity

When your programs allocate memory from the heap, there may be times when an error in your program corrupts the heap, overwriting your program data. For example, assume that your program allocates a fifty and one-hundred byte buffer as shown in Figure 15.5.

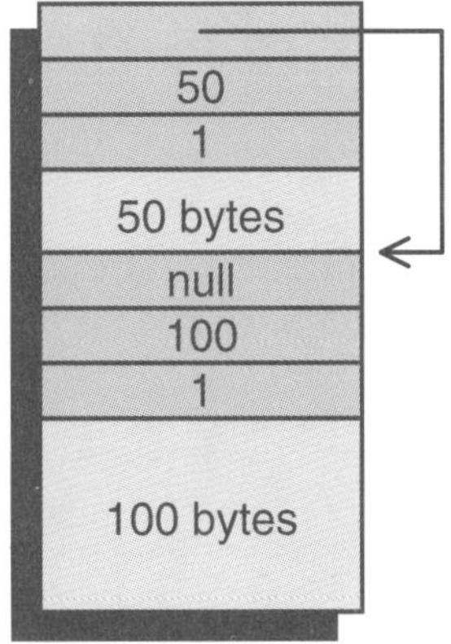

Figure 15.5 Allocating two memory regions from the heap.

Next, assume that your program uses the following *for* loop to assign 0s to the fifty-byte buffer:

```
for (i = 0; i <= 50; i++)
   fifty[i] = 0;
```

Because the loop loops until the variable *i* is less than or equal to 50, the loop assigns the value 0 to a memory location outside of buffer. As Figure 15.6 shows, this assignment overwrites a byte of the node pointer for the second heap entry.

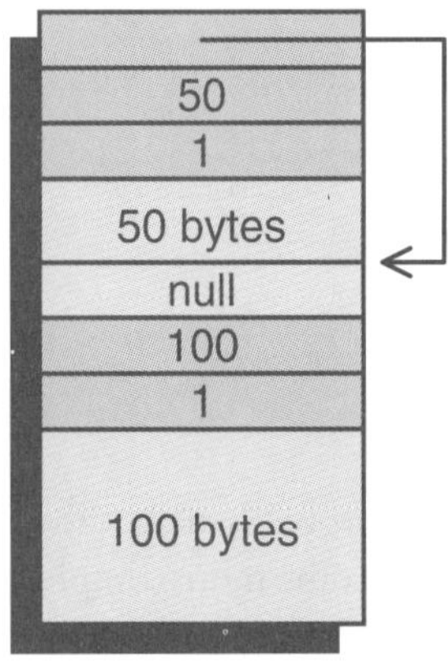

Figure 15.6 Overwriting a byte of the node pointer due to a program error.

The following program, OVERWRIT.CPP, illustrates a similar programming error:

```
#include <iostream.h>
#include <string.h>

void main(void)
 {
   char *fifty = new char[50];
   char *string = new char[100];

   strcpy(string, "Success with C++");

   for (int i = 0; i <= 60; i++)
     fifty[i] = 0;

   cout << string << endl;
 }
```

As you can see, the program allocates the two memory buffers and then assigns a character string to the second buffer. Next, the program uses the *for* loop to assign 0s to the first buffer. As Figure 15.7 shows, the program overwrites a portion of the second buffer.

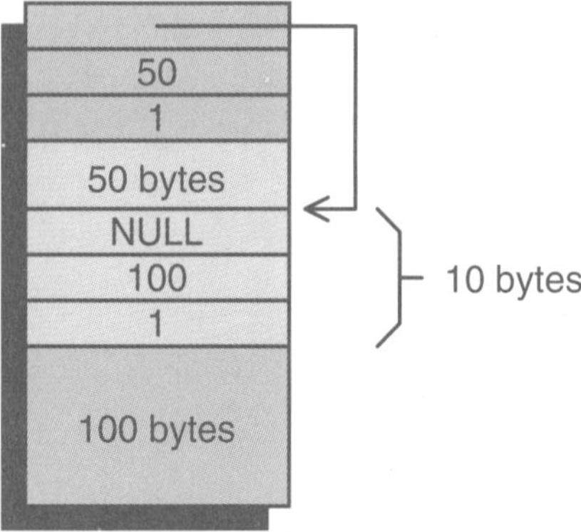

Figure 15.7 Overwriting a region within the heap.

Because this program is short, you can probably detect the cause of the error using standard debugging techniques. As your programs become more complex, however, you might need to examine the heap entries periodically to determine the where the error occurs. The following sections present several techniques your programs can use to test the state of the heap.

Understanding the Heap State

To track memory within the heap, most programming languages use a linked list. Unfortunately, should a program contain a bug and overwrite memory, the program can overwrite one or more nodes within the heap. In such cases, the heap is corrupt. To help you determine the state of the heap, many run-time libraries provide functions that let you examine all of the heap entries, as well as specific entries.

Using these functions, your program can quickly determine if the entire heap is valid or which entry or entries are invalid.

Performing a Quick Heap-State Check

Depending on the error you are trying to detect, there may be times when you simply need to know if the heap entries are valid. In such cases, your programs can use the *heapcheck* run-time library function. Depending on the state of the heap, the function returns one of the values listed in Table 15.1.

Return Value	Meaning
_HEAPEMPTY	No heap
_HEAPOK	Heap entries are valid
_HEAPCORRUPT	One or more heap entries are corrupt

***Table 15.1** Heap-state values returned by heapcheck function.*

The following program, HEAPCHK.CPP, uses the *heapcheck* function to determine that the heap has been corrupted:

```
#include <iostream.h>
#include <string.h>
#include <alloc.h>

void main(void)
 {
   char *fifty = new char[50];
   char *string = new char[100];
```

```
   strcpy(string, "Success with C++");

   switch (heapcheck()) {
    case _HEAPEMPTY:   cout << "No heap" << endl;
                       break;
    case _HEAPOK:      cout << "Heap is valid" << endl;
                       break;
    case _HEAPCORRUPT: cout << "Heap is corrupted" << endl;
                       break;
   };

   for (int i = 0; i <= 60; i++)
     fifty[i] = 0;

   switch (heapcheck()) {
    case _HEAPEMPTY:   cout << "No heap" << endl;
                       break;
    case _HEAPOK:      cout << "Heap is valid" << endl;
                       break;
    case _HEAPCORRUPT: cout << "Heap is corrupted" << endl;
                       break;
   };

   cout << string << endl;
 }
```

As you can see, the program uses the *heapcheck* function before and after the heap corrupting *for* loop. When you compile and execute this program, your screen will display the following:

```
C:\> HEAPCHK  <ENTER>
Heap is valid
Heap is corrupted
```

Using the *heapcheck* function in this way, you may be able to detect the location within your program where the heap becomes corrupted.

Validating a Specific Heap Entry

As you try to debug heap corruptions, there may be times when your program needs to examine pointers one by one. To examine the validity of a heap entry, your programs can use the *heapchecknode* function. The function returns one of the values listed in Table 15.2.

Return Value	Meaning
_HEAPEMPTY	No heap
_HEAPOK	Heap entries are valid
_HEAPCORRUPT	One or more heap entries are corrupt
_BADNODE	Current node is corrupt
_FREEENTRY	Block is free
_USEDENTRY	Block is valid and in use

*Table 15.2 Heap status values returned by **_heapchecknode**.*

The following program, NODECHK.CPP, uses the *heapchecknode* function to examine the program's pointers:

```
#include <iostream.h>
#include <string.h>
#include <alloc.h>

void main(void)
 {
   char *fifty = new char[50];
   char *string = new char[100];

   strcpy(string, "Success with C++");

   for (int i = 0; i <= 60; i++)
     fifty[i] = 0;

   switch (heapchecknode(fifty)) {
    case _HEAPEMPTY:   cout << "No heap" << endl;
                       break;
    case _HEAPOK:      cout << "Heap is valid" << endl;
                       break;
    case _HEAPCORRUPT: cout << "Heap is corrupted" << endl;
                       break;
    case _BADNODE:     cout << "Node is corrupted" << endl;
                       break;
    case _FREEENTRY:   cout << "Entry is not in use" << endl;
                       break;
    case _USEDENTRY:   cout << "Entry is valid and in use" << endl;
                       break;
   };
```

```
   switch (heapchecknode(string)) {
    case _HEAPEMPTY:    cout << "No heap" << endl;
                        break;
    case _HEAPOK:       cout << "Heap is valid" << endl;
                        break;
    case _HEAPCORRUPT: cout << "Heap is corrupted" << endl;
                        break;
    case _BADNODE:      cout << "Node is corrupted" << endl;
                        break;
    case _FREEENTRY:    cout << "Entry is not in use" << endl;
                        break;
    case _USEDENTRY:    cout << "Entry is valid and in use" << endl;
                        break;
   };

   cout << string << endl;
 }
```

As you can see, the program uses the *heapchecknode* function with each of its pointer variables. When you compile and execute this program, your screen will display the following output:

```
C:\> NODECHK  <ENTER>
Entry is valid and in use
Heap is corrupted
```

Testing Free Heap Space

As your programs allocate and release memory over time, the heap's free space may become fragmented, with free and allocated space intermixed, as shown in Figure 15.8.

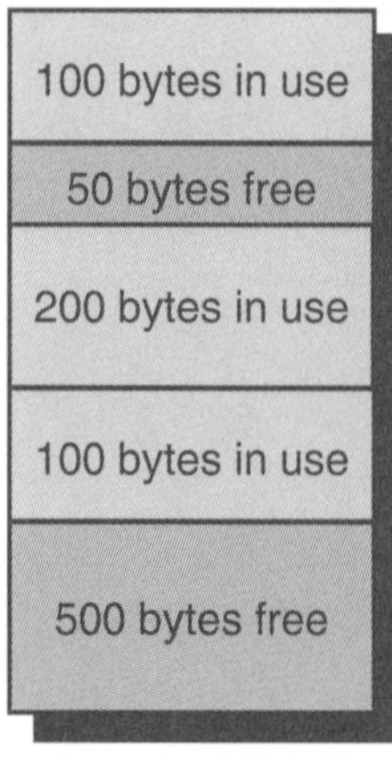

***Figure 15.8** Fragmented free space within the heap.*

Should your program's overwrite a region of heap space that is free, you may not be aware that an error has occurred within your program until the program later tries to allocate the free memory region. To help your programs detect such errors, your programs can use the *heapfillfree* and *heapcheckfree* functions. The *heapfillfree* function assigns a specific value to all of free space within the heap. For example, your program might assign the value –1 to each available memory region. Later, the *heapcheckfree* examines the heap's free space to ensure that each location still contains the specified value. If the program has overwritten a location in available memory, the *heapcheckfree* function will detect the change, letting your program detect the error. The *heapcheckfree* function returns one of the values listed in Table 15.3.

Return Value	Meaning
_HEAPEMPTY	No heap
_HEAPOK	Heap entries are valid
_HEAPCORRUPT	One or more heap entries are corrupt
_BADVALUE	A different value was encountered in a free space location

Table 15.3 *Heap status values returned by the* ***heapcheckfree*** *function.*

The following program, CHKFREE.CPP, uses the *heapfillfree* function to assign the value –1 to the heap free space. The program then uses an errant *for* loop to overwrite a buffer (into the free space). When the *for* loop ends, the program detects the error using the *heapcheckfree* function:

```
#include <iostream.h>
#include <alloc.h>

void main(void)
 {
   char *start, *middle, *end;
   int state;

   start = new char[50];
   middle = new char[50];
   end = new char[50];

   delete middle;    // Create free space in the middle

   state = heapfillfree(-1);

   if (state == _HEAPOK)
     cout << "Heap is ok" << endl;
   else if (state == _HEAPCORRUPT)
     cout << "Heap is corrupt" << endl;

   for (int i = 0; i <= 60; i++)
```

```
    start[i] = i;

  state = heapcheckfree('A');

  if (state == _HEAPOK)
    cout << "Heap is ok" << endl;
  else if (state == _HEAPCORRUPT)
    cout << "Heap is corrupt" << endl;
  else if (state == _BADVALUE)
    cout << "Value has been changed in free space" << endl;
}
```

As you can see, the program allocates three memory buffers, releasing the middle buffer to create free space. When you compile and execute this program your screen will display the following output:

```
C:\> CHKFREE  <ENTER>
Heap is ok
Value has been changed in free space
```

Understanding Garbage Collection

Over time, the heap's free and allocated space can become fragmented. Assume, for example, that your heap appears as previously shown in Figure 15.8. If your program releases the 200-byte region, the heap-management functions will consolidate the two free regions into one region, as shown in Figure 15.9.

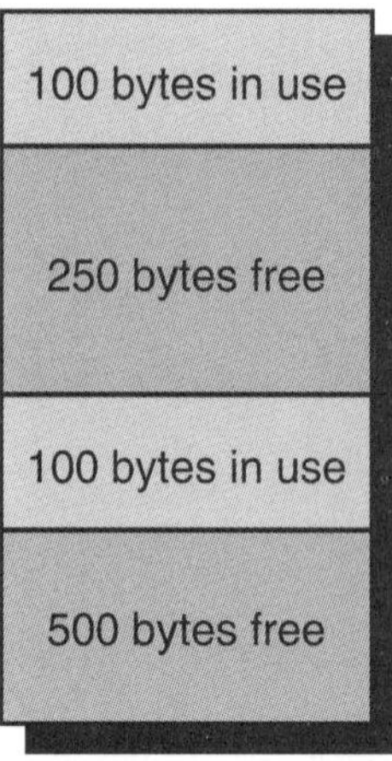

Figure 15.9 *Consolidating free space within the heap.*

As Figure 15.9 shows, the heap contains 750 bytes of available space. Because the space is fragmented, however, the largest piece of memory the program can allocate is 500 bytes. Unfortunately, the C++ programming, however, does not perform *garbage collection*, which would periodically consolidate all the free space, as shown in Figure 15.10.

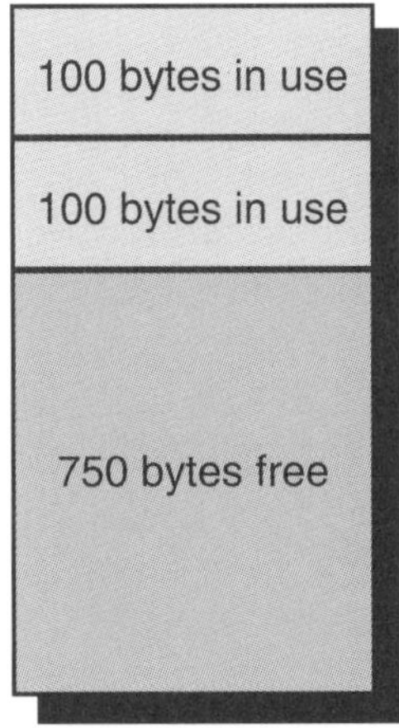

Figure 15.10 *Garbage collection is the process of consolidating free heap space.*

Because your programs have pointers to specific regions in memory, the heap-management routines cannot move the memory regions to consolidate available space (the heap-management functions have no knowledge of the variables to which you may have assigned the pointer values—thus, if the memory is moved, the pointers will be in error). If your program cannot allocate heap space due to fragmentation, your programs will need to release and reallocate memory, essentially performing their own garbage collection.

Putting It All Together

As your programs allocate and free memory dynamically using the *new* and *delete* operators, there may be times when your programs encounter errors that are difficult to detect. To help you debug such errors, most compilers or operating systems provide a set of run-time library functions you can use to test the state of the heap. If you are having trouble detecting such errors within your programs, you should use these functions. Before you continue with Chapter 16, make sure that you have learned the following:

- ✓ The heap is a memory region from which your program can allocate memory dynamically. Depending on your operating system or compiler memory model, the size of your heap can vary.
- ✓ To manage free and allocated memory regions, the heap uses a linked list. For each entry, the heap tracks the entry's size and availability (in use or available).
- ✓ To detect a memory allocation error, your programs can traverse the heap list entries.
- ✓ By examining the heap entries in this way, your programs might be able to detect quickly heap corruptions caused by programming errors.

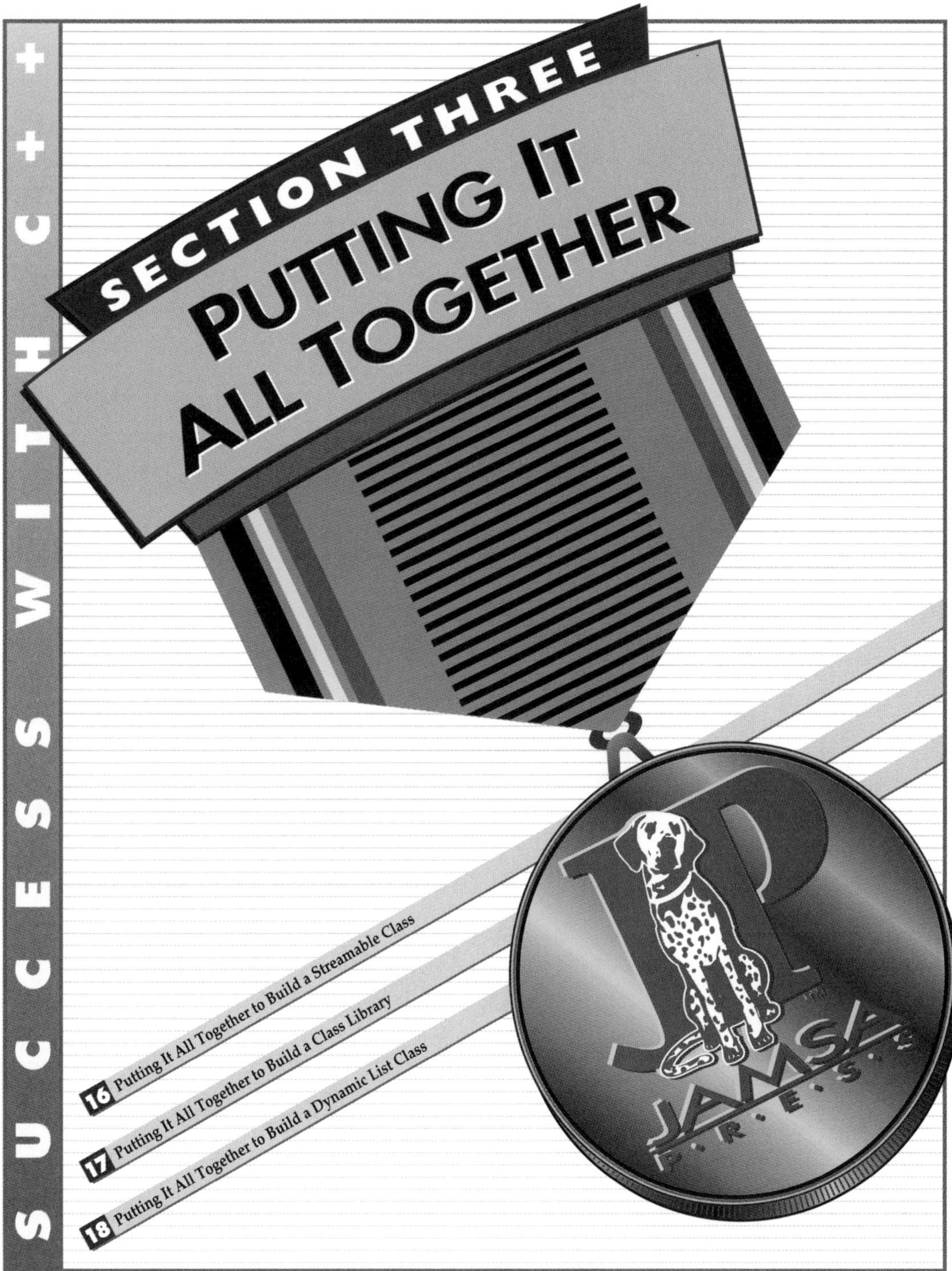
SUCCESS WITH C++
SECTION THREE
PUTTING IT ALL TOGETHER
16 Putting It All Together to Build a Streamable Class
17 Putting It All Together to Build a Class Library
18 Putting It All Together to Build a Dynamic List Class
JAMSA PRESS

Chapter 16
Putting It All Together to Build a Streamable Class

Throughout this book, many of the programs have used member classes functions such as *show_class*, *show_book*, *show_employee* and so on to display class member variables. following this pattern, your programs would use member functions as *file_class* or *file_employee* to write class members to a file stream. When you design your programs, you may find that by building *streamable classes*, your programs become easier to understand.

In the simplest sense, a streamable class is a class with built-in I/O operators—in other words, a class that supports the insertion (<<) and extraction (>>) operators. Using these I/O operators, your programs can easily perform class-based keyboard, screen, or file I/O, just as you use the *cin* and *cout* I/O streams. This chapter examines streamable classes in detail. In particular, you will learn:

- What a streamable class is and how to create it
- The requirements on overloaded operators
- How overloading operators in order to create streamable classes is similar to creating a manipulator
- Where the function called by the overloaded operator is declared
- What must be used for the return value and first parameter of the function called by the overloaded operator
- How the class type of a streamable class is defined
- About streamable classes and stream-based file I/O
- How to use insertion and extraction operators

Performing Class Member I/O the Old-Fashioned Way

Most C++ programs use member functions to perform keyboard, screen, and file I/O. For example, the following program, TRAVEL.CPP, uses the *travel* class, shown here:

```
class travel {
  public:
    travel(char *destination, int distance);
    void display_trip(void);
    int file_trip(ofstream& file);
  private:
    char destination[64];
    int distance;
};
```

As you can see, the class uses the *display_trip* and *file_trip* member functions to perform screen and file output operations. The source code that follows implements TRAVEL.CPP:

```
#include <fstream.h>
#include <string.h>

class travel {
  public:
    travel(char *destination, int distance);
    void display_trip(void);
    int file_trip(ofstream& file);
  private:
    char destination[64];
    int distance;
};

travel::travel(char *destination, int distance)
 {
   strcpy(travel::destination, destination);
   travel::distance = distance;
 }

void travel::display_trip(void)
 {
   cout << "Destination: " << destination << " Distance: " <<
        distance << endl;
 }

int travel::file_trip(ofstream& out_file)
  {
    out_file << destination << endl;
    out_file << distance << endl;
    return(1);
  }

void main(void)
 {
   travel vacation("Maui", 2500);
```

```
  vacation.display_trip();

  ofstream trip_file("TRAVEL.DAT");

  vacation.file_trip(trip_file);
}
```

As you can see, the program invokes the two member functions to perform I/O operations. When you compile and execute this program, your screen will display the following:

```
C:\> TRAVEL  <ENTER>
Destination: Maui Distance: 2500
```

It is important to note that most C++ programs use member functions to perform such class-based I/O in this way. The problem in using such member functions is that they require programmers who are reading your program code to understand additional functions.

A streamable class, on the other hand, uses the insertion operator to perform such I/O:

```
cout  <<  vacation;

output_file << business_trip;
```

To perform stream I/O operations in this way, your programs must overload the insertion (<<) operator for each class type. For example, the following program, STREAM.CPP, uses the insertion operator to display the *travel* object and to write the trip information to a file:

```
#include <fstream.h>
#include <string.h>

class travel {
  public:
    travel(char *destination, int distance);
    friend ostream& operator <<(ostream& stream, travel object);
    friend ofstream& operator <<(ofstream& stream, travel object);
  private:
    char destination[64];
    int distance;
};

travel::travel(char *destination, int distance)
 {
   strcpy(travel::destination, destination);
   travel::distance = distance;
 }
```

```
ostream& operator <<(ostream& stream, travel object)
 {
   stream << "Destination: " << object.destination <<
        " Distance: " << object.distance << endl;

   return(stream);
 }

ofstream& operator <<(ofstream& stream, travel object)
 {
   stream << object.destination << endl;
   stream << object.distance << endl;

   return(stream);
 }


void main(void)
 {
   travel vacation("Maui", 2500);

   cout << vacation;

   ofstream trip_file("TRAVEL.DAT");

   trip_file << vacation;
 }
```

When you compile and execute this program, your screen will display the following output:

```
C:\> STREAM   <ENTER>
Destination: Maui  Distance: 2500
```

Most of the operations this program performs have been discussed in the previous chapters. However, if you don't fully understand the program's processing, don't worry. we will discuss each step in detail throughout this chapter. For now, however, simply understand that a streamable class is a class that uses the insertion and extraction operators to perform stream-based I/O operations.

*Note: When you overload the insertion or extraction operator for a specific class type, you do not change the operator's function for other classes. Thus, the previous program can use the insertion operator, for example, to write characters to the screen, despite the fact that the program has overloaded the operator for the **travel** class. In this way, overloading the insertion for a specific class is no different than overloading the addition or subtraction operators—the overload only affects a specific type.*

Understanding Streamable Classes

Most C++ programs use special member functions to perform class-based keyboard, screen, and file I/O. Unfortunately, such functions introduce additional functions that other programmers who are reading your program must understand. A streamable class, on the other hand, provides built-in functions that provide support for the insertion (<<) and extraction (>>) operators. By creating streamable classes, your programs can perform class-based I/O in a natural way—normally using the insertion and extraction operators.

Creating a Streamable Class

To create a streamable class, your programs overload the insertion (<<) and extraction (>>) operators for specific I/O streams. For example, assume that your program uses the *date* class shown here:

```
class date {
   public:
       date(int month, int day, int year);
   private:
       int month;
       int day;
       int year;
};
```

To overload the insertion operator for output operations to streams such as *cout*, you would overload the *ostream* insertion operator, as shown here:

```
class date {
  public:
    date(int month, int day, int year);
    friend ostream& operator <<(ostream& stream, date date_object);
  private:
    int month;
    int day;
    int year;
};
```

As you can see, overloading the insertion operator is very similar to creating a manipulator, as discussed in Chapter 11. When you overload an insertion or extraction operator, you simply define a function that executes when the operator is used with a specific data type. The first parameter to the function and the function return type are always the stream type:

Function return type
First parameter to the function

```
ostream& operator <<(ostream& stream, date date_object)
 {
      // Statements
 }
```

The function's second parameter specifies the data type for which you are overloading the operator:

```
ostream& operator <<(ostream& stream, date date_object)
 {
      // Statements
 }
```

Second parameter specifying the data type

Note that the function is not class based—in other words, it is not a class member function. However, within the class, you need to declare the operator as a *friend*, as shown here:

```
class date {
  public:
    date(int month, int day, int year);
    friend ostream& operator <<(ostream& stream, date date_object);
  private:
    int month;
    int day;
    int year;
};
```

Specifying the operator is a **friend**

By declaring the operator as a friend, the class provides the operator with access to its private members. The following program, DATE_STR.CPP, for example, uses stream-based output to display the *date* class members:

```
#include <iostream.h>

class date {
  public:
    date(int month, int day, int year);
    friend ostream& operator <<(ostream& stream, date date_object);
  private:
    int month;
    int day;
    int year;
};
```

```
date::date(int month, int day, int year)
 {
   date::month = month;
   date::day = day;
   date::year = year;
 }

ostream& operator <<(ostream& stream, date date_object)
 {
   switch (date_object.month) {
     case  1: stream << "January ";
              break;
     case  2: stream << "February ";
              break;
     case  3: stream << "March ";
              break;
     case  4: stream << "April ";
              break;
     case  5: stream << "May ";
              break;
     case  6: stream << "June ";
              break;
     case  7: stream << "July ";
              break;
     case  8: stream << "August ";
              break;
     case  9: stream << "September ";
              break;
     case 10: stream << "October ";
              break;
     case 11: stream << "November ";
              break;
     case 12: stream << "December ";
              break;
    };

   stream << date_object.day << ", " << date_object.year << endl;

   return(stream);
 }

void main(void)
 {
   date birthday(9, 30, 94);

   cout << birthday;
 }
```

When you compile and execute this program, your screen will display the following output:

```
C:\> DATE_STR  <ENTER>
September 30, 94
```

Rules for Creating Streamable Classes

To create a streamable class, your programs overload the insertion (<<) or extraction (>>) operators for a specific class type. To overload the operators, you define a function that is called each time the operator is used with the specific class type. As you create the function, keep the following rules in mind:

- Declare the function outside of the class—the operator function is not a class-based member function.
- The first parameter to the function, as well as the function's return type, must be a stream.
- The function's second parameter is the class type.
- If the operator will access private class members, the operator must be declared as a friend within the class.

Performing Stream-Based Input Operations

The steps your program must perform for stream-based input operations are very similar to those just discussed. In this case, however, your program must overload the extraction (>>) operator. The following statements illustrate how your program might overload the extraction operator for the *date* class:

```
istream& operator >>(istream& stream, date *date_object)
 {
   cout << "Please type in mm dd yy: " ;

   stream >> date_object->month;
   stream >> date_object->day;
   stream >> date_object->year;

   return(stream);
 }
```

As you can see, the statements follow the rules previously discussed. The following program, GET_DATE.CPP, uses stream-based input to get the month, day, and year that correspond to a *date* object:

```
#include <iostream.h>

class date {
  public:
    date(int month, int day, int year);
    friend ostream& operator <<(ostream& stream, date date_object);
    friend istream& operator >>(istream& stream, date *date_object);
  private:
    int month;
    int day;
    int year;
};

date::date(int month, int day, int year)
 {
   date::month = month;
   date::day = day;
   date::year = year;
 }

ostream& operator <<(ostream& stream, date date_object)
 {
   stream << date_object.month << '/' << date_object.day << '/' <<
     date_object.year << endl;

   return(stream);
 }

istream& operator >>(istream& stream, date *date_object)
 {
   cout << "Please type in mm dd yy: " ;

   stream >> date_object->month;
   stream >> date_object->day;
   stream >> date_object->year;

   return(stream);
 }

void main(void)
 {
   date birthday(9, 30, 94);

   cin >> &birthday;

   cout << birthday;
 }
```

When you compile and execute this program, your screen will prompt you to enter a date. The program then performs the input operation using the extraction operator.

File-Based Stream I/O

When you create streamable classes, your streams are not constrained to those used by *cout* and *cin*. For example, the following program, FILEDATE.CPP, uses stream-based file I/O operations to write several dates to the file DATES.DAT. In this case, the program overloads the insertion (<<) operator for *ofstream* class objects:

```
#include <fstream.h>

class date {
  public:
    date(int month, int day, int year);
    friend ofstream& operator <<(ofstream& stream,
      date date_object);
  private:
    int month;
    int day;
    int year;
};

date::date(int month, int day, int year)
 {
   date::month = month;
   date::day = day;
   date::year = year;
 }

ofstream& operator <<(ofstream& stream, date date_object)
 {

   stream << date_object.month << ' ' << date_object.day << ' ' <<
     date_object.year << endl;

   return(stream);
 }

void main(void)
 {
   date birthday(9, 30, 94);
   date christmas(12, 25, 94);
   date new_years(1, 1, 95);

   ofstream datefile("DATES.DAT");

   datefile << birthday;
   datefile << christmas;
   datefile << new_years;
 }
```

When you compile and execute this program, the program will write three dates to the file DATES.DAT. In a similar way, the following program, READDATE.CPP, overloads the extraction operator to read dates from the file until the end of file is encountered. In this case, the program overloads the extraction operator for *ifstream* objects:

```
#include <fstream.h>

class date {
  public:
    date(void) { };
    friend ifstream& operator >>(ifstream& stream,
      date *date_object);
    friend ostream& operator <<(ostream& stream, date date_object);
  private:
    int month;
    int day;
    int year;
};

ifstream& operator >>(ifstream& stream, date *date_object)
 {
   stream >> date_object->month >> date_object->day >>
      date_object->year;

   return(stream);
 }

ostream& operator <<(ostream& stream, date date_object)
 {
   stream << date_object.month << '/' << date_object.day << '/' <<
     date_object.year << endl;

   return(stream);
 }

void main(void)
 {
   ifstream datefile("DATES.DAT");
   date dateinfo;

   while (! datefile.eof())
     {
       datefile >> &dateinfo;
       if (! datefile.eof())
         cout << dateinfo;
     }
 }
```

As you can see, the steps to overload the insertion and extraction operators for file-based I/O are very easy.

Be Aware of Binary Files

Keep in mind that you should not use the insertion and extraction operators to write binary (typically floating-point) values to a file. As you have read, the insertion operator will convert such values to their ASCII representation, which in turn, can cause errors when you later try to input the values. Instead, your programs should use the *read* and *write* member functions to perform the I/O operation. For example, the following program, FLOATVAL.CPP, overloads the insertion operator to write several structures that contain floating-point values to the file FLOATVAL.DAT. To output the values, the program uses the *write* member function:

```
#include <fstream.h>

class values {
  public:
    values(float a, float b, float c);
    friend ofstream& operator <<(ofstream& stream,
      values *value_object);
  private:
    float a;
    float b;
    float c;
};

values::values(float a, float b, float c)
 {
  values::a = a;
  values::b = b;
  values::c = c;
 }

ofstream& operator <<(ofstream& stream, values *value_object)
 {
   stream.write((char *) value_object, sizeof(class values));

   return(stream);
 }

void main(void)
 {
   ofstream value_file("FLOATVAL.DAT");

   values a(1.1, 2.2, 3.3);
   values b(11.11, 22.22, 33.33);
   values c(111.111, 222.222, 333.333);

   value_file << &a;
   value_file << &b;
   value_file << &c;
 }
```

In a similar way, the following program, FLOATIN.CPP, overloads the extraction operator to read the floating-point values contained in the file FLOATVAL.DAT into a structure variable. The program continues to read and display the structure member values until the end of file is encountered:

```
#include <fstream.h>

class values {
  public:
    values(void) {};
    friend ifstream& operator >>(ifstream& stream,
      values *value_object);
    friend ostream& operator <<(ostream& stream,
      values *value_object);
  private:
    float a;
    float b;
    float c;
};

ifstream& operator >>(ifstream& stream, values *value_object)
 {
   stream.read((char *) value_object, sizeof(class values));

   return(stream);
 }

ostream& operator <<(ostream& stream, values *value_object)
 {
   stream << value_object->a << ' ' << value_object->b << ' ' <<
     value_object->c << endl;

   return(stream);
 }

void main(void)
 {
   ifstream value_file("FLOATVAL.DAT");

   values a, b, c;

   value_file >> &a;
   cout << &a;

   value_file >> &b;
   cout << &b;

   value_file >> &c;
   cout << &c;
 }
```

When you compile and execute this program, your screen will display the following output:

```
C:\> FLOATIN  <ENTER>
1.1 2.2 3.3
11.11 22.22 33.33
111.111 222.222 333.333
```

Putting It All Together

Streamable classes can make your programs easier to understand. As you have seen, creating and using such classes is not difficult. Before continuing with the next chapter, make sure you have learned the following:

- ✓ To create a streamable class, simply overload the insertion (<<) or extraction (>>) operators for a specific class of I/O streams.
- ✓ Operator overloading for the purpose of creating a streamable class is no different than overloading addition and subtraction operators—the overload only affects a specific data type.
- ✓ The overloaded operator must be declared a friend within the class if it will access private class members.
- ✓ Overloading operators in order to create streamable classes is similar to creating a manipulator—you define a function that executes when the operator is used for a specific data type.
- ✓ The function called by the overloaded operator is not a class-based member function—it is declared outside of the class.
- ✓ A stream data type must be used for the return value and first parameter of the function called by the overloaded operator.
- ✓ The class type of a streamable class is defined by the second parameter of the function called by the overloaded operator.
- ✓ Streamable classes can use stream-based file I/O, as well *cin* and *cout*, by simply overloading the operators for *ofstream* class objects.
- ✓ Insertion and extraction operators should not be used to write binary data—use *read* and *write* member functions instead.

Chapter 17
Putting It All Together to Build a Class Library

In the simplest sense, a *library* is a collection of functions your program can use to accomplish specific tasks. The standard C/C++ run-time library, for example, contains functions that let your programs manipulate strings, work with files, allocate memory, and so on. To use a library, you normally include a header file at the start of your program which specifies function prototypes. Next, when you link your program—you specify the library filename, allowing the linker to locate the functions. In the case of the standard run-time library, the linker automatically uses the correct library files. By using libraries, you eliminate the need to write and test considerable amounts of code. Because the functions in the library should have already been thoroughly tested and known to work.

A *class library* is a library that contains the member functions for a specific class. As you build class definitions, you will often find that a class you create for one program is often ideal for use in another. By placing the class member functions into a class library, you make it very easy to reuse classes in two or more programs. Many software developers provide class libraries. For example, if you program in C++ for Windows, there are class libraries that let you perform window-based operations. Likewise, there are class libraries for multimedia applications. In each case, the libraries are simply member functions and related definitions specific to a C++ class.

This chapter examines the steps you must perform to create you own class libraries. By the time you finish this chapter, you will understand the following:

- What an object library is and how to create and use one
- What a class library is and how to create and use one

Creating and Using a Simple Object Library

Before you examine the steps required to build a class library, it will be helpful if you understand the steps to building an *object library*. An object library is a file that contains the compiled code that corresponds to a set of functions. When you create your programs, you can use these prebuilt functions to save time, coding, and testing. In this case, you will build the object library STRFUNC.LIB that contains the *string_copy* and *string_length* functions. To begin, create the file STRFUNC.CPP, which contains the following:

```
void string_copy(char *target, char *source)
 {
   while (*target++ = *source++)
     ;
 }

int string_length(char *string)
 {
   for (int length = 0; *string++; length++)
     ;

   return(length);
 }
```

Next, compile the file to create the object file STRFUNC.OBJ. If you are using Borland C++, use the following command line to create the object file:

```
C:\> BCC  -c  STRFUNC.CPP  <ENTER>
```

Likewise, if you are using Microsoft Visual C++, use the following command line:

```
C:\> CL  -c  STRFUNC.CPP  <ENTER>
```

Next, using the library program provided by your compiler, create the library file STRFUNC.LIB. If you are using Borland C++, you can use the TLIB command as follows to create the library:

```
C:\> TLIB  STRFUNC.LIB  +STRFUNC.OBJ  <ENTER>
```

Likewise, if you are using Microsoft Visual C++, use the LIB command as follows:

```
C:\> LIB  STRFUNC.LIB  +STRFUNC.OBJ;  <ENTER>
```

Note: When you use Microsoft's LIB utility, remember to include the semicolon at the end of your command line. This will cause LIB to use default values. Otherwise, you will be prompted for various filenames.

Before your programs can use the functions a library contains, the programs must specify the corresponding function prototypes. To make specifying function prototypes easy, you should create a header file that contains the prototypes for each library function. Therefore, create the header file STRFUNC.H, which contains the following prototypes:

```
void string_copy(char *target, char *source);

int string_length(char *string);
```

The following program, STRDEMO.CPP, uses the library's *string_length* and *string_copy* functions:

```
#include <iostream.h>
#include "strfunc.h"          // string library header

void main(void)
 {
   char source[64] = "Success with C++";
   char target[64];
   char chapter[64];

   cout << "The string " << source << " has " <<
           string_length(source) << " characters" << endl;

   string_copy(chapter, "Chapter 17");

   cout << "This is " << chapter << endl;

   string_copy(target, source);

   cout << "I am reading " << target << endl;
 }
```

When you compile (or link) this program, you must specify the STRFUNC.LIB library filename. If you are using the Borland C++ compiler, you can compile and link the program using the following command:

```
C:\> BCC  STRDEMO.CPP  STRFUNC.LIB  <ENTER>
```

Likewise, if you are using Microsoft Visual C++, you can compile and link the program as follows:

```
C:\> CL  STRDEMO.CPP  STRFUNC.LIB  <ENTER>
```

When you execute this program, your screen will display the following output:

```
C:\> STRDEMO  <ENTER>
The string Success with C++ has 16 characters
This is Chapter 17
I am reading Success with C++
```

Building an Object Library

An object library is a file that contains the compiled code corresponding to a set of functions. When you create your programs, you can use prebuilt functions to save time, coding, and testing. To build your own object library, perform these steps:

1. Create a source file that contains related functions.
2. Compile the source code to produce an object file.
3. Use a library utility to create the library file.
4. Create a header file that contains the prototypes for each library function.

To use the library functions within your program, perform these steps:

1. Include the corresponding header file at the start of your program.
2. Use one or more library functions within your program's source code.
3. Link your program with the library file.

Creating a Class Library

As you just learned, an object code library contains one or more functions to which your programs can link. In a similar way, a class library contains the object code for one or more functions. In the case of a class library, however, the functions correspond to a specific class or to a set of related classes. As you will learn, the steps you must perform to create a class library are really no different than those just discussed for an object file:

1. Place the class declaration and member functions within a source file.
2. Compile the source file to create an object file.
3. Use a library program to create a library file.
4. Create a header file that contains the class declaration.

To use the class library within your program, you perform the following steps:

1. Include the corresponding header file at the start of your program.
2. Instantiate one or more class objects within the program.
3. Compile the program source file and link it to the class library file.

As you know, many programs use a menu-driven interface. Thus, you might create a *menu* class library that can be used by many different programs. The following declaration, for example, creates a *menu* class:

```
struct option {                // each menu option has option
  char menu_text[64];          // text and a related keystroke
  char keystroke;
 };

class menu {
  public:
    menu(char *title, option *menu_options, int foreground,
      int background);
    void show_menu(void);
    int get_option(void);
  private:
    char title[64];            // menu title
    option options[7];         // array of menu option strings
    int number_of_options;     // number of menu options
    int foreground;            // menu foreground color
    int background;            // menu background color
    int row;                   // row to start menu display
    int column;                // column to start menu display
    void set_colors(int foreground, int background);
    void set_row_and_column(int row, int column);
 };
```

The *menu* class supports menus that contain up to seven options. To instantiate a *menu* object, your program must specify an array of options, an array of keystrokes, and a menu color, as shown here:

```
   option menu_a_options[7] = {{"Option One", 'A'},
                               {"Option Two", 'B'},
                               {"Option Three", 'C'}};

   menu a("Very Long Menu Title", menu_a_options, 37, 44);
```

In this case, the menu will use white text (37) on a blue background (44). These color values are defined by the ANSI driver.

*Note: The program uses ANSI escape sequences to select the screen color and perform cursor positioning. If you are working in a PC environment, you must first install the ANSI.SYS device driver before your system will correctly respond to the color escape sequences. For more information on using ANSI escape sequences within your C++ programs, refer to the book **Jamsa's 1001 C/C++ Tips**, Jamsa Press, 1993.*

Within the *menu* class constructor function, the function code determines the correct row and column placement to center the menu options on your screen. To determine the row and column, the code determines the number of menu options and the length of each option's text.

To create the *menu* class library, place the *menu* class declaration in the file MENU.CPP, as shown here:

```
#include <iostream.h>
#include <string.h>
#include <ctype.h>

struct option {
  char menu_text[64];
  char keystroke;
 };

class menu {
  public:
    menu(char *title, option *menu_options,
        int foreground, int background);
    void show_menu(void);
    int get_option(void);
  private:
    char title[64];           // menu title
    option options[7];        // array of menu option strings
    int number_of_options;    // number of menu options
    int foreground;           // menu foreground color
    int background;           // menu background color
    int row;                  // row to start menu display
    int column;               // column to start menu display
    void set_colors(int foreground, int background);
    void set_row_and_column(int row, int column);
 };

menu::menu(char *title, option *menu_options,
        int foreground, int background)
 {
    strcpy(menu::title, title);

    int number_of_options = 0;
    int longest_option = strlen(title);
```

```
    for (int i = 0; i < 7; i++)
     {
       int option_length = strlen(menu_options[i].menu_text);

       if (option_length > longest_option)
         longest_option = option_length;

       strcpy(menu::options[i].menu_text,
         menu_options[i].menu_text);
       menu::options[i].keystroke = menu_options[i].keystroke;
       if (options[i].menu_text)
         number_of_options++;
     }

    menu::number_of_options = number_of_options;
    menu::foreground = foreground;
    menu::background = background;

    column = (79 - longest_option) / 2;

    // Center options plus title, prompt and 2 blank lines
    row = (24 - (4 + number_of_options)) / 2;
 }

void menu::set_colors(int foreground, int background)
 {
   cout << "\033[" << foreground << ';' << background << 'm' <<
           endl;
   cout << "\033[2J";
 }

void menu::set_row_and_column(int row, int column)
 {
    cout << "\033[" << row << ';' << column << 'H';
 }

void menu::show_menu(void)
 {
    set_colors(foreground, background);
    set_row_and_column(row, column);

    cout << title << endl;

    for (int i = 0; i < number_of_options; i++)
      {
         set_row_and_column(row + 2 + i, column);
         cout << options[i].keystroke << ' ' <<
                 options[i].menu_text;
      }
```

```
    set_row_and_column(row + i, column);
    cout << "Enter choice: ";
  }

int menu::get_option(void)
  {
    char option;
    int done = 0, choice;

    while (! done)
      {
        show_menu();
        option = cin.get();
        option = toupper(option);

        for (int i = 0; i < number_of_options; i++)
          if (option == options[i].keystroke)
            {
              choice = i;
              done = 1;
            }

        while (cin.get() != '\n')
          ;  // Eat characters up to and including \n
      }

    return (choice);
  }
```

Next, compile the file to create object files. As before, if you are using Borland C++, you can compile the file using the following command:

```
C:\> BCC  -c  MENU.CPP  <ENTER>
```

Likewise, if you're using Microsoft Visual C++, use the following command line to compile the file:

```
C:\> CL  -C  MENU.CPP  <ENTER>
```

Next, using TLIB or LIB, depending on your compiler, create the library file using one of the following commands:

```
C:\> TLIB  MENU.LIB  +MENU.OBJ  <ENTER>

C:\> LIB  MENU.LIB  +MENU.OBJ;  <ENTER>
```

Note: Remember to include the semicolon at the end of the LIB command line in order to avoid having to specify filenames.

The following program, MENUDEMO.CPP, creates and displays several different menu options using the *menu* class library:

```
#include <iostream.h>
#include "menu.h"

void main(void)
 {
   int choice;

   option menu_a_options[7] = {{"Option One", 'A'},
                               {"Option Two", 'B'},
                               {"Option Three", 'C'}};

   menu a("Very Long Menu Title", menu_a_options, 37, 44);

   choice = a.get_option();

   cout << endl << "You selected option " << choice+1 << endl;
   cout << "Press Enter to continue...";
   while (cin.get() != '\n')
     ;

   option menu_b_options[7] = {{"Perform Payroll", 'P'},
                               {"Update Accounts Payable", 'A'},
                               {"Print Checks", 'C'},
                               {"Quit", 'Q'}};

   menu b("Not So Quicken", menu_b_options, 37, 41);

   choice = b.get_option();

   cout << endl << "You selected option " << choice+1 << endl;
   cout << "Press Enter to continue...";
   while (cin.get() != '\n')
     ;

   // Restore white on black screen
   cout << "\033[37;40m\033[2J";
 }
```

To compile your program, linking the menu-class library, using Borland C++, issue the following command:

```
C:\> BCC  MENUDEMO.CPP  MENU.LIB
```

Likewise, if you are using Microsoft Visual C issue the following command:

```
C:\> CL  MENUDEMO.CPP  MENU.LIB
```

Putting It All Together

A library is a collection of precompiled functions your programs can use to accomplish a specific task. In the case of a class library, the functions correspond to a specific class or to a set of related classes. This chapter examined the steps you must perform to create a class library, as well as the steps you must perform to use library within your program. In Chapter 18 you will use these steps to build a dynamic-list class library. Before you continue with Chapter 18, make sure that you have learned the following:

- ✓ An object library is a file that contains the compiled code that corresponds to a set of functions.
- ✓ To create an object library, write or assemble the functions in a file, compile the file, use the library program that comes with your compiler to create the library file, and create a header file that contains the function prototypes.
- ✓ To use the library functions within your program, include the corresponding header file at the start of your program, use one or more library functions within your program's source code, and link your program with the library file.
- ✓ To create a class library, place the class declaration and member functions within a source file, compile the source file to create an object file, use a library program to create a library file, and create a header file that contains the class declaration.
- ✓ To use the class library, include the corresponding header file at the start of your program, instantiate one or more class objects within the program, and compile the program source file and link it to the class library file.

Chapter 18
Putting It All Together to Build a Dynamic List Class

Most application programs, regardless of their purpose, need to track information that can be stored using dynamic lists. As you read briefly in Chapter 7, dynamic lists are desirable (over arrays) because they make efficient use of your computer's available memory. If you have worked with singly or doubly linked lists in the past, you know that such lists consist of *nodes*, which contain data, and *pointers*, which connect one node in the list to another. Because of the frequency of linked-list use, programmers always search for ways to create *generic lists* that they can quickly adapt to meet the needs of a different data set for use in the current program or even within a different program.

This chapter helps you create such a generic linked list. To help you move the list from one application to another, this chapter shows you how to create dynamic-list class templates. This chapter uses concepts presented throughout the previous chapters. Take time to experiment with each program presented. You might find the C++ syntax used to create the generic lists to be intimidating at first. However, if you read the text that accompanies each example, you will find that the actual processing is really quite simple. By the time you finish this chapter, you will have learned

- What a singly linked list is
- How to use a class template to support variables of different types
- What a doubly linked list is
- How to search your list and count occurrences of an event
- How to deal with using template-based class libraries

Looking at a Simple Linked List

A *linked list* is a group of items that is arranged in a sequence, and *linked* together, so that each member, or node, points to the next item in the list. These are particularly useful for list-type applications, such as databases.

Before we dive into the complexities of a generic linked list, let's look at a sample example that should get everyone up to speed with linked lists. To begin, we will create a singly linked list whose nodes will store the numbers 1 through 100.

The create the linked list, the program uses one class named *list* and one structure name *node*. The list class contains the member variables *first* and *last*, which point to the start and end of the list:

```
class list {
  public:
    list(void) { first.next = NULL; last = &first; };
    void show_list(void);
    void append_node(node *new_node);
  private:
    node first;
    node *last;
};
```

As you can see, the class supports the member functions *append_node* and *display_list*. The *append_node* function appends the specified node to the end of the linked list. Likewise, the *display_list* function simply traverses the list, displaying each node's value. The *node* structure, in this case, holds data (a value of type *int*) and a pointer to the next node in the list:

```
struct node {
   int data;
   struct node *next;
};
```

The following program, SIMPLE.CPP, implements the singly linked list using the *list* class and *node* structure:

```
#include <iostream.h>

struct node {
  int value;
  struct node *next;
};

class list {
  public:
    list(void) { first.next = NULL; last = &first; };
    void show_list(void);
    void append_node(node *new_node);
  private:
    node first;
    node *last;
};

void list::show_list(void)
 {
   node *current_node = first.next;
```

```
   while (current_node)
     {
       cout << current_node->value << endl;
       current_node = current_node->next;
     }
 }

void list::append_node(node *new_node)
 {
   last->next = new_node;
   last = new_node;
   last->next = NULL;
 }

void main(void)
 {
   list single;
   node *new_node;

   for (int i = 1; i <= 100; i++)
     {
       new_node = new node;
       new_node->value = i;
       single.append_node(new_node);
     }
   single.show_list();
 }
```

As you can see, the program simply appends values to the list using the *append_node* function. After all the values have been assigned to the list, the program displays the list contents.

UNDERSTANDING APPEND_NODE

At first glance, the *append_node* function can seem confusing but it is really quite simple. First, remember that the *list* class member variable, *last*, points to the end of the list. Also, remember that the pointer variable *next*, in the *node* structure, always points to the next node in the list.

When we append a new node to the list, the new node must become the last node in the list. We do this by assigning our new node to the class member variable, *last:*

```
last = new_node;
```

However, as you will note, this is not the first statement in the *append_node* function. Again, keep in mind that the new node is going to become the last node in our list. This means, what was the last node in the list is becoming the *next-to-the-last* node. For this reason, the *old* last node must point to the *new* node as the *next* node in the list. To do this, we must make *next* point to *new_node* **before** we make *new_node* the *last* node:

```
last->next = new_node;
```

In every linked list, there must always be something to tell us when we have reached the last node in the list. A common programming practice is to use NULL to indicate the end of a list. SIMPLE.CPP does that by assigning NULL to the *next* pointer for *new_node*, which has now become our *last* node:

```
last->next = NULL;
```

By now, understanding the *list* constructor function should be easier:

NULL indicates there is not a next node

Last node is the same as the first node

```
list(void) { first.next = NULL; last = &first; };
```

When you initialize the list, the *last* node is the same as the *first* node. Also, the *next* pointer is NULL because there is no next node. The first node is the first, last, and only node in the list when it is initialized by the constructor function.

To assign values to the linked list, the previous program used the following statements to allocate a node and then to assign a node value:

```
for (int i = 1; i <= 100; i++)
  {
    new_node = new node;
    new_node->value = i;
    single.append_node(new_node);
  }
```

If you change *node* from a structure to a class, you can reduce the number of statements required to build the list to those shown here:

```
for (int i = 1; i <= 100; i++)
  single.append_node(new node(i));
```

In this case, the program appends the initialized pointer object to the end of the linked list in one step. The following program, NODECLAS.CPP, uses the *node* class to construct the linked list:

```
#include <iostream.h>

class node {
  public:
    node(int value) { node::value = value; };
    node(void) { };
    void show_value(void) { cout << value << endl; };
    struct node *next;
  private:
    int value;
};

class list {
  public:
    list(void) { first.next = NULL; last = &first; };
    void show_list(void);
    void append_node(node *new_node);
  private:
    node first;
    node *last;
};

void list::show_list(void)
 {
   node *current_node = first.next;

   while (current_node)
     {
       current_node->show_value();
       current_node = current_node->next;
     }
 }

void list::append_node(node *new_node)
 {
   last->next = new_node;
   last = new_node;
   last->next = NULL;
 }

void main(void)
 {
   list single;

   for (int i = 1; i <= 100; i++)
     single.append_node(new node(i));

   single.show_list();
 }
```

As you can see, the *node* class provides constructor functions, as well as a function to display the node value.

Using a Class Template

In the previous programs, the linked list held only values of type *int*. Using the following template, however, you can change the *node* structure to support values of type *int*, *float*, *long*, and so on:

```
template<class T> class node {
  public:
    node(T value) { node::value = value; };
    node(void) { };
    void show_value(void) { cout << value << endl; };
    struct node<T> *next;
  private:
    T value;
};
```

The following program, NEW_LIST.CPP, uses the *node* template to create three lists, one to hold values of type *int*, one for values of type *float*, and one for values of type *long*:

```
#include <iostream.h>

template<class T> class node {
  public:
    node(T value) { node::value = value; };
    node(void) { };
    void show_value(void) { cout << value << endl; };
    struct node<T> *next;
  private:
    T value;
};

template<class T> class list {
  public:
    list(void) { first.next = NULL; last = &first; };
    void show_list(void);
    void append_node(node<T> *new_node);
  private:
    node<T> first;
    node<T> *last;
};

template<class T> void list<T>::show_list(void)
 {
   node<T> *current_node = first.next;

   while (current_node)
     {
       current_node->show_value();
       current_node = current_node->next;
     }
 }
```

```
template<class T> void list<T>::append_node(node<T> *new_node)
 {
   last->next = new_node;
   last = new_node;
   last->next = NULL;
 }

void main(void)
 {
   list<int> single;
   list<float> values;
   list<char> letters;

   for (int i = 1; i <= 10; i++)
     single.append_node(new node<int> (i));

   single.show_list();

   for (i = 0; i < 10; i++)
     values.append_node(new node<float> (0.1 * i));

   values.show_list();

   for (i = 'A'; i <= 'Z'; i++)
     letters.append_node(new node<char> (i));

   letters.show_list();
 }
```

You can see that, using the *node* template, the program can quickly create linked lists capable of storing integer, floating-point, or character data.

Note: If you are having trouble understanding the templates in NEW_LIST.CPP, read Chapter 6 again. The only real difference between NEW_LIST.CPP and NODECLAS.CPP is in the ***main*** *function. Everything else in NEW_LIST.CPP is* identical *to NODECLAS.CPP, except that classes and functions are implemented using template specifications. Try reading NEW_LIST.CPP and ignoring everything related to templates.*

Supporting a Doubly Linked List

When your programs insert or remove elements from a linked list, you can simplify many operations by using a *doubly linked list.* In the simplest sense, a doubly linked list contains data values and two pointers, one that points to the next node and one that points to the previous node:

```
template<class T> class node {
  public:
    node(T value) { node::value = value; };
    node(void) { };
    void show_value(void) { cout << value << endl; };
    struct node<T> *next;
    struct node<T> *previous;
  private:
    T value;
};
```

Note the only difference between this template and the *node* template in NEW_LIST.CPP is the addition of the *previous* pointer:

```
    struct node<T> *previous;
```

The following program, DOUBLY.CPP, changes the *node* structure and *list* member functions to support a doubly linked list:

```
#include <iostream.h>

template<class T> class node {
  public:
    node(T value) { node::value = value; };
    node(void) { };
    void show_value(void) { cout << value << endl; };
    struct node<T> *next;
    struct node<T> *previous;
  private:
    T value;
};

template<class T> class list {
  public:
    list(void) { first.next = NULL; last = &first;
      first.previous = NULL; };
    void show_list(void);
    void append_node(node<T> *new_node);
    void show_reverse(void);
  private:
    node<T> first;
    node<T> *last;
};

template<class T> void list<T>::show_list(void)
 {
   node<T> *current_node = first.next;
```

```
   while (current_node)
     {
       current_node->show_value();
       current_node = current_node->next;
     }
 }

template<class T> void list<T>::show_reverse(void)
 {
   node<T> *current_node = last;

   while (current_node->previous)
     {
       current_node->show_value();
       current_node = current_node->previous;
     }
 }

template<class T> void list<T>::append_node(node<T> *new_node)
 {
   last->next = new_node;
   new_node->previous = last;
   last = new_node;
   last->next = NULL;
 }

void main(void)
 {
   list<int> single;
   list<float> values;
   list<char> letters;

   for (int i = 1; i <= 10; i++)
     single.append_node(new node<int> (i));

   single.show_list();

   for (i = 0; i < 10; i++)
     values.append_node(new node<float> (0.1 * i));

   values.show_list();

   for (i = 'A'; i <= 'Z'; i++)
     letters.append_node(new node<char> (i));

   letters.show_list();

   letters.show_reverse();
 }
```

As you can see, the class adds the *show_reverse* function, which displays a list's contents from last to first. Because each node now contains a pointer to the previous note, traversing the list in reverse is very easy.

The *append_node* function is identical to those in the previous programs, except now we must make our new pointer, *previous,* point to the previous node in the list.

Also, note that the *list* constructor must now initialize *previous,* as well as *next,* to a NULL value. Like a singly linked list when initialized by the *list* constructor, the first node of a doubly linked list is the first, last, and only node in the list—there are no *previous* or *next* nodes.

Each of the previous programs added elements to the linked list by simply appending a new element to the end of the list. The following program, INSERT.CPP, however, adds the *insert_node* member function to the *list* class, which lets the program insert values into the list in ascending order: Using a doubly linked list, it is easy for the program to insert an element within a list:

```
#include <iostream.h>
#include <stdlib.h>

template<class T> class node {
  public:
    node(T value) { node::value = value; };
    node(void) { };
    void show_value(void) { cout << value << endl; };
    T get_value(void) { return(value); };
    struct node<T> *next;
    struct node<T> *previous;
  private:
    T value;
};

template<class T> class list {
  public:
    list(void) { first.next = NULL; last = &first;
      first.previous = NULL; };
    void show_list(void);
    void append_node(node<T> *new_node);
    void show_reverse(void);
    void insert_node(node<T> *new_node);
  private:
    node<T> first;
    node<T> *last;
};

template<class T> void list<T>::show_list(void)
 {
   node<T> *current_node = first.next;
```

```
    while (current_node)
      {
        current_node->show_value();
        current_node = current_node->next;
      }
  }

template<class T> void list<T>::show_reverse(void)
  {
    node<T> *current_node = last;

    while (current_node->previous)
      {
        current_node->show_value();
        current_node = current_node->previous;
      }
  }

template<class T> void list<T>::append_node(node<T> *new_node)
  {
    last->next = new_node;
    new_node->previous = last;
    last = new_node;
    last->next = NULL;
  }

template<class T> void list<T>::insert_node(node<T> *new_node)
  {
    node<T> *current_node = first.next;
    node<T> *previous_node = &first;

    while ((current_node) &&
        (current_node->get_value() < new_node->get_value()))
      {
        current_node = current_node->next;
        previous_node = previous_node->next;
      }

    previous_node->next = new_node;
    new_node->previous = previous_node;
    new_node->next = current_node;
   }

void main(void)
  {
    list<float> values;

    for (int i = 0; i < 10; i++)
      values.insert_node(new node<float> (rand()));

    values.show_list();
  }
```

The *insert_node* function is straightforward. The *while* statement traverses the list one node at a time and compares the *new_node* value:

```
while ((current_node) &&
    (current_node->get_value() < new_node->get_value()))
  {
    current_node = current_node->next;
    previous_node = previous_node->next;
  }
```

When a *current_node* value is found to be less than the *new_node* value, the *while* statement ends. The new node is inserted with the following statements:

```
previous_node->next = new_node;
new_node->previous = previous_node;
new_node->next = current_node;
```

If all of the node values are less than the *new_node* value *insert_node*, in effect, *appends* the new node to the end of the list.

Adding Class Members

The previous programs have performed simple list operations, inserting or appending nodes or listing the node contents. In many cases, however, your programs will need to search a linked list for a specific value or will need to perform a specific operation on each node's data value. The following program, SEARCH.CPP, for example, uses the *search* member function to search the linked list for the first occurrence of a specific value. In addition, the program uses the *count* member function to count the number of times a specific value appears within the list:

```
#include <iostream.h>
#include <stdlib.h>

template<class T> class node {
  public:
    node(T value) { node::value = value; };
    node(void) { };
    void show_value(void) { cout << value << endl; };
    T get_value(void) { return(value); };
    struct node<T> *next;
    struct node<T> *previous;
  private:
    T value;
};
```

```
template<class T> class list {
  public:
    list(void) { first.next = NULL; last = &first;
      first.previous = NULL; };
    void show_list(void);
    void append_node(node<T> *new_node);
    void show_reverse(void);
    void insert_node(node<T> *new_node);
    node<T> *search(T value);
    int count(T value);
  private:
    node<T> first;
    node<T> *last;
};

template<class T> void list<T>::show_list(void)
 {
   node<T> *current_node = first.next;

   while (current_node)
     {
       current_node->show_value();
       current_node = current_node->next;
     }
 }

template<class T> void list<T>::show_reverse(void)
 {
   node<T> *current_node = last;

   while (current_node->previous)
     {
       current_node->show_value();
       current_node = current_node->previous;
     }
 }

template<class T> void list<T>::append_node(node<T> *new_node)
 {
   last->next = new_node;
   new_node->previous = last;
   last = new_node;
   last->next = NULL;
 }

template<class T> void list<T>::insert_node(node<T> *new_node)
 {
   node<T> *current_node = first.next;
   node<T> *previous_node = &first;
```

```
   while ((current_node) &&
       (current_node->get_value() < new_node->get_value()))
     {
       current_node = current_node->next;
       previous_node = previous_node->next;
     }

   previous_node->next = new_node;
   new_node->previous = previous_node;
   new_node->next = current_node;
  }

template<class T> node<T> *list<T>::search(T value)
 {
   node<T> *current_node = first.next;

   while (current_node)
     if (current_node->get_value() == value)
       return(current_node);
     else
       current_node = current_node->next;

   return(NULL);
 }

template<class T> int list<T>::count(T value)
 {
   node<T> *current_node = first.next;

   int count = 0;

   while (current_node)
    {
      if (current_node->get_value() == value)
        count++;
      current_node = current_node->next;
    }
   return(count);
 }

void main(void)
 {
   list<float> values;

   for (int i = 0; i < 10; i++)
     values.insert_node(new node<float> (2.5 * i));

   values.show_list();
```

```
    if (values.search(7.5))
      cout << "Found the value 7.5" << endl;
    else
      cout << "The value 7.5 was not found" << endl;

    cout << "7.5 was found " << values.count(7.5) << " times" <<
            endl;
  }
```

As you can see, the program uses the *search* function to search the list for the value 7.5. Likewise, the program uses the count function to *count* the number of occurrences of the value 7.5 within the list.

In a similar fashion to the *insert_node* function found in the previous program, the *search* function simply walks through our list:

```
while (current_node)
  if (current_node->get_value() == value)
    return(current_node);
  else
    current_node = current_node->next;

return(NULL);
```

Only now, rather than looking for a value that is less than our function parameter, as we were in *insert_node*, we are looking for an equivalent *current_node* value. If an equivalent value is found, *search* immediately returns the value of the node:

```
  if (current_node->get_value() == value)
    return(current_node);
```

If no matching value is found, *search* returns a NULL.

The *count* function is almost identical to *search*. However, instead of immediately returning when a matching value is found, *count* increments a counter variable of type *int:*

```
while (current_node)
 {
   if (current_node->get_value() == value)
     count++; ———————————————— Counter variable
   current_node = current_node->next;      incremented
 }
return(count);
```

Unlike the other member functions we have just examined, *count* always traverses the *entire* list before returning. The value of the counter variable, which can be zero, is always returned by *count.*

Templates and Class Libraries

In Chapter 17 you learned how to create a class library. The programs presented in this chapter have made extensive use of templates to create generic lists. As you learned in Chapter 6, during compilation, the C++ compiler creates the correct classes and class functions, based on the types specified in an object declaration. Unfortunately, because templates are used by the compiler, it is very difficult for your programs to create template-based class libraries. In the case of the programs just shown, you might find that placing the templates and functions into a header file is easier and more flexible than trying to create a class library file.

Putting It All Together

This chapter has examined ways you can use templates to create a generic linked-list class. The programs presented in this chapter illustrate many of the concepts discussed throughout this book. Take time to experiment with each program. Before you continue on your way with C++, make sure that you have learned the following:

- ✓ In singly linked list, each node points forward to the next node; the last points to NULL.
- ✓ The **list** <*type*> statement in the class template supports variables of different types, depending on *type*.
- ✓ A doubly linked list, each node has a pointer to the next node and the previous node.
- ✓ You can place the *search* member function the *count* member function into your class template to search your list and count occurrences of a value.
- ✓ It is very difficult for your programs to create template-based class libraries. You might find that placing the templates and functions into a header file is easier and more flexible than trying to create a class library file.

Index

D

E

F

G

H

I

J

K

L

M

N

O

P

Q

R

S